BEST FRIENDS

TEACHER'S GUIDE

1

Janice L. Baillie

McGraw-Hill

MEXICO • BUENOS AIRES • CARACAS • GUATEMALA • LISBON • MADRID • NEW YORK
SAN JUAN • BOGOTA • SANTIAGO • SAO PAULO • AUCKLAND
LONDON • MILAN • NEW DELHI • SAN FRANCISCO • SINGAPORE
ST. LOUIS • SYDNEY • TORONTO

McGraw-Hill/Contemporary

A Division of The McGraw-Hill Companies

Best Friends Teacher's Guide 1, 1st Edition

Published by McGraw-Hill Contemporary, a business unit of The McGraw-Hill Companies, Inc., 1221 Avenue of the Americas, New York, NY 10020.

ISBN 0-07-254350-7 (USE)
ISBN 0-07-121185-3 (ISE)

Editorial director: Tina Carver
Editorial coordinator: Judy MacDonald
Editor: Lenore Cohen
Production coordinator: Alfonso Reyes G.
Art direction: Lilia Barajas
Design and layout: X-Libris
Lilia Barajas
Flor Barajas
Maritza Ramírez
Fernando García
Illustrations: Rubén Feria
Claudia Navarro
Lilia Barajas
Cover: Lilia Barajas

INTERNATIONAL EDITION ISBN 0-07-121185-3 (ISE)

10 09 08 07 06 05 04 03 02 01
20 09 08 07 06 05 04 03 02
CTP SLP

Printed in Singapore

TABLE OF CONTENTS

Scope and Sequence

	Vocabulary	Spelling	Phonics
	Number words 1-10, boy(s), girl(s), *Passive* friends, happy, little, CD Happy birthday.	cake, ball, balloon, candle, present, doll, party hat, kite, teddy bear, book	/b/ /d/
	Colors: red, blue, yellow, black, white, pink, gray, purple, orange, green *Passive* favorite color, toy chest	pencil, ruler, backpack, pen, crayon, notebook, pencil case, chair, desk	/p/ /b/
	brown, house, bathroom, bedroom, living room, kitchen, garage, car *Passive* animals, beautiful, small, big Come here now. I'm sorry.	brother, sister, mother, father, turtle(s), dog(s), cat(s), bird(s), fish	/t/ /th/
	monster, happy, smart, funny, friends, tall, short, cute, pretty, ugly, great, toy *Passive* vowels, shoulders, knees I love you.	legs, head, hands, finger(s), arm(s), mouth, eye(s), nose, ear(s), feet	/h/ /r/
	hot, cold, clean, mess(y), sad, picnic, umbrella, snowman, crazy, sunny, rainy, windy, snowy, cloudy *Passive* wet, warm, snowflake, yummy	window, floor, clock, poster, computer, eraser, blackboard, flag, apple	/c/ /g/
	surprise, shelf, bus, train, plane, taxi, bike, car, home, school, fine, sick *Passive* babies	teacher, dentist, vet, homemaker, pilot, nurse, doctor, bus driver, taxi driver, police officer, student	/s/ /sh/
	Number words 11-20, square, circle, triangle, rectangle *Passive* horse, chicken, bear, parrot, cage Good night. How many...?	seal, tiger, sheep, lion, giraffe, elephant, monkey, zebra, duck, cow	/ch/ /sh/
	boat, restaurant, toy store, bookstore, comic book, brave, box, food *Passive* cookie	lollipop, hot dog, candy, apple, banana, sandwich, chocolate, hamburger, ice cream	/b/ /v/

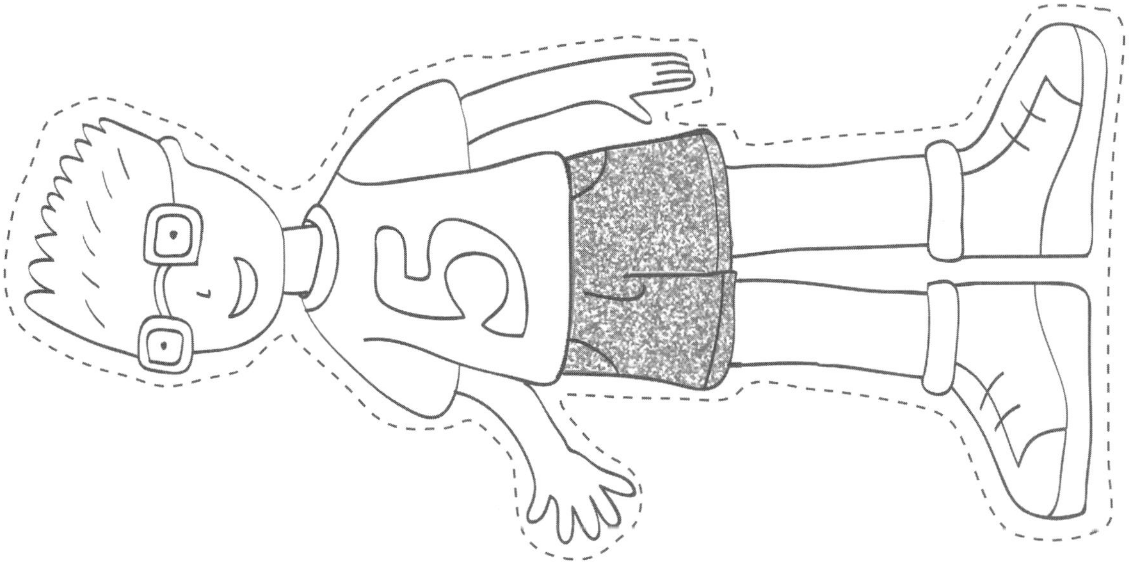
5

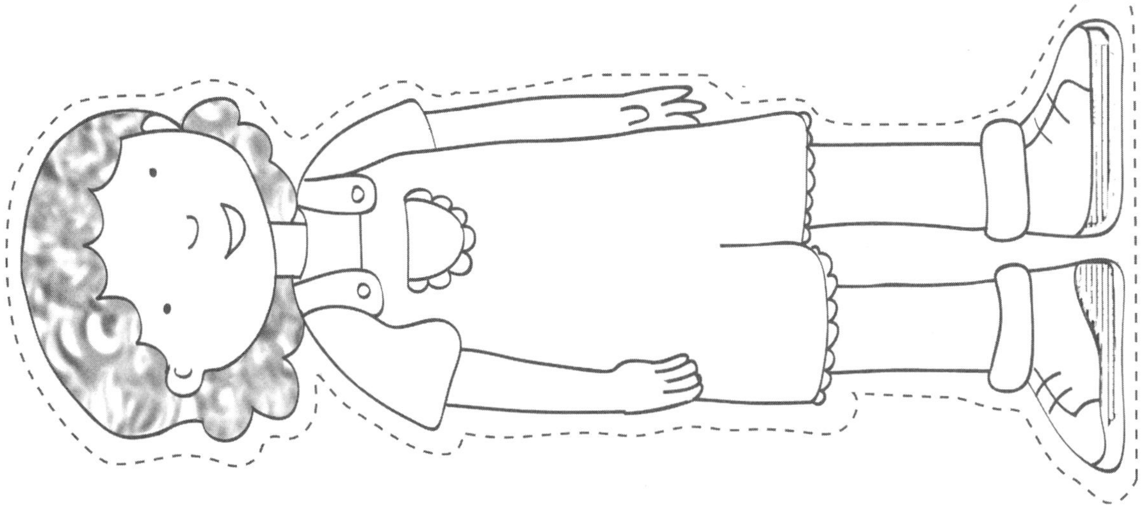

Meet your Best Friends!

Unit 1

Objectives

Students will:
- learn greetings
- introduce themselves and others

Lesson 1 Hi! I'm Mariana.

Materials
Best Friends Student Book 1 pages 2-5
Other Materials
Teacher's Guide blackline master 1, index cards, crayons, scissors, glue, pictures of students, old magazines

New Language
Hi!/Hello! I'm..., This is...
Passive Vocabulary
friends

1. **Getting Started**
(Before starting the class, photocopy the blackline masters of the characters and create stick puppets for each character in *Best Friends 1*.) Introduce the story characters to the class with the stick puppets. Hold up a character and say *Hi! I'm (Daniel).* or *Hello! I'm (Daniel).* Repeat the procedure for each character. Then introduce yourself, saying *Hi! I'm (name)* and *Hello. I'm (name),* exaggerating the *Hi/Hello* gesture with one hand and then pointing to yourself. Show students that the greeting can go at the beginning or the end of the statement by saying *I'm (name). Hi!,* and *Hi, I'm (name);* also *I'm (name). Hello!,* and *Hello, I'm (name).*

   Ask students to look at the picture on page 2 in their Student Book. Point to and name each character again. Say, *(Daniel.) This is (Daniel)* and repeat the name several times. Do the same with the other characters. Then explain to students that the story characters are friends.

   Play the tape for **Exercise 1**. As each character speaks, students should trace with a finger under the words in the speech bubble.

   Play the tape for **Exercise 2**. Repeat several times as necessary until students repeat with confidence and reasonably good pronunciation.

2. **Working Together**
Invite students to look at **Exercise 3** on page 3 in the Student Book. Do the first example together to make sure students understand it and the concept of matching. Point to the example shown and to the corresponding child in the scene on page 2. Repeat the procedure for the other characters as necessary or ask volunteers to show the correlation.

   Then pair students and have them do the exercise. Check answers as a class.

Grammar Tips

- Emphasize that you use *I'm (name)* when the person is speaking about himself or herself, but that you use *This is (name)* when the person is speaking about another person.
- When people are speaking in English, they use contractions. A contraction happens when one or more letters in a word are replaced with an apostrophe ('). The contraction for *I am* is *I'm*.

Ask students which children in the scene on page 2 introduce themselves (all of them do, except Steve) and which one talks about a friend (Mariana does). For more practice, have them talk about these characters or the stick puppets, e.g., *This is Melba, This is Natalie,* etc.

Finally, prompt several students to introduce themselves saying *Hi! I'm (name)* or *Hello! I'm (name.)* After each student says his or her name, say to the class *This is (name).*

Ask students to look at the pictures in **Exercise 4**. Mention that the children are friends. Read aloud the speech bubbles for each dialogue and tell students to repeat. Then distribute three index cards to each student. Have each student make a word card with his or her first name; then on the second card they can choose to write *Hi! I'm (name),* or *Hello! I'm (name);* and on the third card they write *This is* (blank space). (Write the structures on the board for students' reference or have students look at the speech bubbles in their books.) Let the class practice talking to their friends by introducing themselves and others by holding up the appropriate word cards.

3. **Finishing Up**

Pair students and have them work on **Exercise 5** together. First point to each scene and pronounce the names of the characters for students' reference (*Mike, Sarah, Rex, Julia, Poppi, Betsy*). Go over the example, checking that students understand why that is the correct answer. When students are done, check answers together.

For **Exercise 6**, distribute crayons, scissors, and glue. Help students find the correct page at the back of their books (page 147) and follow the directions for the activity. Tell them that the friend they draw can be someone who is not in the classroom; they can draw anyone they consider their friend. Help them with the spelling of names if they want to label their pictures.

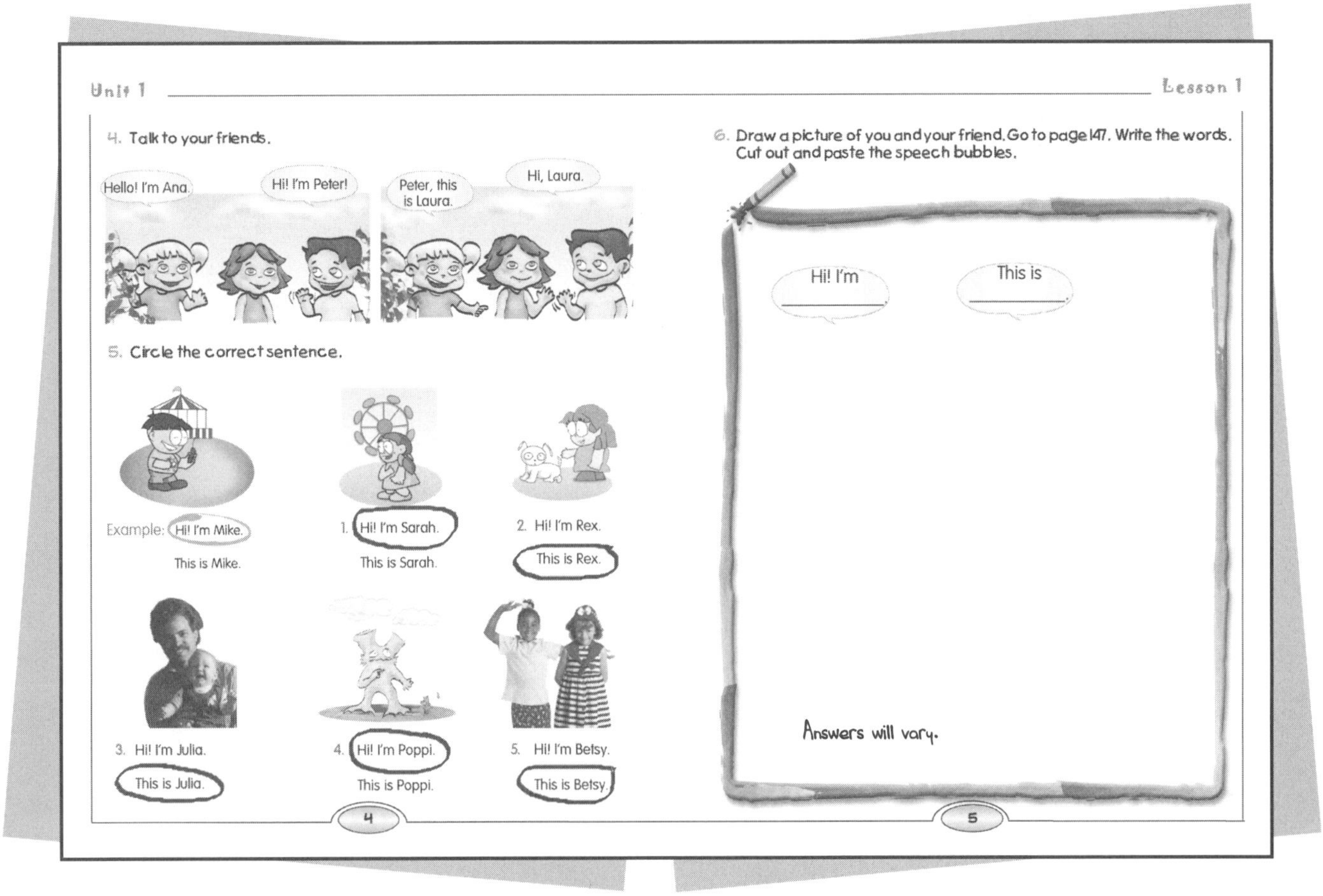
Unit 1 Lesson 1

4. Talk to your friends.

5. Circle the correct sentence.

Example: Hi! I'm Mike. / This is Mike.

1. Hi! I'm Sarah. / This is Sarah.

2. Hi! I'm Rex. / This is Rex.

3. Hi! I'm Julia. / This is Julia.

4. Hi! I'm Poppi. / This is Poppi.

5. Hi! I'm Betsy. / This is Betsy.

6. Draw a picture of you and your friend. Go to page 147. Write the words. Cut out and paste the speech bubbles.

Answers will vary.

4 5

Fun and Games

A. **What's his/her favorite color? Poppi and a friend.** Have students draw a picture of Poppi (they can refer to Exercise 4 on page 4 in the Student Book) and another "monster" friend for Poppi. Encourage them to say the new monster's name or write it on the picture. As an alternative they can cut out and glue speech bubbles similar to those in Exercise 6. Help with writing and cutting out as necessary. Display the pictures on a bulletin board.

B. **Introductions.** Ask students to bring pictures of themselves from home. Divide the class into groups of five students each. Each student should "introduce" himself or herself to the group, using the lesson target language while holding up their picture.

A variation on this activity is to have each group put their pictures into a cap or box and choose one randomly. The first student introduces the person whose picture he or she is holding by saying *This is (name).* Each one takes a turn until everyone is introduced.

C. **Famous people.** Distribute magazines, scissors, and two index cards to pairs of students. Have each one cut out a person from the magazine and invent a name for the person, writing it on a card. Tell each pair to role-play meeting and introducing themselves for the first time as they hold up their cutouts and cards.

Tapescript

Unit 1 Lesson 1 Page 2

Exercise 1: Look and listen.

Daniel: I'm Daniel. Hello!
Melba: Hi! I'm Melba.
Natalie: Hello! I'm Natalie.
Ken: Hello. I'm Ken.
Mariana: Hi! I'm Mariana. This is Steve.
Steve: Hi!

Exercise 2: Listen and repeat.
(See Exercise 1 above.)

Lesson 2 Is it a kite?

Objectives

Students will:
- develop vocabulary related to toys and party objects
- listen for a purpose
- differentiate between /b/ and /d/

Materials
Best Friends Student Book 1 pages 6-9
Other Materials
ball or picture of a ball, index cards

New Language
Is it a…?
Yes it is./No, it isn't.
Passive Vocabulary
CD
Spelling
ball, balloon, book, cake, candle, doll, kite, party hat, present, teddy bear

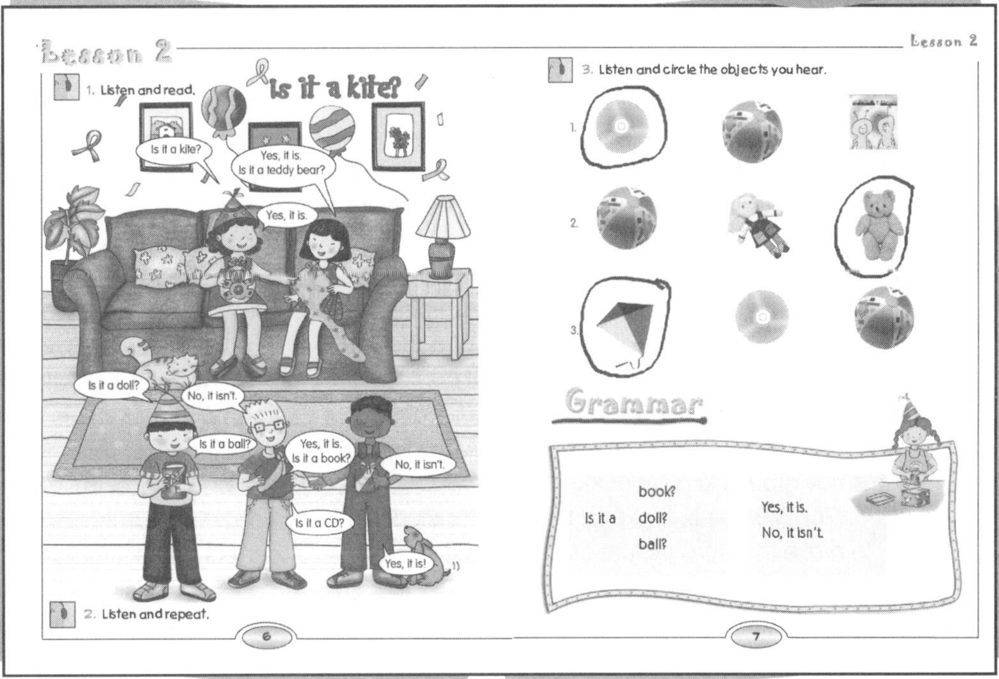

1. **Getting Started**
To introduce new vocabulary, distribute index cards and ask students to draw on one side the following objects as you do the same on your own set of cards or on the board: *balloon, teddy bear, kite, doll, ball, CD.* Then name each object, prompting students to hold up the appropriate picture card and repeat with you. (If these objects are also in the classroom, ask volunteers to find them.)

   Present the question and answer structure *Is it a…?/Yes, it is.* or *No, it isn't.*, using your set of picture cards or pictures on the board. Name an object, e.g., *ball,* then ask *Is it a ball?* Nod your head yes and say *Yes, it is.* Repeat the procedure for the other pictures. Then point to the kite picture card, saying *Is it a ball?* Shake your head no, and say *No, it isn't.* Ask about other cards in the same way in order to get the answer *No, it isn't.*

   Play the tape for **Exercise 1**. Go over the title and dialogues, pointing to each speech balloon and tracing from left to right with a finger under the words as you read aloud.

   For **Exercise 2**, repeat as necessary until students know the vocabulary and say it with confidence and reasonably good pronunciation. As each character speaks, students should trace with a finger under the words in the speech bubble.

2. **Working Together**
Have students look at the pictures in **Exercise 3** on page 7 in the Student Book. Review the structure *This is…* by pointing to and naming objects in the rows, e.g., *This is a CD, This is a ball, This is a book.* Then play the tape for students to just listen. Repeat the tape and have them complete the activity. (Be sure they understand that they must identify the object by circling the correct one in each row. Draw an object on the board and a circle around it, if necessary. Finally, ask pairs to compare answers, then check answers as a class.

Grammar Tips

- A question mark is used as punctuation at the end of a question, and a period is used at the end of a sentence.
- The contraction *isn't* stands for *is not*. In this case, the contraction is formed by joining *is* and *not* and replacing the *o* in *not* with an apostrophe.

Ask students to practice the structures using the chart and their picture cards. Pair students and have partners point to pictures randomly, asking *Is it a (CD)?* Partners answer accordingly *Yes, it is.* or *No, it isn't.*

For **Exercise 4**, first play the tape for students to just listen as they look at the pictures. Point out that the first answer is given on the tape as a model for students to follow. Be sure they are looking at the correct scene on page 8 in each case. They should answer together as a group. Then repeat the tape several times, asking small groups to answer together.

For **Exercise 5**, first play the tape for students to make the word-picture association as they follow in their books. Go over the new vocabulary (*cake, book, party hat, candle*, and *present*), repeating each several times. Reinforce the meaning of *present* by pointing to the objects that Mariana is holding in the scenes in Exercise 4. Say *This is a present* in each case. Finally, have students repeat after the tape and then trace the words.

As reinforcement, hand out five index cards to each student, asking them to draw the new vocabulary objects on one side. Then have the class gather all their picture cards from the lesson. Say each word randomly and have students hold up the corresponding picture card, repeating after you.

Tell students to do **Exercise 6**, helping as necessary with the instructions. Students may work in pairs if they wish. Have pairs compare answers with other pairs or individuals.

Assign **Exercise 7**. Play the tape several times before students trace the letters and words.

3. Finishing Up

For **Exercise 8**, write the example on the board but without the letter *b*, then fill in the blank with a large *b*. Ask students to trace over the *b* in the example in their books. Then play the entire tape as students listen and "trace in" the missing letters in their books. Finally, repeat the tape and have students write in the correct letters. Pairs can check each other's work.

Then ask students to take out all their Lesson 2 picture cards. They should label the pictures neatly on the back side of each card, using previous exercises as a spelling reference, so that one side is a picture card and the other is a word card.

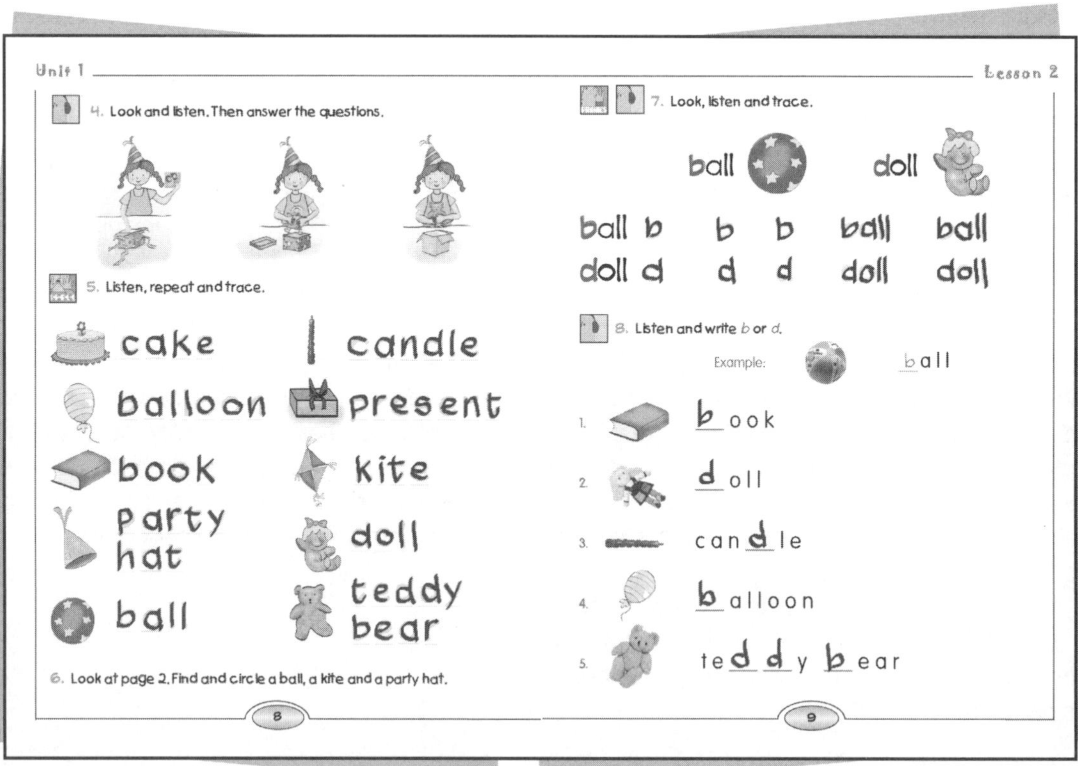

Fun and Games

A. **Picture Concentration.** Have two volunteers bring to the front of the classroom their complete sets of Lesson 2 cards. Using a large, flat surface such as table, place all of the cards with the picture side face down in random order. Explain that the object of the game is to find two pictures that match. Have one volunteer demonstrate by randomly picking up two cards at a time to see if they match. If they do, he or she places them together in a pile to the side and continues. If they don't match, he or she puts them back face down where they were. Then it is the other volunteer's turn. Then pair students and have them play against each other to see who gets the most cards. When they finish playing, ask them to put their cards in order so that each student gets his or her cards back again.

B. **Word Concentration.** Pairs could play Concentration searching for matched pairs of word cards. Follow the procedure for Picture Concentration above.

C. **Dictation.** Use one set of lesson word cards. Divide the class into two teams. The first person on Team A reads a word card aloud, and the first person on Team B writes it on the board. If the word is spelled correctly, Team B gets a point; if it is wrong, Team A gets a point. Teams switch roles. Go through the cards as often as necessary to give everyone a chance to dictate and write. The team with the most points at the end wins.

Tapescript

Unit 1 Lesson 2 Page 6

Exercise 1: Listen and read.

Melba: Is it a kite?
Natalie: Yes, it is. Is it a teddy bear?
Melba: Yes, it is.
Ken: Is it a doll?
Steve: No, it isn't.
Ken: Is it a ball?
Steve: Yes, it is. Is it a book?
Daniel: No, it isn't.
Steve: Is it a CD?
Daniel: Yes, it is!

Unit 1 Lesson 2 Page 6

Exercise 2: Listen and repeat.

(See Exercise 2 above.)

Unit 1 Lesson 2 Page 7

Exercise 3: Listen and circle the objects you hear.

Number 1: This is a CD.
Number 2: This is a teddy bear.
Number 3: This is a kite.

Unit 1 Lesson 2 Page 8

Exercise 4: Look and listen. Then answer the questions.

Mariana: What is it? Is it a book? *(Pause)* No, it isn't. It's a CD. Thank you!
Mariana: What is it? Is it a doll? *(Pause for students to complete.)*
Mariana: What is it? Is it a kite? *(Pause for students to complete.)*

Unit 1 Lesson 2 Page 8

Exercise 5: Listen, repeat and trace.

cake cake
balloon balloon
book book
party hat party hat
ball ball
candle candle
present present
kite kite
doll doll
teddy bear teddy bear

Unit 1 Lesson 2 Page 9

Exercise 7: Look, listen and trace.

ball
doll
ball /b/ /b/ /b/ ball ball
doll /d/ /d/ /d/ doll doll

Unit 1 Lesson 2 Page 9

Exercise 8: Listen and write *b* or *d*.

1. book
2. doll
3. candle
4. balloon
5. teddy bear

Lesson 3 I'm six.

Objectives

Students will:
- learn the number words one through ten
- recognize singular and plural nouns

Lesson 3 I'm six. Lesson 3

1. Listen and read the dialogue. Practice with a friend.

Happy birthday, Mariana! How old are you?

I'm six.

2. Look at the pictures. Count and write the numbers.

1 one 2 two 3 three 4 four 5 five
6 six 7 seven 8 eight 9 nine 10 ten

I'm seven I'm six I'm one I'm ten

3. Listen and repeat.

One little, two little, three little friends,
Four little, five little, six little friends,
Seven little, eight little, nine little friends,
Ten little happy friends.

One little, two little, three little friends,
Four little, five little, six little friends,
Seven little, eight little, nine little friends,
Ten little happy friends.

4. Match and draw different objects.

Example: 3 seven
1. 7 five
2. 1 one
3. 8 three
4. 5 eight

10 11

Materials
Best Friends Student Book 1 pages 10-13
Other Materials
The Mariana and Melba stick puppets, index cards, crayons or colored pencils

New Language
How old are you?/I'm (six).
Passive Vocabulary
boy(s)
girl(s)
happy
Happy birthday!
little

1. **Getting Started**
Introduce the structure *How old are you?* by asking students to look back at the birthday party scene on page 2 in their books. Review *cake* and *candle* by pointing and repeating. Count the candles on the cake as you hold up a finger for each one: *One, two, three, four, five, six! Six candles.* Then use the Mariana and Melba stick puppets to act out the dialogue on page 10.
Play the tape for **Exercise 1**. Go over the instructions and dialogue, pointing to each speech balloon and tracing from left to right with a finger under the words as you read aloud. Repeat until students are comfortable with the new language.
For **Exercise 2**, introduce the numbers one through ten. Pronounce each one slowly as you point to the numerals and number words. Repeat as necessary until students know the vocabulary and repeat with confidence and reasonably good pronunciation. Then count together the number of fingers each child on page 10 is holding up. (This indicates his or her age). Do the first one as an example (*I'm seven*). Then have students fill in the others, working in pairs. Circulate to check that students are writing the number words in the blanks and not the numerals. Check answers as a class, writing the number words on the board for students' reference.

2. **Working Together**
Have students look at **Exercise 3** on page 11 in the Student Book. Tell them that that they are going to listen to a song about *numbers* and *friends*. Play the tape and clap loudly as each number word is pronounced. Then repeat the tape, this time holding up the correct number of fingers in ascending order as each number is said. Repeat the procedure so that students chant along, tap loudly as each number word comes up, and hold up fingers as appropriate.
For **Exercise 4**, explain the example. Be sure students understand why each column matches across. Suggest that they draw party objects in the boxes, but accept any objects as long as the correct number is shown. Have students exchange books with a classmate and check one another's work.

Grammar Tips

- Regular singular nouns generally become plural by adding an *s: friend/friends, candle/candles, book/books.*
- In English, the final *s* is pronounced /z/ after voiced consonants such as /b/, /d/, and /l /: *tabs, toads,* and *balls.* It is pronounced /s/ after voiceless consonants such as /k/, /p/, and /t/: *books, caps,* and *presents.*

Go over the structures in the Grammar Box, emphasizing the pronunciation of the final *s* in *boys* and *girls.* Then present the example in **Exercise 5**. Help anyone who does not understand well how to add in his or her native language. Encourage students to say what they have drawn in their boxes, e.g., *seven kites.*

Distribute ten index cards to each student and have them write the numerals 1 through 10 on one side and the corresponding number words on the other side, as large as possible. They can refer to page 10 on their books for spelling reference as necessary. Make your own set of cards as well. Circulate to check the spelling and that the handwriting on all cards is easy to read. Using your set of cards with the numeral side showing, demonstrate the following activity: Point to a numeral randomly and ask *Is it a two?* Answer as appropriate *Yes, it is.* or *No, it isn't.* Then have pairs practice with their cards. If anyone asks about the numeral eight, provide the structure *Is it an eight?* However, do not get into a discussion about the use of *a* vs. *an* at this stage.

3. **Finishing Up**

For **Exercise 6**, distribute crayons or colored pencils. Indicate to students that they should write *Happy birthday, Mariana!* in the card. Guide students to first trace the letter *a* in the words and then the rest of the letters. Ask them to finish the card by drawing objects or a scene related to birthdays.

After they finish the birthday cards, have students exchange books. Each student could circle all the letter *a*'s in their partner's signature. Then check whose name has the most *a*'s in it and whose name has the fewest *a*'s.

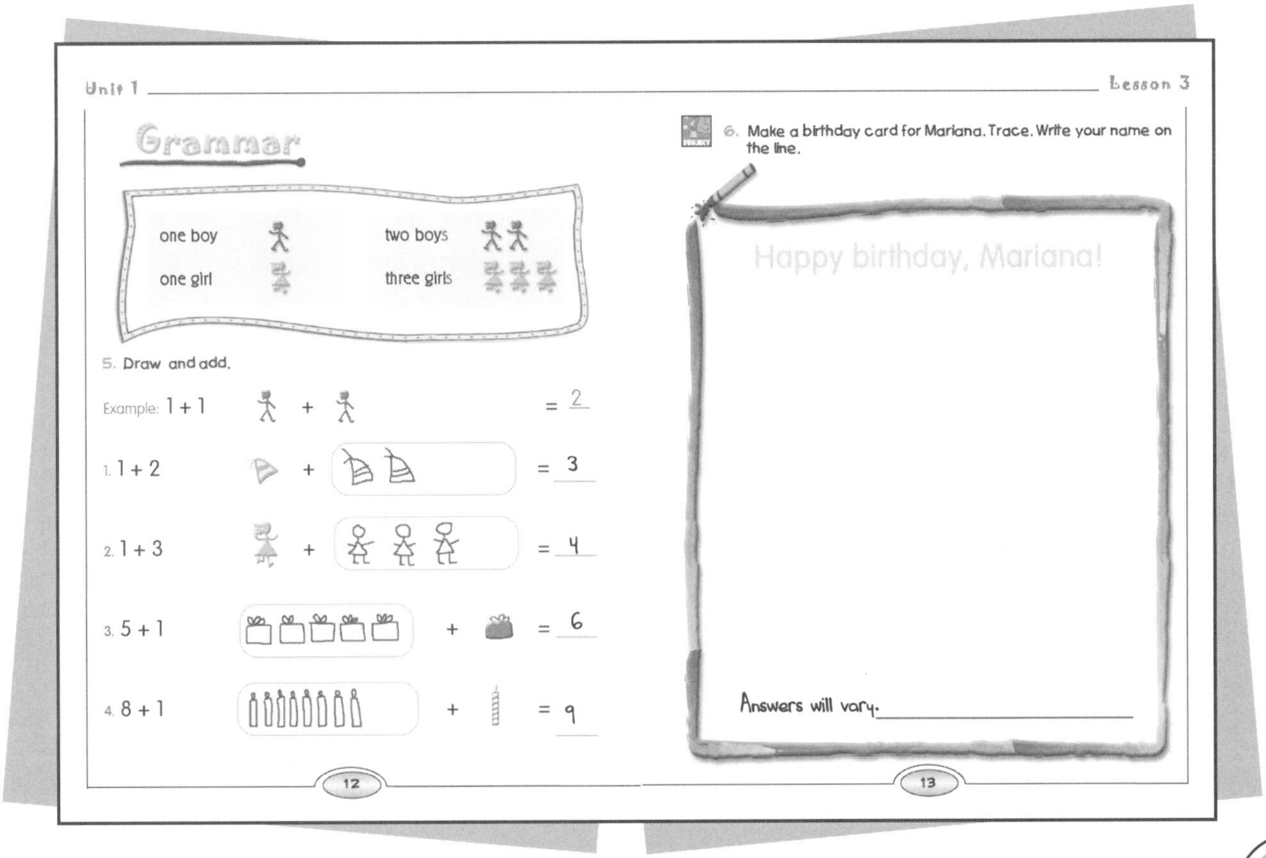
Unit 1 Lesson 3

Grammar

one boy — two boys

one girl — three girls

5. Draw and add.

Example: 1 + 1 = 2

1. 1 + 2 = 3
2. 1 + 3 = 4
3. 5 + 1 = 6
4. 8 + 1 = 9

6. Make a birthday card for Mariana. Trace. Write your name on the line.

Happy birthday, Mariana!

Answers will vary.

12 13

Fun and Games

A. **How old are you?** Prompt students to tell the class their names and ages by having the Melba and Mariana stick puppets say *Hi! I'm (name). I'm (six).*, then pointing to the students. As students say their ages, mark on the board how many are six years old, seven years old, or other.

B. **Say the number.** Be sure all students have their sets of picture-word cards for numbers one through ten. Divide the class into groups of five or six. Ask students to stand up. Alternate holding up any numeral, then any number-word, and have students hold up the exact same card as quickly as possible. When everyone is holding up a card, say the number together loudly. Then check that everyone has the same card. Any student who isn't showing the correct card must sit down. Repeat the procedure faster and faster until only one student is left standing in each group.

C. **Draw!** Divide the class into five teams and have them stand far away from the board. Using all the lesson vocabulary, tell the first student in each team what to draw on the board and how many, e.g., *four boys.* The first student who finishes correctly gets a point for his or her team. Give everyone a chance to draw. The team with the most points wins.

Tapescript

Unit 1 Lesson 3 Page 10
Exercise 1: Listen and read the dialogue. Practice with a friend.

Melba: Happy birthday, Mariana!
How old are you?

Mariana: I'm six.

Unit 1 Lesson 3 Page 11
Exercise 3: Listen and repeat.

One little, two little, three little friends,
Four little, five little, six little friends,
Seven little, eight little, nine little friends,
Ten little happy friends.
One little, two little, three little friends,
Four little, five little, six little friends,
Seven little, eight little, nine little friends,
Ten little happy friends.

Lesson 4 Review

Objectives

Students will:
- read a dialogue
- review language from Lessons 1-3

Materials

Best Friends Student Book 1 pages 14-17

Other Materials

stick puppets, picture and word cards from Lessons 1-3, bits of paper for game markers

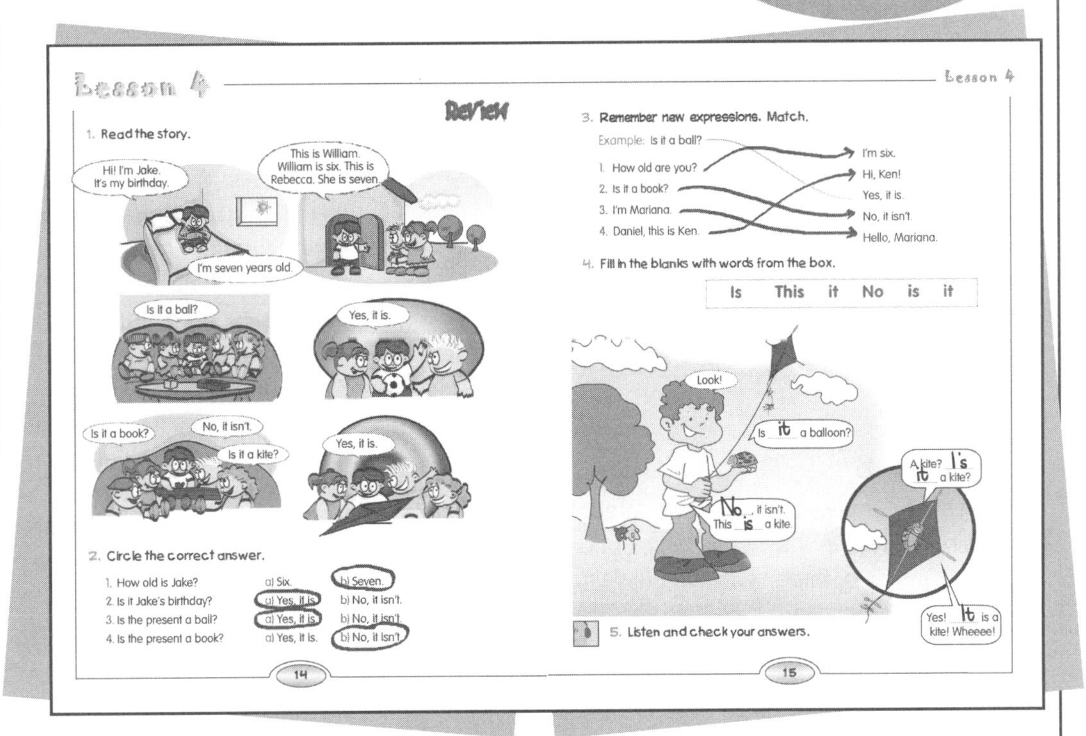

Lesson 4 — Review

1. Read the story.

Hi! I'm Jake. It's my birthday.

This is William. William is six. This is Rebecca. She is seven.

I'm seven years old.

Is it a ball?

Yes, it is.

Is it a book?

No, it isn't.

Is it a kite?

Yes, it is.

2. Circle the correct answer.

1. How old is Jake? a) Six. b) Seven.
2. Is it Jake's birthday? a) Yes, it is. b) No, it isn't.
3. Is the present a ball? a) Yes, it is. b) No, it isn't.
4. Is the present a book? a) Yes, it is. b) No, it isn't.

14

Lesson 4

3. Remember new expressions. Match.

Example: Is it a ball? — I'm six.

1. How old are you? — Hi, Ken!
2. Is it a book? — Yes, it is.
3. I'm Mariana. — No, it isn't.
4. Daniel, this is Ken. — Hello, Mariana.

4. Fill in the blanks with words from the box.

Is	This	it	No	is	it

Look!

Is it a balloon?

No, it isn't. This is a kite.

A kite? Is it a kite?

Yes! It is a kite! Wheeee!

5. Listen and check your answers.

15

Read

Exercise 1: Dialogue summary. A story in dialogue format tells about Jake and his friends, how old they all are, and what presents these friends are giving Jake. Jake is guessing what the presents are, and his friends are telling him if he is right or not. He gets a ball and a kite as birthday presents.

Read the dialogue aloud, pointing to each speech bubble as you read. Ask students to listen and follow in their books. For fun, change voices to represent different speakers. Then read the dialogue again and encourage students to read aloud with you. Finally, assign the roles of Jake and the other two speakers to three capable students. They can use the book to read their parts or they can try to memorize and recite their parts.

Story Comprehension

Exercise 2: Do number 1 together: *How old is Jake? Seven.* Then read all the questions aloud for students, allowing time for them to circle their answers. When everyone has finished, check answers as a class.

Vocabulary

Exercise 3: Review the concepts of matching and asking/answering questions logically by reading aloud the example. Be sure to use a rising intonation for the question. Then read the numbered objects one at a time and ask students to find the logical match to it, e.g., *How old are you?/I'm six.* They can read the answer aloud or point to it in their books. Give everyone a chance to answer a question.

Then have students practice the structures by handing out the Mariana, Ken, and Daniel stick puppets to three capable students. Encourage them to role-play the situations in numbers 3 and 4: For number 3, the Mariana puppet introduces herself to the Ken and Daniel puppets by saying *I'm Mariana.*, and they say *Hello, Mariana*; for number 4, the Mariana puppet stands next to the Ken puppet and introduces Ken to Daniel (who is standing in front of them). Give several groups of three students turns at using the puppets.

Exercise 4: Start the exercise by asking students to read aloud the words or phrases in the word box. Tell them they should use them only once to fill in the blanks. Then ask them to decide which word or phrase goes best in the first blank. Tell them the first answer, if necessary, and ask students to write it in their books. (Have them also cross it out in the box so they know they have used it already.) Then allow students to continue on their own until all the blanks are filled. They may work in pairs, if they wish.

Listen

Exercise 5: Play the tape so that students can check their answers. Play it several times for them to compare and, if necessary, change their answers.

Write

Exercise 6: Review numbers one through ten by counting together things in the Student Book and also in the classroom: One, two, three, four, five boys and girls (on the sofa on page 14, Exercise 1); *One, two kites* (on page 15, Exercise 4); *One, two, three, four, etc. books* (or other objects in the classroom).

Then have students count the objects listed below the birthday party scene on page 16. They can write the numeral or the number words for their answers. As extra credit, ask them to count how many answers they had to write (*eight*).

Exercise 7: Play a game! Tell students to look at page 17 in their books. Tell them they are going to play a game. Ask them to make themselves game markers out of small bits of paper. Give directions to play. The object is for students to move the number of steps you say and also name the object or number that they land on: Four. Four. (Students move four steps and say *ball*.)

A variation of the game is for students to count aloud how many steps it takes to get to the object or number you name: *Ball, ball.* (Students count four steps to the ball, saying *one, two, three, four*.)

Finally, allow groups of three students to play the game, with one as the caller and the other two as the players. The student who follows the caller's instructions correctly and gets to the finish line first wins.

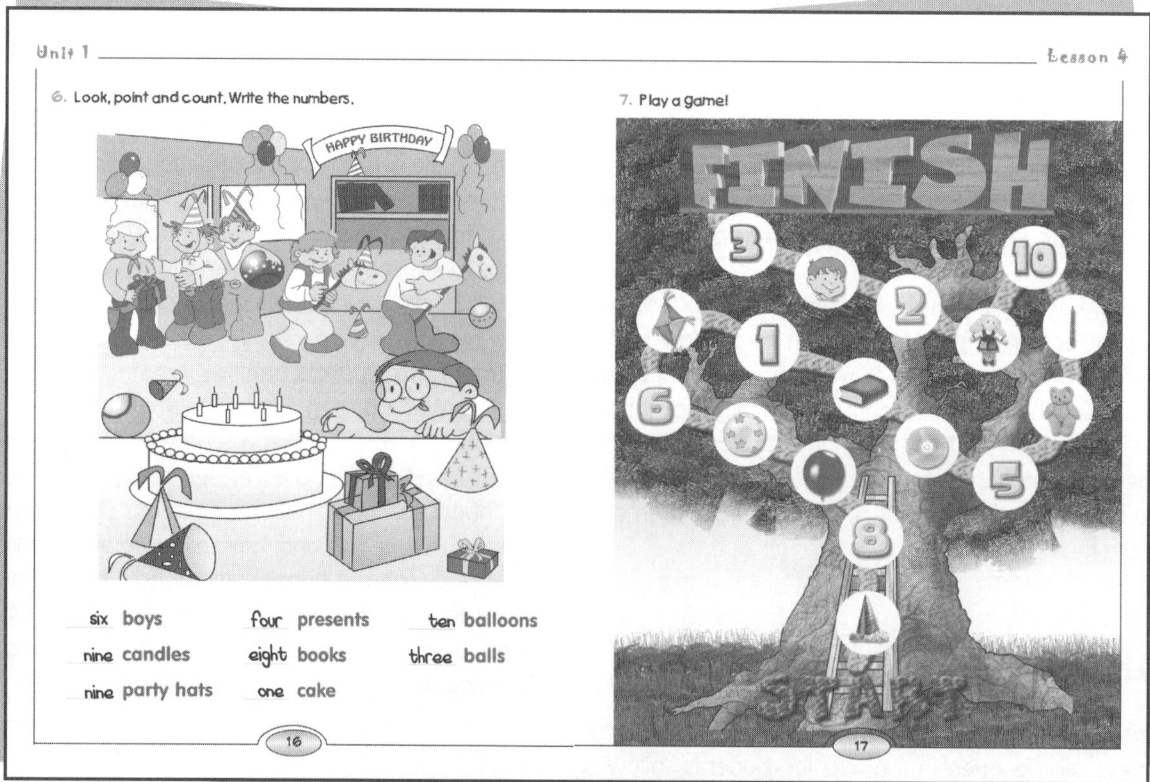

Fun and Games

A. **Picture and Word Concentration.** Have two volunteers bring to the front of the classroom their complete sets of Unit 1 picture and word cards. Using a large, flat surface such as table, place all the cards with either the picture side or the word side face down in random order (for numbers, the numerals are the "picture side"). Remind students that the object of the game is to find two pictures or words that match. Have one volunteer demonstrate by randomly picking up two cards at a time to see if they match. If they do, he or she places them together in a pile to the side and continues. If they don't match, he or she puts them back face down where they were. Then it is the other volunteer's turn. Pair students and have them play against each other with their sets of Unit 1 cards to see who gets the most cards. When they are finished playing, ask them to put their cards in order so that each student gets his or her cards back again.

B. **Happy Birthday!** Divide students into groups of four or five. Assign one student in each group to be the "birthday boy" or the "birthday girl." The others in the group should role-play giving them presents by handing over a picture card and saying *Happy Birthday, (name)! This is a (kite).* Encourage use of all Unit 1 vocabulary.

C. **Dictation.** Pair students and have them open one of the partner's Student Book to the game on page 17. One partner points to an object or number and "dictates" it for the other to write down on a separate sheet of paper. Then they reverse roles, alternating dictating and writing, until all the objects have been read and written by both students (*party hat, eight, balloon, ball, six, kite, one, book, CD, five, teddy bear,candle, ten, doll, two, boy, three*). Have students sign their names and hand in their papers. Check their spelling and return the lists for feedback.

Tapescript

Unit 1 Lesson 4 Page 15

Exercise 5: Listen and check your answers.

Boy: Look!
Bug: Is it a balloon?
Boy: No, it isn't. This is a kite.
Bug: A kite? Is it a kite?
Yes! This is a kite! Wheeee!

Unit 1 Test

Name______________________________ Date______________

1. Draw a birthday party. How old is this girl? ____________ Draw candles on the cake.

2. Match.

   1. party hat
   2. This is Steve.
   3. four dolls
   4. Hi! I'm Natalie.
   5. Is it a cake?

Yes, it is.

3. Write.

Example:  three books

1. 

____

2. 

____

3.  ______________________________

4. 

____

Unit 2

Lesson 1 It's a notebook.

Objectives

Students will:
- develop vocabulary related to school supplies
- learn colors

Materials
Best Friends Student Book 1 pages 18-21
Other Materials
index cards, colored construction paper, crayons or colored pencils, stick puppets; red, blue, yellow paint, stick puppet of a purple monster wearing a gray sweater

New Language
black, blue, gray, green, pink, purple, red, yellow
What's this/that? It's a...
Passive vocabulary
favorite color, monster
Spelling
backpack, crayons, desk, notebook, pencil case
pencil sharpener, pencils
pens, ruler

1. **Getting Started**

Ask students to look at the picture on page 18 in their Student Book. Talk about the people in the scene. Say *This is Mrs. Williams. This is Ken. This is Melba.* Then point to and name the labeled objects to introduce new vocabulary. Repeat several times and ask students to repeat with you.

Review numbers by counting aloud from one to ten. Then find objects in your classroom that are the same as the new vocabulary items, but mention *how many* items you see; for example, *one ruler, two notebooks, eight desks, ten crayons*. Ask students to repeat with you.

Play the audio for **Exercise 1**. Point to the vocabulary on page 18 as each item is mentioned.

Play the audio for **Exercise 2**. This time, students should point to the items as they are mentioned. Finally, play the audio a few more times for students to repeat along with it.

2. **Working Together**

Grammar Tips

- Note that *this* refers to a singular item that is very close to the person or persons talking about it, whereas *that* refers to a singular item that is further away from the person or persons talking about it.
- The contraction for *It is* is *It's*. In this case, a contraction is formed by replacing the first letter of the third-person singular verb *is* with an apostrophe. The question *What's this/that?* is another example of a contraction (*What's...? = What is...?*).

Introduce the structures in the Grammar Box by asking *What's this?* about a classroom vocabulary item that is close to you, and answer *It's a (desk).* Then point to the same item further away and ask and answer *What's that? It's a (desk).* Present a few more examples to contrast *this* and *that.* Be sure you only talk about singular items.

Invite students to look at **Exercise 3** on page 19 in the Student Book. Relate the ruler shown in number 1 to the labeled ruler in the scene on page 18 and also the word *ruler* in the word box. Pair students and have them do the exercise. Check answers as a class.

Then hand out seven index cards to each student and tell them to draw picture cards for all the items on page 18. They should show just one of each item, i.e., one crayon, one pen, etc. Then ask them to label each picture neatly on the back side, using page 18 as a spelling reference. Make your own set of cards. Then model asking *What's this?* by touching a random picture card; elicit an appropriate answer such as *It's a (pencil).* Model asking *What's that?* by placing a picture card on the chalk ledge and standing a distance from it. Elicit an appropriate answer. Finally, prompt students to ask and answer using their picture cards in the same way.

For **Exercise 4**, introduce the color words *red, blue, yellow,* and *green* by distributing four index cards to each student and making "picture" cards of these colors. (Color the card completely or color a large rectangle or other simple shape). Then hold up a card and say the color word several times, e.g., *red, red, red.* Ask students to repeat. Do the same for all the colors. Check comprehension by saying a color word and having students hold up the appropriate picture card.

Have students look at the pictures in **Exercise 4**. Play the audio, asking students to repeat.

Before playing the tape for **Exercise 5**, distribute index cards to make a picture card for each new color shown on page 20. Show and name all the color picture cards. Then play the audio, doing number 1 as an example together so that it is clear to students that they are listening for a purpose. Repeat tape as many times as necessary, until students finish the exercise. Then check the answers together as a class.

To introduce colors *gray* and *purple,* show students a stick puppet of a purple monster wearing a gray sweater. Pretend that the monster is speaking by making a "monster voice" and say *Hello, I'm Purpgray.. I like purple and gray.* As the monster mentions the two new colors, point to the monster and his sweater. Tell students to repeat these lines after you, until they learn the new colors. Then, let each student make a stick puppet of a monster and invent its name. They color it with the colors they like and then say to each other *Hello, I'm (name). I like (colors).*

3. **Finishing Up**

For **Exercise 6**, be sure everyone has several crayons. Read aloud the question in the first speech bubble, stressing the word *red.* Point to the blue crayon and shake your head no, vigorously, as you read the answer *No, it isn't.* Read the next question and then stress the word *blue* as you read the answer and point to the crayon. Then have students play the guessing game with crayons.

After students complete the color-by-number activity in **Exercise 7,** tell them that they can use pages 20 and 21 as a reference to write the color words on the back of their color picture cards. An alternative is to write the color words on the board for reference. Double-check spelling on the cards.

Fun and Games

A. **Make colors.** Demonstrate mixing certain colors to get other colors. Slowly name the colors you are using while mixing one paint with another: *Red... blue...purple! Blue...yellow...green! Red...white...pink! Black...white...gray!,* and so on. Repeat several times, encouraging students to say the colors along with you. (A messy alternative is to allow students to mix and name colors.)

B. **Color by number.** Have students create their own color-by-number drawings. They can draw individual lesson vocabulary items or entire scenes. Ask them to refer to (but not copy) the number-color key in Exercise 7 on page 21 in the Student Book. Invite each student to describe his or her artwork to the class, e.g., *This is a (desk). It's a (pink and blue) desk.*

C. **Dictation.** Use your set of Lesson 1 picture-word cards. Show the picture side of a random card and ask students to write the word you dictate. Indicate a number first, for listing purposes: *Number 1: pencil. Number 2: purple.,* and so on. Place the cards across a desk or table with the word side facing up from left to right for students to come up and check their spelling.

Tapescript

Unit 2 Lesson 1 Page 18
Exercise 1: Listen, point and count.

Mrs. Williams:	Please, for tomorrow...one box of ten crayons.
Melba	... One box of ten crayons.
Mrs. Williams:	Two pens and two pencils, please.
Ken:	Blue pens?
Mrs. Williams:	Blue or black pens. And a notebook.
Melba:	Is that a notebook?
Mrs. Williams:	Yes, this is a notebook. One notebook. Oh! And a pencil case and a pencil sharpener.
Ken:	... A pencil case and a pencil sharpener.
Mrs. Williams:	Yes. And one ruler, please.
Melba:	... One ruler. For tomorrow?
Mrs. Williams:	For tomorrow.

Unit 2 Lesson 1 Page 18
Exercise 2: Listen and repeat.
(See Exercise 1 above.)

Unit 2 Lesson 1 Page 20
Exercise 4: Listen and repeat.

1. Girl:	What's this?
Little boy:	It's a red crayon.
2. Girl:	What's that?
Little boy:	It's a blue crayon.
3. Girl:	What's this?
Little boy:	It's a yellow crayon.
4. Girl:	What's that?
Little boy:	It's a green crayon.

Unit 2 Lesson 1 Page 20
Exercise 5: Listen and circle.

1. Mariana:	My favorite color is pink.
2. Daniel:	My favorite color is red.
3. Melba:	My favorite color is green.
4. Natalie:	My favorite color is yellow.

Lesson 2 What's your favorite color?

Objectives

Students will:
- practice greetings
- listen for a purpose

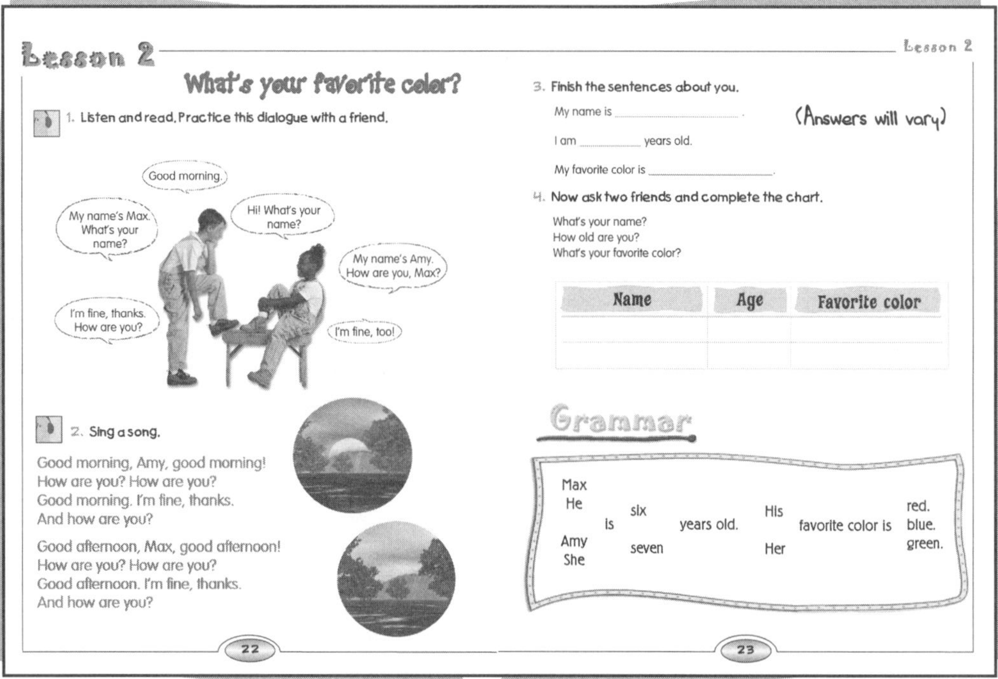

Lesson 2 — Lesson 2

What's your favorite color?

1. Listen and read. Practice this dialogue with a friend.

Good morning.
My name's Max. What's your name?
Hi! What's your name?
My name's Amy. How are you, Max?
I'm fine, thanks. How are you?
I'm fine, too!

2. Sing a song.

Good morning, Amy, good morning!
How are you? How are you?
Good morning. I'm fine, thanks.
And how are you?

Good afternoon, Max, good afternoon!
How are you? How are you?
Good afternoon. I'm fine, thanks.
And how are you?

3. Finish the sentences about you.

My name is ________.
I am ______ years old.
My favorite color is ________.

(Answers will vary)

4. Now ask two friends and complete the chart.

What's your name?
How old are you?
What's your favorite color?

Name	Age	Favorite color

Grammar

Max / He / Amy / She	is	six / seven	years old.	His / Her	favorite color is	red. / blue. / green.

22 — 23

Materials
Best Friends Student Book 1 pages 22-25
Other Materials
stick puppets, index cards, Lesson 1 color picture-word cards

New Language
Good morning/afternoon.
How are you? I'm fine, thanks.
What's your/his/her name?
My/your/his/her name is…
Passive Vocabulary
favorite color

1. **Getting Started**
Say *Hi (Hello), I'm (name). My name's (name).* Encourage students to return your greeting using this structure. Then present the statement and question *My name's (name). What's your name?* Stress *my* and *your* as you point to yourself and then to a student. Repeat the procedure with several students.

Play the audio for **Exercise 1** pointing to each speech balloon and tracing from left to right with a finger under the words as you read aloud. Ask students to listen the first time and trace with you. Then play the dialogue several times. Students should guess from the word order in the speech bubbles that *Good morning* and *Good afternoon* are also greetings. Finally, have pairs practice on their own.

Play the audio for **Exercise 2**. Every time *Good morning* is said, point to the morning scene next to the lyrics. Have students do the same. Repeat for *Good afternoon* in the second stanza of the song but this time pointing to the afternoon scene. Play the song several times and ask students to trace with a finger under the words in each line.

2. **Working Together**
For **Exercise 3**, use the Mariana stick puppet to model the information each student should fill in. Hold up six fingers as Mariana says her age, and move the puppet close to something that is pink as she says *I like (color). My favorite color is (pink).* Make sure everyone understands the concept of *favorite color* before doing the exercise. If students don't understand, show them several color cards. As you do this, express which ones you like and don't like, by smiling, frowning, and shaking your head yes or no. At the end, show the card with the color you like best, and with a big smile say *My favorite color is (red).* Then have students complete Exercise 3 and some of them read it aloud to check their answers.

For **Exercise 4**, model the activity by borrowing a volunteer's book and filling in his or her chart with one friend's name. (Spell out the number word for the age category; do not use numerals.) Let him or her continue with the second friend's information. Circulate to check that everyone is doing the activity correctly. You can then write the different colors on the board. Ask students what their favorite colors are and make a line on the board for each student to see what the favorite color of the class is.

Grammar Tips

- The personal pronoun *he* refers to third-person singular male subjects of sentences: *Max/he, a boy/he, a lion/he.* The personal pronoun she refers to third-person singular female subjects of sentences: *Amy/she, a girl/she, a lioness/she.* A sentence will have either the subject or the personal pronoun, never both at the same time: Correct: Max is a boy. He is a boy. Incorrect: Max, he is a boy.
- The possessive adjective his refers to third-person singular male subjects of sentences: *Max/his teddy bear, a boy/his favorite color.* The possessive adjective *her* refers to third-person singular female subjects of sentences: *Amy/her pencil, a lioness/her name.*

Point to Max, on page 22, and combine the words and phrases in the Grammar Chart on page 23 to show how *Max* and *He* are interchangeable and how *his* refers to a male: *Max is six (seven) years old. He is six (seven) years old. His favorite color is (red).* Repeat the procedure for Amy.

Distribute four index cards to each student and invite them to make word cards for *he, she, his,* and *her.* Practice the use of *he* and *she* by holding up a stick puppet, saying the name, e.g., *Natalie,* and eliciting the card *she.* Switch back and forth between male and female puppets to practice *he* and *she.* Encourage students to say the pronouns as they hold up the cards. Repeat the procedure for *his* and *her* by placing a stick puppet, e.g., Natalie, next to a desk and saying *Her name's Natalie. This is her desk.*

For **Exercise 5**, be sure students know whether names are for males or females (male: John, Mark; female: Sophia, Sandra, Anna).

Assign **Exercise 6**, helping as necessary with the instructions. Have students show their work to the two friends they drew to see if they agree with what they wrote.

3. Finishing Up

Play the audio for **Exercise 7** several times before students color the picture. If they have trouble getting the key color words, hold up the appropriate color picture card as an aid.

For **Exercise 8**, be sure students understand they have to choose either the *a* or *b* answer. If necessary, do the first one as an example together. Have partners exchange books and correct each other's work.

For **Exercise 7**, distribute crayons, scissors, and glue. Tell students their friends don't have to be someone in the classroom; they can draw anyone. Help them with the spelling of names as necessary.

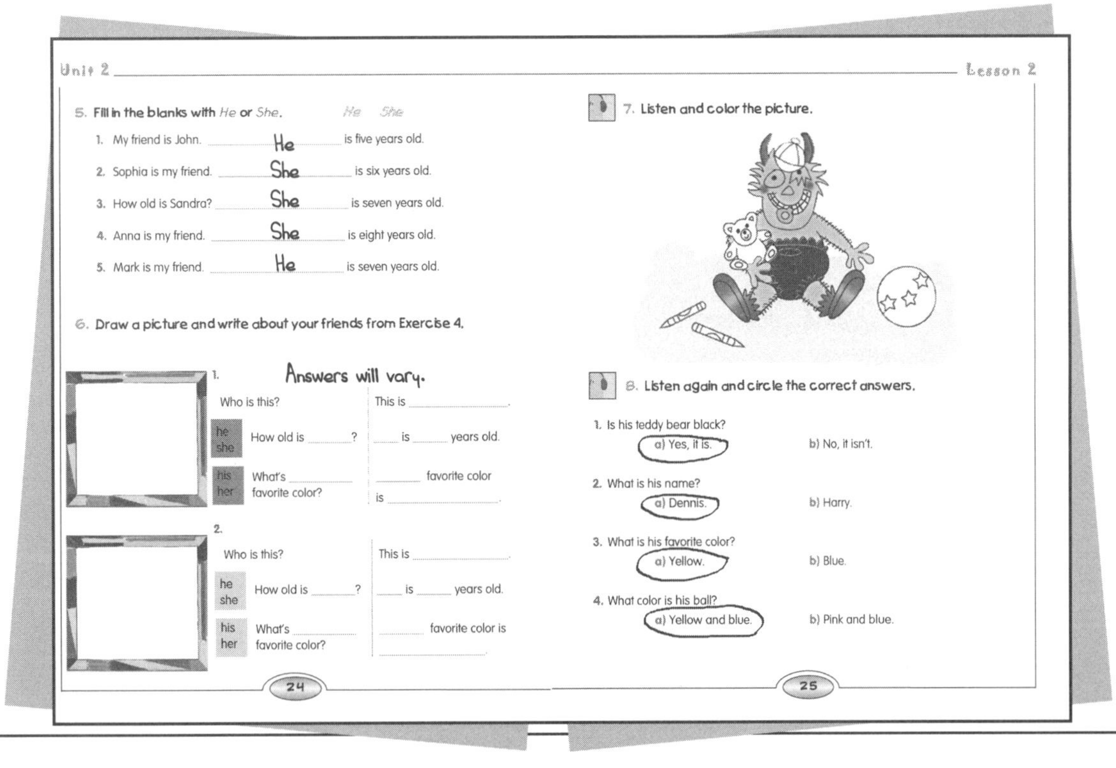
Unit 2 — Lesson 2

5. Fill in the blanks with *He* or *She*. He She

1. My friend is John. He is five years old.
2. Sophia is my friend. She is six years old.
3. How old is Sandra? She is seven years old.
4. Anna is my friend. She is eight years old.
5. Mark is my friend. He is seven years old.

6. Draw a picture and write about your friends from Exercise 4.

Answers will vary.

1. Who is this? This is ______. he/she How old is ______? ______ is ______ years old. his/her What's ______ favorite color? ______ favorite color is ______.

2. Who is this? This is ______. he/she How old is ______? ______ is ______ years old. his/her What's ______ favorite color? ______ favorite color is ______.

7. Listen and color the picture.

8. Listen again and circle the correct answers.

1. Is his teddy bear black? a) Yes, it is. b) No, it isn't.
2. What is his name? a) Dennis. b) Harry.
3. What is his favorite color? a) Yellow. b) Blue.
4. What color is his ball? a) Yellow and blue. b) Pink and blue.

24 25

Fun and Games

A. **What's his/her favorite color?** Place the stick puppets spread out on the chalk ledge. Ask students to indicate what they think each puppet's favorite color is by either saying the color word or placing a color picture card next to the puppet. Write the color words on the board as they are mentioned and mark how many puppets "prefer" blue versus red versus green, etc.

B. **Chain.** Have everyone stand in a circle. Ask the student to your right *What's your name?* Elicit *My name's (name).* Have that student ask the person to his or her right the same question, going around in a chain until the last student asks you *What's your name?* An alternative chain is to ask and answer *What's your favorite color?/My favorite color is (pink).*

C. ***Good morning* or *Good afternoon*?** Pair students and have them role-play the use of *Good morning* or *Good afternoon* as appropriate to the time your English class meets. One partner is the teacher sitting at a desk, and the other is the student. Emphasize that each should say the same thing. For more practice, one partner can draw on the board the sun coming up, as seen on page 22 in the Student Book, to elicit *Good morning.* A picture of a darkening sky could indicate afternoon, as could a clock showing the *p.m.* designation.

Tapescript

Unit 2 Lesson 2 Page 22

Exercise 1: Listen and read.

Max: Good morning.
Amy: Hi. What's your name?
Max: My name is Max. What's your name?
Amy: My name is Amy. How are you, Max?
Max: I'm fine, thanks. How are you?
Amy: I'm fine, too!

Unit 2 Lesson 2 Page 22

Exercise 2: Sing a song.

Max : Good morning, Amy, good morning!
How are you? How are you?
Amy: Good morning. I'm fine, thanks.
And how are you?
Amy: Good afternoon, Max, good afternoon!
How are you? How are you?
Max: Good afternoon. I'm fine, thanks.
And how are you?

Unit 2 Lesson 2 Page 25

Exercise 7: Listen and color the picture.

This is Dennis! He is one year old. His favorite color is yellow. His ball is yellow and blue and his hat is red. His teddy bear is black. His crayons are yellow and pink. He is happy!

Unit 2 Lesson 2 Page 25

Exercise 8: Listen again and circle the correct answers.

(See Exercise 7 above.)

Lesson 3 Where's the pencil?

Objectives

Students will:
- learn place prepositions
- recognize the alphabet

Materials
Best Friends Student Book 1 pages 26-29
Other Materials
index cards, scissors, glue, the Mariana stick puppet

New Language
chair
table
Where's the…?
It's in/on/under…

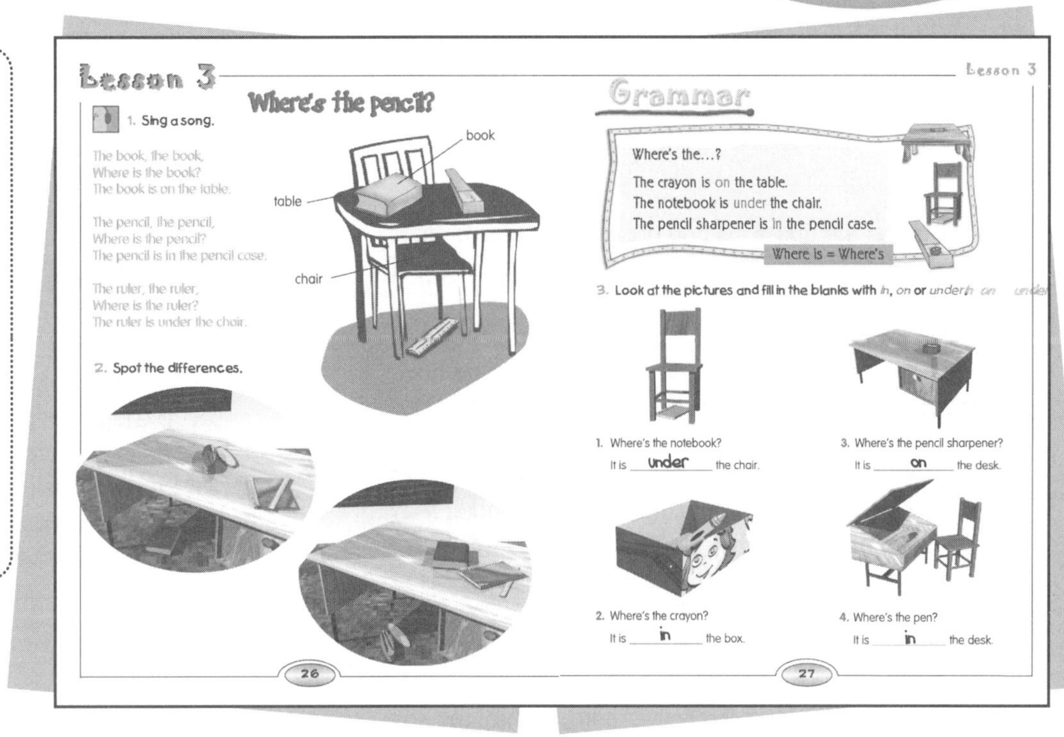

1. **Getting Started**
(Do the following every day that the class meets from now to the end of the school year: Greet students with *Good morning* or *Good afternoon*, depending on the time the class meets. Encourage them to respond to you and also greet one another.

Introduce the structure *Where is (the ruler)?* by placing a ruler on a desk, for example, asking the question, and answering *It's on the desk.* Repeat the procedure, substituting the prepositions *in* and *under* and placing the ruler correctly with respect to the desk (*in, on,* or *under*).

Review *book* and *chair,* and introduce the new vocabulary, *table*, by pointing to and naming the same objects in the classroom. Ask students to repeat.

Play the audio for **Exercise 1**. Go over the song, pointing to each line and tracing from left to right with a finger under the words as you read aloud. Ask students to do the same. Then play the song stanza by stanza and point to the book and table (pencil and pencil case, ruler and chair) in Exercise 1 as each one is mentioned. Finally, play the song again and encourage students to point to each object and its label as mentioned.

2. **Working Together**
For **Exercise 2**, ask students to point to objects in the scenes when you point to a specific item in the first picture and ask, e.g., *Where is the (notebook)?* Repeat the question for the second picture. Check that students identify the "pairs" and realize the position is different. Depending on how capable students are in English, ask them to answer in complete sentences, phrases, or one-word answers. For example, (first picture) *The pencil case is on the table; on the table; on;* (second picture) *The pencil case is under the table; under the table; under.*

Grammar Tips

- The definite article *the* precedes nouns that have been determined (that is, when we have mentioned the noun before, or when there is only one), e.g., *the table in the classroom.* We are talking about a specific table in a specific classroom.
- The article *the* is used for both singular and plural nouns: *the ruler, the rulers.*

- ✤ Prepositions such as *in, on,* and *under* show how an item or items are positioned with respect to one another or to another item: *The teddy bear is on the table. The teddy bears are in the desks. The blue teddy bear is under the chair.*
- ✤ The question *Where's the...?* is another example of a contraction (*Where's...? = Where is...?*).

Go over the questions and answers in the Grammar Box, making sure students understand the placement of the objects.

For **Exercise 3**, do number 1 together as an example. Write the prepositions on the board if students have trouble identifying them in the instructions. Have students exchange books and check one another's work.

Then distribute three index cards to each student and have them create word cards for *in, on, under*. They can go to page 27 in their books for spelling reference. Make your own set of cards as well. Using your set of cards, demonstrate the following activity: Place any object in, on, and under some other object, e.g., a pen in a backpack, a pen on your head, a pen under a book. Have students hold up the correct card, or they can say the preposition aloud. Then have pairs practice with their cards.

For **Exercise 4**, pair students and distribute scissors and glue. Help them find the correct page at the back of their books (page 149). At this point, ask students to make picture-word cards for *table*.

For **Exercise 5**, students should already be familiar with the concept of an alphabet and a system of writing for their native language. Encourage them to recognize the English-language letter names by playing the audio several times as students follow in their books and attempt to chant along. When you are sure they recognize the letters, play the tape again and ask them to point to each letter as it is chanted in the tape.

Then distribute twenty-six index cards to each student to create their own alphabet letter cards using Exercise 5 as a reference. Tell them to keep them in a pile in order from *A* to *Z*. Say the alphabet in groups of three consecutive letters, e.g., *A, B, C* or *D, E, F*, and have students hold up those cards.

For **Exercise 6**, tell students to listen to the tape and fill in the blanks. If they have problems, tell them to refer to the alphabet on page 28 for order reference.

3. Finishing Up

For **Exercise 7** students can work in groups, sharing scissors and glue. Tell them to paste the objects that go in the backpack in the first column and the objects that go in the toy chest in the second column. When they finish, tell them to show you their work to check them.

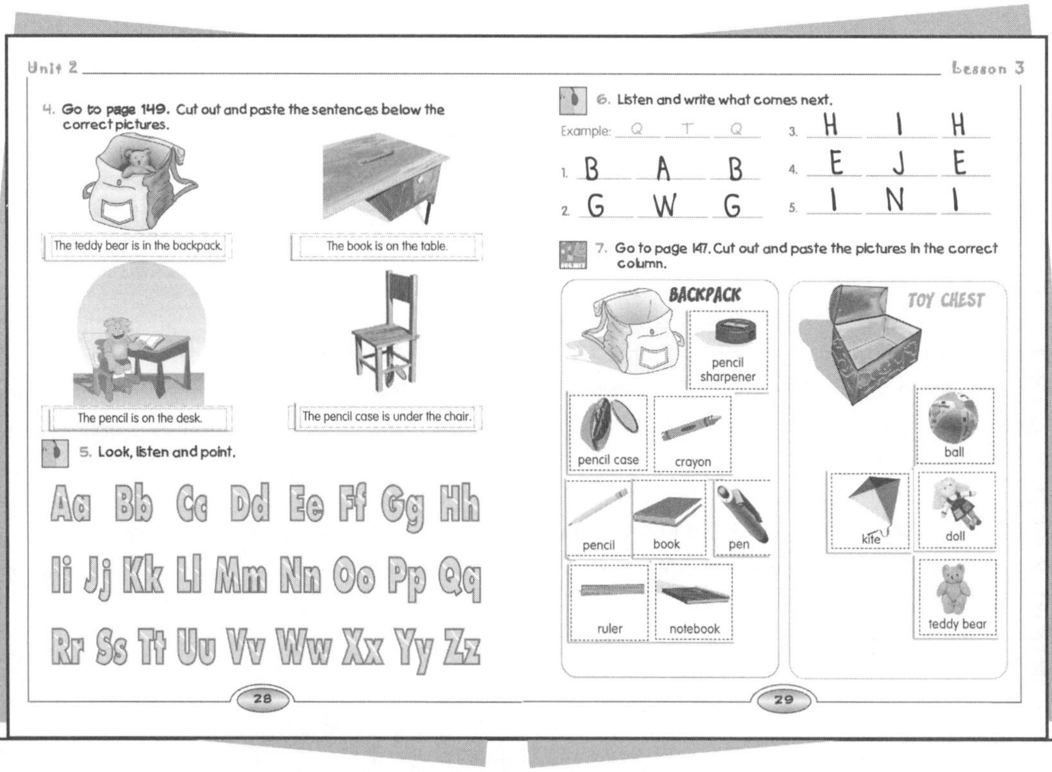

Unit 2 — Lesson 3

4. Go to page 149. Cut out and paste the sentences below the correct pictures.

The teddy bear is in the backpack. | The book is on the table. | The pencil is on the desk. | The pencil case is under the chair.

5. Look, listen and point.

Aa Bb Cc Dd Ee Ff Gg Hh
Ii Jj Kk Ll Mm Nn Oo Pp Qq
Rr Ss Tt Uu Vv Ww Xx Yy Zz

6. Listen and write what comes next.

Example: Q T Q
1. B A B
2. G W G
3. H I H
4. E J E
5. I N I

7. Go to page 147. Cut out and paste the pictures in the correct column.

BACKPACK: pencil sharpener, pencil case, crayon, pencil, book, pen, ruler, notebook

TOY CHEST: ball, kite, doll, teddy bear

28 29

Fun and Games

A. **Where is Mariana?** Place the Mariana stick puppet in a box. Ask and answer *Where's Mariana? She's in the box.* Put the puppet in other places, such as on the box or under the box, or in someone's backpack, and encourage a chorus of the question and answer each time. Do the activity faster and faster, and finally make the puppet "collapse" in exhaustion on a desk to end the game.

B. **Say the letter.** Be sure all students have their sets of alphabet cards. Divide the class into groups of five or six. Students must stand up for this activity. Alternate holding up letters and have students hold up the exact same card as quickly as possible. When everyone is holding up a card, name the letter together loudly. Then check that everyone has the same card. Any student who isn't showing the correct card must sit down. Repeat the procedure faster and faster until only one student is left standing in each group.

C. **Dictation.** Use one set of word cards for *in, on,* and *under.* Divide the class into two teams. The first person on Team A reads a word card aloud, and the first person on Team B writes it on the board. If the word is spelled correctly, Team B gets a point; if it is wrong, Team A gets a point. Teams switch roles. Go through the cards as often as necessary to give everyone a chance to dictate and write. The team with the most points at the end wins.

Tapescript

Unit 2 Lesson 3 Page 26

Exercise 1: Sing and song.

The book, the book
Where is the book?
The book is on the table.

The pencil, the pencil
Where is the pencil?
The pencil is in the pencil case.

The ruler, the ruler,
Where is the ruler?
The ruler is under the chair.

Unit 2 Lesson 3 Page 28

Exercise 5: Look and listen.

Aa Bb Cc Dd Ee Ff Gg Hh Ii Jj Kk Ll Mm Nn Oo Pp Qq
Rr Ss Tt Uu Vv Ww Xx Yy Zz

Unit 2 Lesson 3 Page 29

Exercise 6: Listen and write what comes next.

Example: Q T Q
1. B A B
2. G W G
3. H I H
4. E J E
5. I N I

Lesson 4 Review

Objectives

Students will:

- read a dialogue
- review language from Lessons 1-3
- differentiate between /p/ and /b/

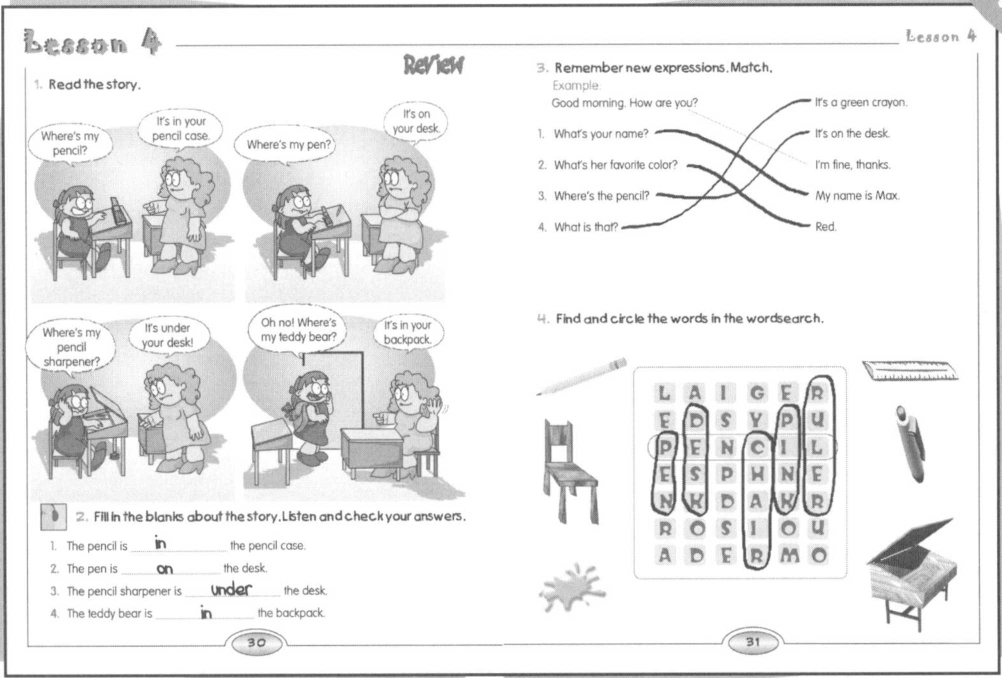

Lesson 4 — Lesson 4

Review

1. Read the story.

2. Fill in the blanks about the story. Listen and check your answers.

1. The pencil is __in__ the pencil case.
2. The pen is __on__ the desk.
3. The pencil sharpener is __under__ the desk.
4. The teddy bear is __in__ the backpack.

3. Remember new expressions. Match.

Example:
Good morning. How are you? — I'm fine, thanks.

1. What's your name? — It's a green crayon.
2. What's her favorite color? — It's on the desk.
3. Where's the pencil? — I'm fine, thanks.
4. What is that? — My name is Max.

Red.

4. Find and circle the words in the wordsearch.

L	A	I	G	E	R
E	D	S	Y	P	U
P	E	N	C	I	L
E	S	P	H	N	E
N	K	D	A	K	R
R	O	S	I	O	U
A	D	E	R	M	O

30 31

Materials

Best Friends Student Book 1 pages 30-33

Other Materials

stick puppets, picture and word cards from Lessons 1-3 for Units 1 and 2, bits of paper for game markers, crayons or colored pencils, paper

Read

Exercise 1: Dialogue summary. A story in dialogue format tells about a girl who can't keep her things in order. She asks her teacher where her pencil is, where her pen is, where her pencil sharpener is, and where her teddy bear is. Each time the teacher tells the girl where the things are because the teacher can see them.

Read the dialogue aloud, pointing to each speech bubble as you read. Ask students to listen and follow in their books. For fun, change voices to represent different speakers. Then read the dialogue again and encourage students to read aloud with you. Finally, assign the roles of the girl and the teacher to pairs of capable students. They can use the book to read their parts or they can try to memorize and recite their parts. If possible, have them role-play the scenes with props.

Story Comprehension

Exercise 2: Do number 1 together as an example: *The pencil is in the pencil case.* Then read all the questions aloud for students, allowing time for them to fill in their answers. When everyone is done, play the audio to check answers as a class.

Vocabulary

Exercise 3: Review the concepts of matching and asking/answering questions logically by reading aloud the example. Be sure to use a rising intonation for the question. Then read the numbered questions one at a time and ask students to find the logical match to it, e.g., *What's your name?/My name is Max.* They can read the answer aloud or point to it in their books. Give everyone a chance to answer a question.

Then have students practice the structures by handing out the stick puppets to volunteers. Encourage them to role-play the situations using the puppets and props in the classroom such as a green crayon, a desk, and something red. Give several groups of students turns at using the puppets.

Exercise 4: Start students off by reviewing the capital letters of the alphabet and reminding them that words are formed by putting together certain letters. Tell them that the pictures represent the words they have to find in the puzzle. Read the circled example aloud letter by letter. (Have them also cross out the picture so they know they have found it already.) Then allow students to continue on their own. They may work in pairs, if they wish.

Listen

Exercise 5: Play the audio for students several times so that they practice the letter pronunciation and tracing. Students should listen and repeat several times. Then tell them to trace the letters as they repeat what they hear in the tape. At the end, they can listen to the tape one more time and repeat while they trace in their books.

Exercise 6: Review /p/ and /b/ words in Units 1 and 2 by showing picture cards: for /p/, *present, pen, pencil, pencil case, pencil sharpener*; for /b/, *ball, balloon, book, boy*. Then divide your class into three teams. Team A is going to answer line one, Team B, line two, and Team C, line three. Go over the example, making sure they understand what they have to do. Then, Team A mentions the three objects in their line and chooses the correct one. Teams B and C do the same. The other two teams say if they are correct or if there is a mistake.

Exercise 7: Play a game! Review vocabulary with all picture-word cards from Units 1 and 2. Hold up either the picture side or the word side and elicit the vocabulary.

Then tell students to look at page 33 in their books. Tell them they are going to play Bingo. Give directions to cut out the "mini" word cards at the back of the book (page 155). The object is for students to paste the words in the boxes in any position they choose. (There are more words than Bingo squares.) Call out random words for students to place markers on until someone has one item marked in each of rows across 1 through 3 or columns down 1 through 3. Continue calling out words until someone completes one column or row. This student shouts out *Bingo!* and becomes the caller.

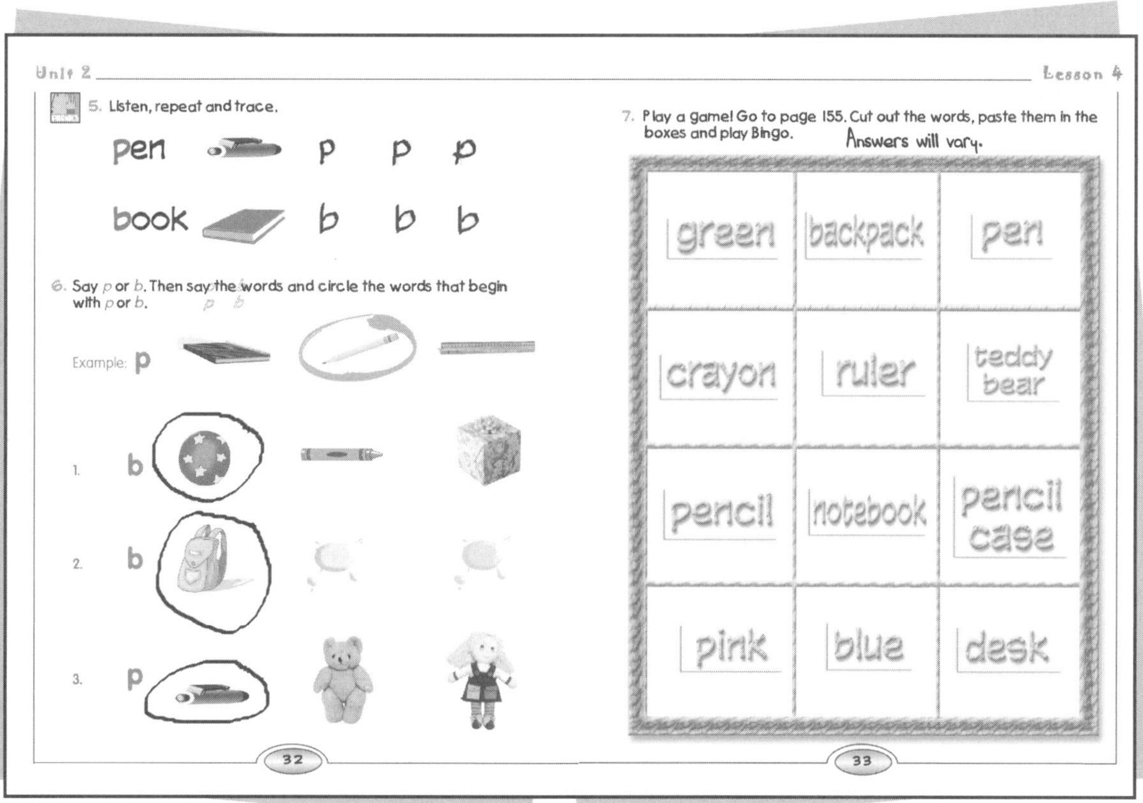

Unit 2

5. Listen, repeat and trace.

pen p p p

book b b b

6. Say *p* or *b*. Then say the words and circle the words that begin with *p* or *b*.

Example: p

1. b

2. b

3. p

32

Lesson 4

7. Play a game! Go to page 155. Cut out the words, paste them in the boxes and play Bingo.

Answers will vary.

green	backpack	pen
crayon	ruler	teddy bear
pencil	notebook	pencil case
pink	blue	desk

33

Fun and Games

A. **Where is he/she?** A variation on the *Where's Mariana* game in Lesson 3 is to ask about students. Have a volunteer stand on a notebook. Ask and answer *Where's (Toni)? He's on the notebook.* Then ask each student to position himself or herself somewhere in the room using available classroom objects and other props. Encourage a chorus of the question and answer each time. Do the activity faster and faster. Accept incomplete answers.

B. **Chain.** Have everyone stand in a circle. Ask the student to *your* right about the student to *his or her* right *What's his/her name?* Elicit *His/Her name's (name).* Have the student to your right do the same, going around in a chain until the last student asks you about the student to your right *What's his/her name?* Give the answer to complete the chain.

C. **Draw!** Divide the class into five teams and distribute crayons or colored pencils of the colors learned and sheets of paper. Using Unit 2 vocabulary, tell the first student in each team what to draw, then the second student, the third, etc. e.g., *a blue notebook on a red chair, boys under backpacks.* Whoever finishes first (and correctly) gets a point for his or her team. The team with the most points wins.

Tapescript

Unit 2 Lesson 4 Page 30

Exercise 2: Listen and check your answers.

1. The pencil is in the pencil case.
2. The pen is on the desk.
3. The pencil sharpener is under the desk.
4. The teddy bear is in the backpack.

Unit 2 Lesson 4 Page 32

Exercise 5: Listen, repeat and trace.

pen /p/ /p/ /p/ pen
book /b/ /b/ /b/ book

Unit 2 Test

Name____________________________________ Date________________

1. Draw:

1. two red pencils
2. four yellow desks.
3. The boy is on the chair.
4. The girl is under the table.

2. Match.

1. her doll
2. his notebooks
3. his ruler
4. her teddy bears

3. Write.

1. The book is _______ the backpack.
2. The pen is _______ the desk.
3. The doll is _______ the notebook.
4. The ball is _______ the toy chest.

Unit 3

Lesson 1 Who are they?

Objectives

Students will:
- learn colors
- listen for a purpose

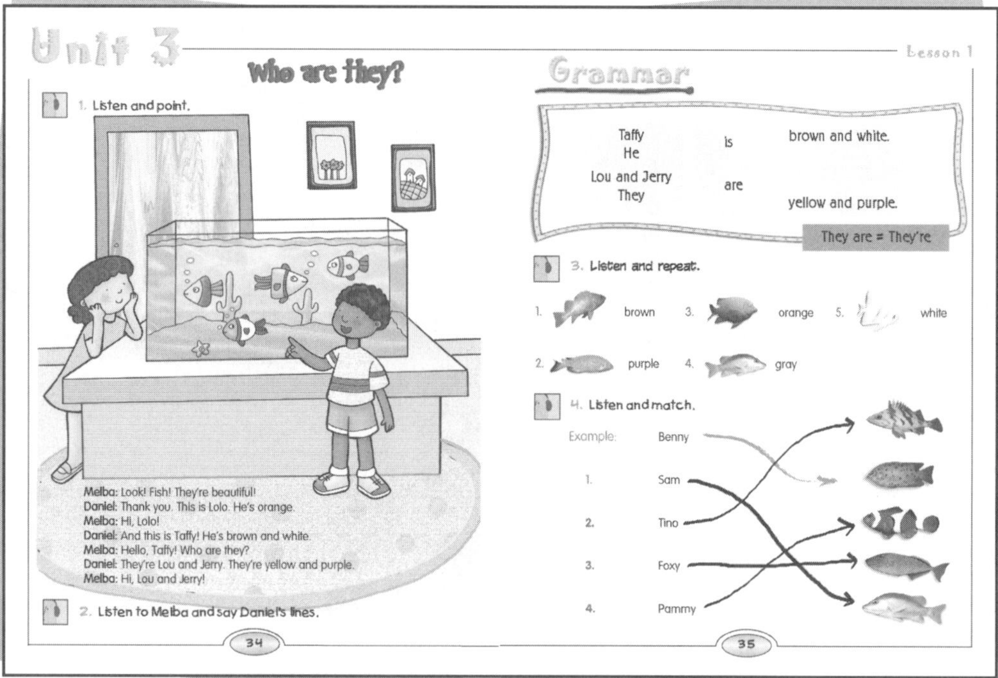
Unit 3 — Lesson 1

Who are they?

1. Listen and point.

Melba: Look! Fish! They're beautiful!
Daniel: Thank you. This is Lolo. He's orange.
Melba: Hi, Lolo!
Daniel: And this is Taffy! He's brown and white.
Melba: Hello, Taffy! Who are they?
Daniel: They're Lou and Jerry. They're yellow and purple.
Melba: Hi, Lou and Jerry!

2. Listen to Melba and say Daniel's lines.

34

Grammar

Taffy He	is	brown and white.
Lou and Jerry They	are	yellow and purple.

They are = They're

3. Listen and repeat.

1. brown 3. orange 5. white
2. purple 4. gray

4. Listen and match.

Example: Benny
1. Sam
2. Tino
3. Foxy
4. Pammy

35

Materials
Best Friends Student Book 1 pages 34-37
Other Materials
index cards, stick puppets, Unit 2 color picture-word cards, crayons or colored pencils, old *National Geographic* (or similar magazines), scissors, glue

New Language
brown
orange
white
Passive Vocabulary
beautiful
Who...?

1. **Getting Started**
Introduce the color words *orange, brown,* and *white* by distributing index cards to each student and making picture cards of these colors. Then hold up a card and say the color word several times, e.g., *orange, orange, orange.* Ask students to repeat. Do the same for all the colors. Check comprehension by saying a color word and having students hold up the appropriate picture card. Finally, show your picture cards and write on the board the color words for students to copy onto the backside.

Present the pronoun *they* in the following way: Show any of the male puppets, for example, the Daniel puppet, and say *He. He's Daniel.* Then show two puppets, male or female, and say *They. They're (Melba) and (Daniel).* Check comprehension by contrasting the Ken puppet with any pair of puppets and elicit from students *He. He's Ken. They. They're (Mariana) and (Natalie).* Repeat for the Steve puppet and another pair of puppets.

Make students understand the concept of *beautiful* by showing pictures of really pretty, colorful scenes of animals, such as those in *National Geographic* magazine, and saying *Look! They're beautiful!* Then ask students to look at the picture on page 34 in their Student Book. Point to the fish in the scene and say *Look! Fish! They're beautiful!* Have students repeat. Depending on students' level, ask them to identify other beautiful objects around them. They can point or say *beautiful.*

Play the audio for **Exercise 1**. As each character speaks, students should trace with a finger under the words in the lines. Play the audio a second time and encourage students to knock on each color word loudly as it is mentioned.

Play the audio for **Exercise 2**. Repeat several times as necessary until students can repeat Daniel's lines with confidence and reasonably correct pronunciation.

2. **Working Together**

Grammar Tips

- The personal pronoun *they* refers to third-person plural male, female, and neutral subjects of sentences: *boys, girls, fish, books = they.* A sentence will have either the subject or the personal pronoun, never both at the same time: Correct-*Max and Daniel are boys. They are boys.* Incorrect-*Max and Daniel, they are boys.*
- The contraction for *They are* is *They're.* In this case, a contraction is formed by replacing the first letter of the third-person plural verb *are* with an apostrophe.
- The position of adjectives such as colors can fall before the nouns they modify or after a conjugated form of the verb *be: the blue chair/The chair is blue. the red books/The books are red.*

Teach the structures in the Grammar Box by pointing to the appropriate fish on page 34 as you read the sentences. Emphasize the substitution of proper names for personal pronouns. Then encourage students to name the colors of items in the classroom. e.g., *Look. (Books.) They are (green) and (orange).*

Play the audio for **Exercise 3**. Tell students to look at their books and repeat. Then practice the new colors by playing the tape again and asking students to hold up and say the appropriate color picture card as each color is mentioned.

Before playing the tape for **Exercise 4**, pronounce all the names, including the example name, for easier audio recognition. Then play the tape up to the end of the example. Be sure students understand the example before continuing.

3. **Finishing Up**
Pair students and have them work on **Exercise 5** together, following the example. When students are done, check answers together. As answers are given, a volunteer could hold up the appropriate color picture card or write on the board the color words as they are mentioned. Finally, have students create a word card of the word *they* to keep with the rest of their word cards.

For **Exercise 6**, distribute crayons or colored pencils. Hold up color picture cards, if necessary, to help students read the sentences and color the fish.

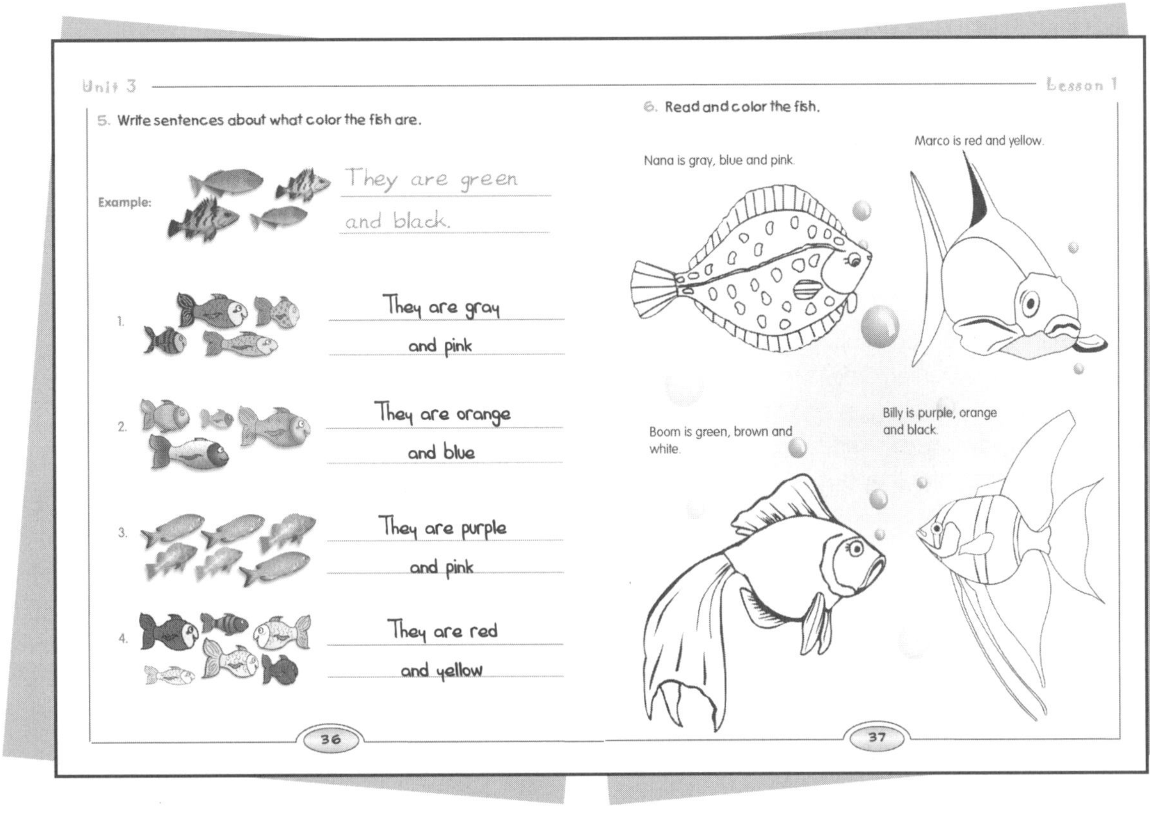

Fun and Games

A. **What's his/her name?** Have students draw a picture of a fish, using as many colors as they like. Encourage them to give the fish a name, which they can write at the top of their artwork. Suggest that students write speech bubbles for their fish, similar to those in Exercise 6, page 5 in their Student Book, saying what color the fish is. For example, *I am red, green, and white.* Help with writing as necessary. Display the pictures on a bulletin board.

B. **Look!** Pair students. Have them color in all the picture cards they have accumulated so far (if they haven't already done so) and combine them with their partner's cards so there are two of each picture card. Then one partner matches up, for example, the two pen picture cards by saying *Look. Pens.* The other partner says the color or colors, e.g., *They are (blue).* or *They are (yellow) and (brown).*

C. **Dictation.** Use your complete set of color picture-word cards. Show the picture side of any card and ask students to write the word you dictate. Indicate a number first, for listing purposes: *number 1: gray; number 2: orange,* and so on until all the colors have been dictated. Place the cards across a desk or table with the word side facing up from left to right for students to come up and check their spelling.

Tapescript

Unit 3 Lesson 1 Page 34

Exercise 1: Listen and point.

Melba: Look! Fish! They're beautiful!
Daniel: Thank you. This is Lolo. He's orange.
Melba: Hi, Lolo.
Daniel: And this is Taffy. He's brown and white.
Melba: Hello, Taffy! Who are they?
Daniel: They're Lou and Jerry. They're yellow and purple.
Melba: Hi, Lou and Jerry!

Unit 3 Lesson 1 Page 34

Exercise 2: Listen to Melba and say Daniel's lines.

Melba: Look! Fish! They're beautiful!
(Pause for students to say Daniel's line.)
Melba: Hi, Lolo!
(Pause for students to say Daniel's line.)
Melba: Hello, Taffy! Who are they?
(Pause for students to say Daniel's line.)
Melba: Hi, Lou and Jerry!

Unit 3 Lesson 1 Page 35

Exercise 3: Listen and repeat.

This is a brown fish.
This is a purple fish.
This is an orange fish.
This is a gray fish.
This is a white fish.

Unit 3 Lesson 1 Page 35

Exercise 4: Listen and match.

Example: Benny is an orange and purple fish.

Sam is a gray and green fish.
Tino is a pink and brown fish.
Foxy is a yellow and purple fish.
Pammy is a red and white fish.

Lesson 2 Look at these dogs!

Objectives

Students will:
- develop vocabulary related to pets

Materials
Best Friends Student Book 1
pages 38-41
Other Materials
index cards, crayons, toy and party picture cards from Unit 1, scissors, paste

New Language
Look at these/those…
Passive Vocabulary
animals
Come here now.
I'm sorry.
Spelling
bird(s)
cat(s)
dog(s)
fish
parrots(s)
turtle(s)

1. **Getting Started**

Present *these* and *those* by holding up or standing near two familiar classroom objects, e.g., books, pencils, or desks. Say *Look at these. They're (books). Look at these (books).* Have students repeat. Then stand further away from the items and say. *Look at those. They're (books). Look at those (books).* Then ask students to look at page 38 in their Student Book. Point to the two dogs, touching the page, and say *Look at these dogs.* Point to the two cats without touching the book page and say *Look at those cats.*

Play the audio for **Exercise 1**. Point to each speech balloon and trace from left to right with a finger under the words as you read aloud. Ask students to listen the first time and trace with you. Then play the dialogue several times and have students repeat.

For **Exercise 2**, review the structures *What's his/her name?* by asking *What's her name?* as you point to Mariana. Elicit *Her name is Mariana.* Then elicit the animals' names (*Rex* or *Pete*; *Bianca* or *Maggie*) by asking *What's his/her name?* Then read the dialogue aloud. Encourage students to knock on their desks when they hear an animal's name. Finally, have them fill in the animal names.

2. **Working Together**

Grammar Tips

- Note that *these* refers to plural items that are very close to the person or persons talking about them, whereas *those* refer to plural items that are at a distance from the person or persons talking about them.
- The question *What are these/those…?* can be contracted in spoken English and dialogues to *What're these/those…?*, but *What are* is not contracted in written English that does not represent a dialogue.

Drill the structures in the Grammar Box using crayons. Place five or six groups of crayons around the room. Model *Look at these crayons.* by standing next to them and pointing. Then model *Look at those crayons.* by standing at some distance. Do this several times to contrast *these* and *those*. Repeat the procedure, but make sure at least two of the crayons in the group are the same color. Say *Look at these crayons.*

They're (green). Look at those crayons. They're (red). Then find objects in the classroom that are two colors and say *Look at these/those (desks). They're (blue and white).*

Have students look at **Exercise 3** on page 39 in the Student Book. Review the colors in the word box by pointing to objects in the classroom that are those colors. Say, for example, *Look at these (pens). They're (orange). Look at those (fish). They're (red) and (blue).* Be sure to reinforce the difference between *these* and *those* by distancing yourself properly from the objects you are mentioning.

Review or introduce vocabulary related to animals and pets. Point to each picture and say the words: *dogs, cats, turtles, fish, birds/parrots.* Have students repeat with you. Then write the words on the board under the heading *Animals.* Point to all the animals on page 38 in the Student Book and say *Look at those cats and dogs. They're animals.* Point to all the animals on page 39 and say *Look at those animals. They're dogs. They're cats. They're turtles. They're fish. They're birds/parrots.* Distribute two index cards to each student to draw picture cards for the new vocabulary *turtle* and *bird.* Be sure students draw only one animal in each case. Have them write the word on the other side. Then ask students to complete the activity. Pairs can compare answers and practice the structures. Finally, play the tape for students to check their answers.

For **Exercise 4,** ask *What are these?* about several crayons. Answer, for example, *They're (green) crayons.* or *They're (green and yellow) crayons.* Repeat for *What are those?,* but stand at a distance from the crayons. Then review all the colors seen in the pictures by holding up crayons of the same color (or color picture cards from Unit 2) and saying the color word. Finally, have students complete the activity. Be sure they know they must circle the best answer based on the picture.

For reinforcement, ask students to separate out all toy and party items (from Unit 1, Lesson 1) from their picture cards. Working in pairs, partners match their cards so that there are pairs of each item. One partner points to any pair of cards right next to him or her and asks *What are these?* The other answers *They're (cakes).* Then they switch roles, alternating asking *What are these/those?* by having the pair of cards near or further away.

3. Finishing Up

Assign **Exercise 5,** helping as necessary with the instructions. Students may work in pairs, if they wish. Have pairs compare answers with other pairs or individuals.

Unit 3 Lesson 2

4. Look at the picture and circle the correct answer.

1. What are these?
a) They're red and yellow fish.
b) They're gray and pink fish.

3. What are these?
a) They're yellow cats.
b) They're gray cats.

2. What are those?
a) They're brown and white dogs.
b) They're brown and white cats.

4. What are those?
a) They're green turtles.
b) They're purple turtles.

5. Go to page 149. Cut out and paste the animals in the right place on the shelf.

40 41

Fun and Games

A. **Look at these/those...!** Divide students into small groups spread out around the classroom. Go to one group, wave your hand over their heads, and say *Look at these fish!* The group must pantomime being fish. The other groups decide if the group represented the animal correctly or not. When everyone agrees, go to another group, stand somewhat away, and point toward them. Say *Look at those cats!* They pantomime this animal, and so on. Alternate animal names *(dogs, cats, turtles, fish, birds/parrots)* and the use of *these* and *those* until every group has had a chance to pantomime.

B. **Animals.** Each student draws a set of his or her favorite animal from this lesson. They can color them as they wish. Encourage them to write about their animals, e.g., *They're (parrots). They're (purple) (parrots).* or *They're (purple) and (pink) (parrots).* Display students' work on the bulletin board under the heading *Animals.*

C. **Picture Dictation.** Distribute large sheets of paper and crayons. Dictate the following sentences for students to draw (not write): *Number 1. They're brown and green turtles. Number 2. They're red dogs. Number 3. They're gray and purple cats. Number 4. They're pink and blue parrots. Number 5. They're orange fish.* Have students switch papers and correct each other's artwork as you read the sentences aloud again.

Tapescript

Unit 3 Lesson 2 Page 38
Exercise 1: Read, listen and repeat.

Neighbor: Mariana! Look at these dogs!
Mariana: I'm sorry! Rex! Bianca! Come here!
Neighbor: And look at those cats!
Mariana: Pete and Maggie! Come here! I'm sorry, Mr. Jones.

Unit 3 Lesson 2 Page 39
Exercise 3: Look at the animals. Listen and practice with a friend.

Look at those dogs. They're black dogs.
Look at these cats. They're gray and brown cats.
Look at those turtles. They're green turtles.
Look at these fish. They're orange and white fish.
Look at those birds. They're parrots. They're green and yellow parrots.

Lesson 3 I have a small family.

Lesson 3 I have a small family. Lesson 3

1. Listen to Melba talking about her family. Then match the names to the people.

This is my family!

Michael
Sally
Paul
Nancy

2. Listen again. Complete the sentences with the words from the box.

brother mother father sister

1. Paul is my father
2. Michael is my brother
3. Nancy is my mother
4. Sally is my sister

3. Read about Steve's family. Then fill in the blanks with the correct numbers.

I have a big family. I have one mother and one father. I have two sisters. I have three brothers.

One mother Two sisters
One father Three brothers

Grammar

I	have	one brother. two sisters.
He She	has	one sister. two brothers.

4. Fill in the blanks with has or have.

1. I have a small family.
2. He has a big family.
3. She has one brother.
4. He has two sisters.
5. I have a mother and father.

5. Listen and fill in the missing letters.

1. m oth e r
2. f a t h e r
3. s i s t er
4. b r o th er
5. c a t
6. d o g

42 43

Objectives

Students will:

- develop vocabulary related to family members and rooms of the house
- listen for a purpose

Materials
Best Friends Student Book 1 pages 42-45
Other Materials
index cards, scissors, glue, stick puppets

New Language
I have…
He/She has…
bathroom, bedroom, car garage, house, kitchen living room
Passive Vocabulary
family, small
Spelling
brother, father, mother, sister

1. **Getting Started**
Introduce the concept of family members by asking students to look at page 42 in their Student Book. Then draw on the board a large simple family tree as follows:

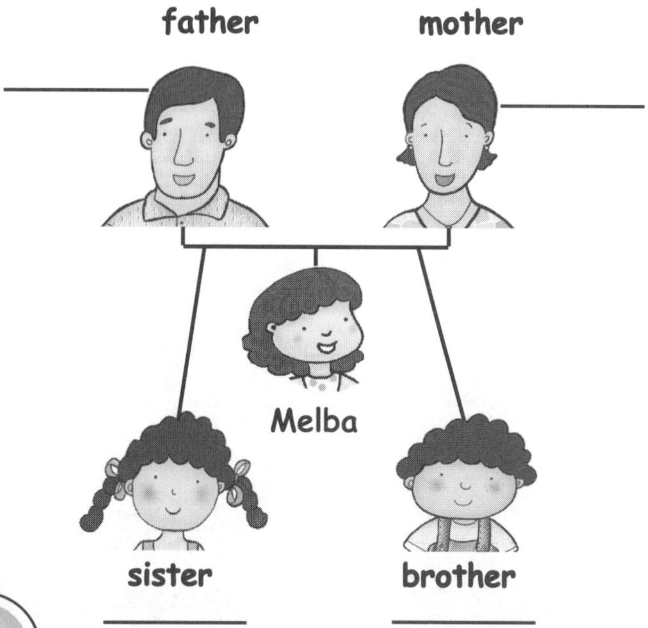

Point to Melba on page 42 and write her name next to the middle figure in the line representing children in the family tree on the board. Point to the top male figure and say *father* several times. Point to the top female figure and say *mother*; say *sister* for the female to the left of the Melba figure (as you face the board) and *brother* for the male to the right.

Play the tape for **Exercise 1**. Fill in the names of Melba's family in the family tree on the board as they are mentioned (*Paul*, etc.). Then play the tape again and point to each figure and name on page 42. Finally, have students complete the activity. Be sure they have the correct matches before continuing.

For **Exercise 2**, pronounce each word in the word box slowly as you point to the family members in Exercise 1: *brother/Michael, mother/Nancy*, etc. Then write the family member words next to the appropriate figure in the family tree on the board. Finally, play the audio and check answers as a class.

For **Exercise 3**, explain the instructions. If necessary, go over the structures in the Grammar Box first. Check the answers as a class.

Grammar Tips

- The verb *have* means "to possess" in either the material sense, or to indicate a relationship between the subject(s) and object(s) of a sentence.
- First-person singular sentences use the *have* form of the verb, third-person singular sentences use the *has* form.

2. **Working Together**

For **Exercise 4**, students should refer to the Grammar Box for reference. Have them exchange books with a classmate and check one another's work.

Then distribute two index cards to make *has* and *have* word cards. Say a pronoun, e.g., *she*, and ask students to hold up the corresponding card (*has*). Practice all the conjugations in the Grammar Box. An alternative is for students to have ready their *he, she,* and they word cards from previous lessons.

For **Exercise 5**, help anyone who does not understand clearly how English words are made up of individual letters. Have students listen to the tape as many times as necessary until everyone has completed the words. Ask individual capable students to write each answer on the board for everyone to check their answers.

Then ask students to make picture-word cards for all family member words, pets included. Distribute as many index cards as each student requests. (Be sensitive to those who may not live in a nuclear family). To represent *sisters* and *brothers*, students can either draw a few girls on the same card, e.g., and label it *sisters*, or they can draw individual sisters on separate cards and label each one *sister*. (Note that *father, mother, brother,* and *sister* each represent that particular family member only. None of them can be used to indicate both members of male/female "pairs," i.e., *father and mother, = parents* ; *brothers and sisters = siblings.*)

For **Exercise 6**, introduce vocabulary by pointing to the picture and naming the house and its parts. For example, *House. This is a house. Bedroom. This is the bedroom,* and so on. Then, as students read the text, they can point to the corresponding place in the picture and word-bank word before they label the rooms in their books..

Play the audio for **Exercise 7** and have students repeat the sentences. Then have students make picture-word cards for the rooms of a house (or other buildings where people live that they are familiar with).

3. **Finishing Up**

Play the audio for **Exercise 8** several times. Encourage students to sing along. For the last stanza, get students to infer *classroom* by spreading your arms out and pointing to things all around the classroom.

For **Exercise 9**, give directions for the activity. When students have finished, check their answers by showing one completed picture.

Unit 3

6. Read the sentences and label the rooms.

bedroom kitchen living room bathroom

I have a beautiful house! I have a yellow kitchen and a pink bedroom. The bathroom is green. The living room is blue and I have a gray car. The garage is purple.

7. Listen and repeat.

44

Lesson 3

8. Sing a song.

My mother's in the kitchen, the kitchen, the kitchen.
My mother's in the kitchen, kitchen now.

My father's in the bedroom, the bedroom, the bedroom.
My father's in the bedroom, bedroom now.

My sister's in the bathroom, the bathroom, the bathroom.
My sister's in the bathroom, bathroom now.

My brother's in the living room, the living room, the living room.
My brother's in the living room, living room now.

9. Listen to the song again. Go to page 149. Cut out and paste the people in the correct rooms.

45

Fun and Games

A. **Sing with cards!** Have students set apart the following picture cards: *mother/kitchen, father/bedroom, sister/bathroom, brother/living room.* Chant or sing the lyrics in Exercise 8 on Student Book page 45. Students should hold up the appropriate pair of cards with each stanza. For more fun, chant or sing faster and faster, encouraging students to follow with their cards.

B. **Puppet families.** Encourage students to talk about the stick puppets and their families. Model with the Ken puppet, for example, and say *This is Ken. Ken has a family. He has a brother. He has a mother. He has two sisters.* Allow each student a turn with a puppet. Accept one-sentence descriptions and incomplete statements.

C. **Puppet families.** Encourage students to talk about the stick puppets and their families. Model with the Ken puppet, for example, and say *This is Ken. Ken has a family. He has a brother. He has a mother. He has two sisters.* Allow each student a turn with a puppet. Accept one-sentence descriptions and incomplete statements.

Tapescript

Unit 3 Lesson 3 Page 42

Exercise 1: Listen to Melba talking about her family. Then match the names to the people.

Melba: This is my family. I have a small family. Paul is my father. Nancy is my mother. Sally is my big sister and Michael is my little brother.

Unit 3 Lesson 3 Page 43

Exercise 5: Listen and fill in the missing letters.

1. mother m-o-t-h-e-r mother.
2. father f-a-t-h-e-r father
3. sister s-i-s-t-e-r sister
4. brother b-r-o-t-h-e-r brother
5. cat c-a-t cat
6. dog d-o-g dog

Unit 3 Lesson 3 Page 44

Exercise 7: Listen and repeat.

Natalie: I have a beautiful house! I have a yellow kitchen and a pink bedroom. The bathroom is green. The living room is blue and I have a gray car. The garage is purple.

Unit 3 Lesson 3 Page 45

Exercise 8: Sing a song.

My mother's in the kitchen, the kitchen, the kitchen.
My mother's in the kitchen, kitchen now.

My father's in the bedroom, the bedroom, the bedroom.
My father's in the bedroom, bedroom now.

My sister's in the bathroom, the bathroom, the bathroom.
My sister's in the bathroom, bathroom now.

My brother's in the living room, the living room, the living room.
My brother's in the living room, living room now.

Unit 3 Lesson 3 Page 45

Exercise 9: Listen to the song again. Go to page 149. Cut out and paste the people in the correct rooms.

(See Exercise 8 above.)

Lesson 4 Review

Objectives

Students will:
- read a dialogue
- review language from Lessons 1-3

Materials
Best Friends Student Book 1 pages 46-49
Other Materials
stick puppets, picture and word cards from Lessons 1-3, crayons or colored pencils, bits of paper for game markers
Passive Vocabulary
big
Differentiate between /th/ and /t/

Read

Exercise 1: Dialogue summary. A story in dialogue format tells about two boys who describe their houses and families. The first boy boasts about having a big house with lots of bathrooms and a big family. The other boy has a small house, but says he has a big family too, with one brother and one sister. The first boy disagrees and makes fun. Then he says he has a lot of pets. The second boy has one pet. However, he also has friends, which the first boy probably doesn't have!

Read the dialogue aloud, pointing to each speech bubble as you read. Ask students to listen and follow in their books. For fun, change voices to represent different speakers. Then read the dialogue again and encourage students to read aloud with you. Finally, assign the roles of the two speakers to a pair of capable students, and ask three "friends" to stand next to the second speaker. The speakers can use the book to read their parts or they can try to memorize and recite their parts.

Story Comprehension

Exercise 2: Do number 1 together: *I have one dog.* (Match to the second boy.) Then read all the statements aloud for students, allowing time for them to indicate their answers. When everyone is done, check answers as a class.

Vocabulary

Exercise 3: Read the numbered items one at a time and ask students to provide the logical match to it, e.g., *I have a big family. I have three sisters and two brothers.* They can read the answer aloud or point to it in their books.

Exercise 4: Play the audio several times for students to practice the letter pronunciation and tracing. Note that the /th/ sound doesn't exist in all languages, so students need a lot of practice listening for and pronouncing this sound and differentiating it from the /t/ sound.

Go over the example for **Exercise 5** together. After students fill in the blanks, ask them to search in their word cards for words that have /t/ or /th/ in any position (initial, middle, and final). A few examples are: *present, party, hat, this, those, they.* Have students hold up cards one at a time. Review the pronunciation and have them repeat.

Exercise 6: Encourage students to label the rooms of their house and their family members. Then ask students to go up to the board one at a time and write their names and the number of brothers and/or sisters each has. Children who have no brothers or sisters can write the number of friends or pets they have.

Exercise 7: Start students off by reading aloud the words in the word boxes. Model pairing one word from each box by saying *I have three brothers.* Remind students of the difference between singular and plural nouns by saying *One ball. Two balls. One house. Two houses.* Tell students they should try to write true sentences about themselves, but they don't have to use every word in every box. Have them cross out words as they use them. Allow students to continue on their own. Check spelling and word order.

Exercise 8: Play a game! Tell students to look at page 49 in their books. Tell them they are going to play a game. Ask them to make themselves game markers out of small bits of paper. Give directions to play. The object is for students to move the number of steps you say from the start line and also name the object(s) and how many: *Five. Five.* (Students move five steps and say *three pens*). Check where players landed. Any student who is in the wrong place must go back to the start line. Play until someone gets to the finish line.

Then allow groups of three students to play the game, with one as the caller and the other two as the players. Whoever follows the caller's commands correctly and gets to the finish line first wins.

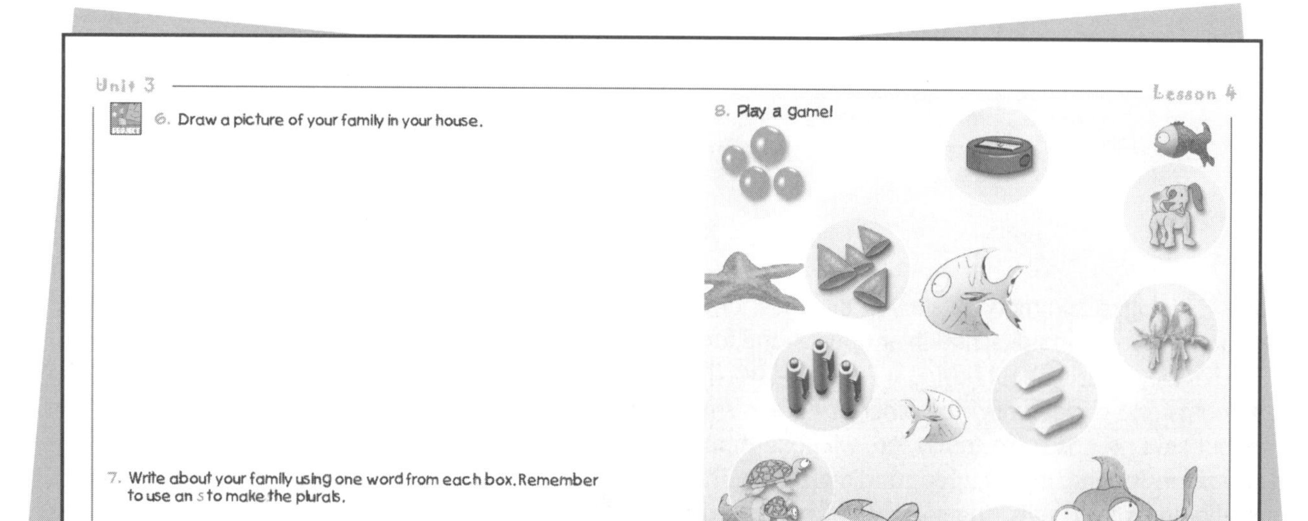
Unit 3

Lesson 4

6. Draw a picture of your family in your house.

7. Write about your family using one word from each box. Remember to use an s to make the plurals.

one two three four five six seven eight nine ten
mother father brother sister dog fish cat parrot turtle

I have ________________.

I have ________________.

I have ________________.

I have ________________.

I have ________________.

I have ________________.

Answers will vary.

8. Play a game!

48 49

Fun and Games

A. **Animal families.** Have students draw a picture of their pets in their pet-houses (e.g., fish bowl, dog house, sofa in a living room). Then they can imagine the pets' families and add them to the scene. Encourage students to label their pets' family members. Or, suggest that students write a speech bubble where their pet says *I have two sisters*, for example. Help with writing as necessary. Display the pictures on a bulletin board.

B. **I have…** Be sure all students have their sets of picture-word cards for all family members and rooms of a house. Divide the class into groups of five or six. Tell students to stand up. Alternate holding up any picture, then any word, and have students hold up the exact same card as quickly as possible. When everyone is holding up a card, identify it together loudly by saying *I have a father (kitchen, brother, etc.)*. Then check that everyone has the same card. Any student who isn't showing the correct card must sit down. Repeat the procedure faster and faster until only one student is left standing in each group.

C. ***Dictation.*** Pair students and have them open one of their books to the game on page 49. One partner points to an object or set of objects and "dictates" it for the other to write down on a separate sheet of paper. Then they reverse roles, alternating dictating and writing, until all the items have been listed by both students: (three fish, one teddy bear, two turtles, three pens, four party hats, four balloons, one pencil sharpener, one dog, two birds, three erasers, one apple, one cat). Have students sign their names and hand in their papers. Check their spelling and return the lists for feedback.

Tapescript

Unit 3 Lesson 4 Page 47

Exercise 4: Listen and repeat. Then trace and say.

Turtle ... t / t / t / ... turtle
Three ... th / th / th / ... three

Unit 3 Test

Name________________________________ Date________________

1. Draw an animal family in this living room. Write the family member words, the animal words, and the color words on your picture.

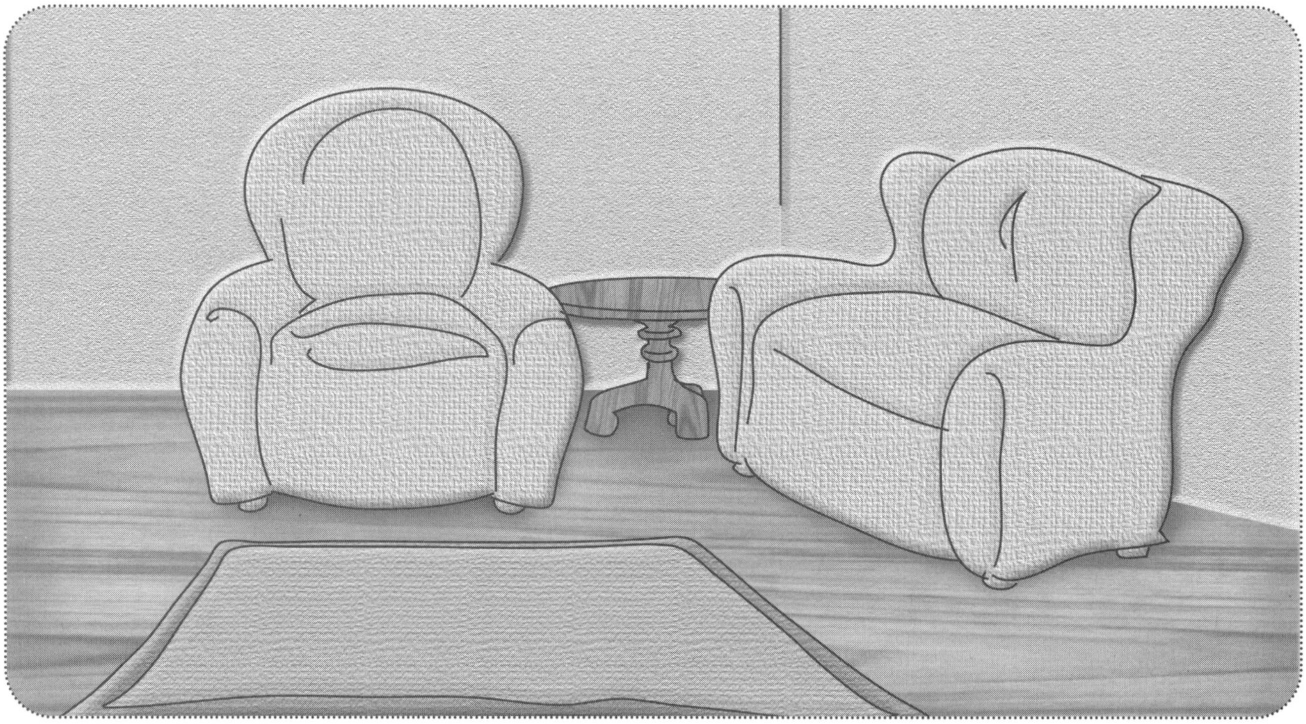

2. Match.

1. He has two sisters.
2. What are these?
3. I have a father.
4. She has a pretty parrot.
5. Those dogs are black.

They're turtles.

3. Write the rooms.

1.  ________________

2.  ________________

3.  ________________

4.  ________________

Unit 4

Lesson 1 I have two feet.

Objectives

Students will:
- learn vocabulary related to parts of the body
- describe people
- learn irregular plural nouns
- listen for a purpose

Materials
Best Friends Student Book 1 pages 50-53
Other Materials
index cards, old *National Geographic* (or similar) magazines, crayons or colored pencils, stick puppet of Purpgray monster

New Language
monster, ugly, wonderful
Spelling
arm(s), ear(s), eye(s), feet, finger(s), hand(s), head(s), leg(s), mouth(s), nose(s)

Unit 4 — Lesson 1

I have two feet.

1. Listen and repeat. Then write the parts of the body next to the monster.

2. Look at the monster. Count the parts of the body.

six eyes — two heads — four legs
four ears — three arms — four feet
two noses — three hands
two mouths — twelve fingers

Grammar

Regular Plurals		Irregular Plurals	
hand	hands	foot	feet
leg	legs	fish	fish
finger	fingers		
head	heads		

3. Complete the sentences about the monster using *has*.

Example: The monster *has* six eyes.
1. The monster
2. The monster — Answers will vary.
3. The monster
4. The monster

50 — 51

1. **Getting Started**
Use the stick puppets to introduce *legs, heads, hands,* and *fingers* by pointing to and naming these parts of the body on the puppets. Then hold up your own hand, then two hands, one finger, then three fingers, etc. and contrast the singular with the plural: *One hand. Two hands. One finger. Three fingers,* and so on.

Explain the vocabulary *monster, ugly,* and *wonderful.* Ask students to look at page 50 in their Student Book and have them repeat *monster* several times. Ask where in their books they can find a monster they already know (Poppi on page 4, Exercise 5, and the Purpgray stick puppet in Unit 2, Lesson 2). Say the word *monster* and point to Poppi, to the stick puppet, and then to the monster on page 50. Remind students of the beautiful fish in Unit 3, and ask for opinions, pointing to each monster and saying *Is this monster beautiful and wonderful? Is he ugly?* (make a face showing disgust). Depending on students' level, ask them to identify other wonderful or ugly objects around them. They can point or say *He's ugly* or *He's wonderful.*

Play the audio for **Exercise 1**. As each character speaks, students should trace with a finger under the words in the lines. Point to your hands, head, etc. as each is mentioned. Play the tape a second time and encourage students to do the same as they repeat the dialogue. Finally, direct them to label some parts of the body on the monster using the words in the word box.

For **Exercise 2**, present the vocabulary by pointing to and naming each picture and word on page 51. Ask students to repeat. Then encourage them to say the parts of the body and touch the same on themselves and then on the monster on page 50. Finally, do the first one together as an example, counting how many eyes the monster has (six). Be sure students write the number word, not the numeral. Check answers as a class.

Grammar Tips

- Regular plural nouns end in *s: hand/hands, nose/noses, mouth/mouths.*
- Irregular plural nouns have many forms. Some don't have a final *s* and are exactly the same as the singular form, such as *fish/fish, sheep/sheep*. Some don't have a final *s* and change their spelling, such as *foot/feet, man/men.*

2. **Working Together**
   For **Exercise 3**, show the Daniel puppet and say *Daniel has two eyes. He has one head. He has two arms,* and so on. Then read the example aloud. Point to the monster on page 50 and count aloud from one to six as you point to each of the monster's eyes. Students can work in pairs or by themselves. Accept any reasonable answers.

   Before playing the audio for **Exercise 4**, read aloud all the labels, from top to bottom and left to right, for easier audio recognition. Encourage students to follow in their books. Then play the audio for students to listen and point to each part of the body as it is mentioned.

3. **Finishing Up**
   Pair students and have them work on **Exercise 5** together, following the example. They can refer to Exercise 4, if necessary. When students are done, check answers together.

Then distribute index cards for students to create the following picture cards: *arm, ear, eye, finger, hand, head, legs, mouth, nose, feet.* Make a set for yourself. Write on the board the words for students to copy onto the backside of the cards. Then check comprehension by saying a word and having students hold up the appropriate picture card.

For **Exercise 6**, preview by describing the monster on page 50. Point to the parts of the body and say *Look! He has two pink heads. Look! He has three green hands,* etc. Then point to number 1 and say *Look! She has yellow hands.* Establish a match between the girl's hands and the pair of hands in the second line. Encourage students to draw a line between them. Then play the audio as many times as necessary for students to make the correct match.

For **Exercise 7**, help less capable students realize that they can "get" the answer from the picture clue if they have trouble with the audio.

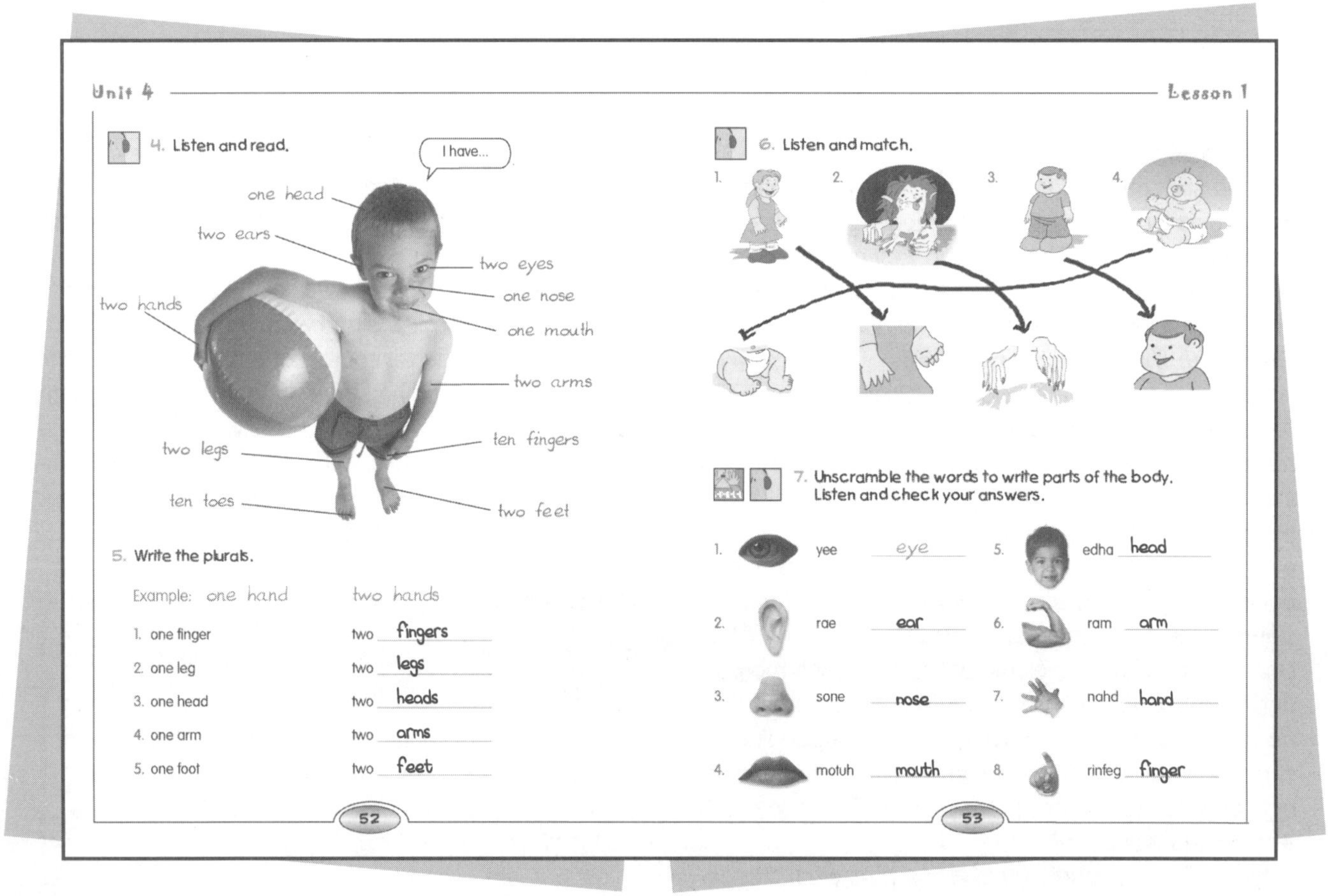
Unit 4 — Lesson 1

4. Listen and read.

5. Write the plurals.

Example: one hand	two hands
1. one finger	two fingers
2. one leg	two legs
3. one head	two heads
4. one arm	two arms
5. one foot	two feet

6. Listen and match.

1. 2. 3. 4.

7. Unscramble the words to write parts of the body. Listen and check your answers.

1.	yee	eye
2.	rae	ear
3.	sone	nose
4.	motuh	mouth
5.	edha	head
6.	ram	arm
7.	nahd	hand
8.	rinfeg	finger

52 53

Fun and Games

A. **It's wonderful/ugly!** Distribute *National Geographic* or similar magazines, one to each group of five. Have students select an animal or animals, or another object or objects from the pages and give their opinions by saying *It's wonderful./ They're wonderful.* or *It's ugly./They're ugly.* Students can cut out their pictures and make one large display for the bulletin board.

B. **Draw!** Divide the class into five teams and have them stand far away from the board. Using all the lesson vocabulary, tell the first student in each team what parts of the body to draw on the board and how many, e.g., *five arms.* The first student to finish correctly gets a point for his or her team. Give everyone a chance to draw. The team with the most points wins.

C. **Teacher Says.** Play a simplified form of Simon Says. Each student should have his or her set of picture-word cards for parts of the body. Demonstrate the game as follows: Hold up any card, e.g., the head card, touch your head with the card, and say *Touch your head!* Student should follow your lead as quickly as possible. Then hold up another card, e.g., the fingers card, touch your leg with the card, and say *Touch your fingers!* If a student touches his or her leg with the card instead of his o her fingers, that student is out. Any student not holding the correct card is also out. Play until a winner is declared.

Tapescript

Unit 4 Lesson 1 Page 50
Exercise 1: Listen and repeat. Then write the body parts next to the monster.

Melba: Look! It has three green hands!
Steve: And two pink heads.
Melba: It has twelve fingers!
Steve: And four yellow legs.
Melba: It's ugly!
Steve: No, it's great!

Unit 4 Lesson 1 Page 52
Exercise 4: Listen and read.

Boy: I have one head. I have two eyes, two ears, one nose and one mouth. I have two arms, two hands and ten fingers. I have two legs, two feet and ten toes.

Unit 4 Lesson 1 Page 53
Exercise 6: Listen and match.

1. I have two small hands.
2. I have nine beautiful fingers!
3. My eyes are black.
4. Look! I have two feet!

Unit 4 Lesson 1 Page 53
Exercise 7: Unscramble the words to write the parts of the body. Listen and check your answers.

1. eye
2. ear
3. nose
4. mouth
5. head
6. arm
7. hand
8. finger

Lesson 2 This is an ear.

Objectives

Students will:
- use indefinite articles correctly
- recognize vowels

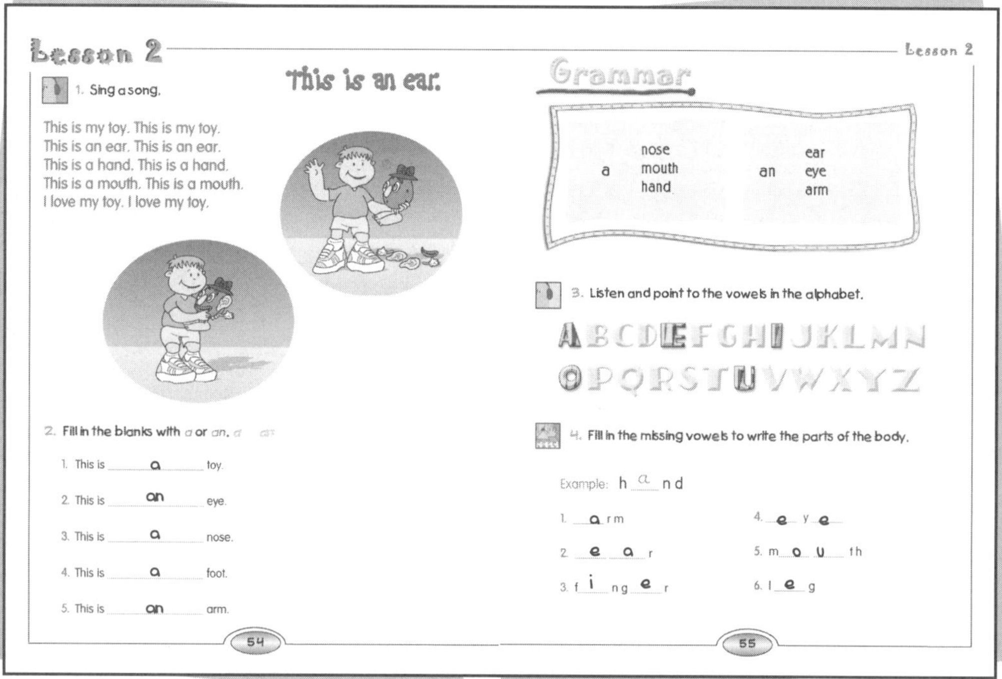

Lesson 2

1. Sing a song.

This is an ear.

This is my toy. This is my toy.
This is an ear. This is an ear.
This is a hand. This is a hand.
This is a mouth. This is a mouth.
I love my toy. I love my toy.

2. Fill in the blanks with a or an.

1. This is a toy.
2. This is an eye.
3. This is a nose.
4. This is a foot.
5. This is an arm.

54

Lesson 2

Grammar

a	nose mouth hand	an	ear eye arm

3. Listen and point to the vowels in the alphabet.

A B C D E F G H I J K L M N
O P Q R S T U V W X Y Z

4. Fill in the missing vowels to write the parts of the body.

Example: h a nd

1. a rm
2. e a r
3. f i ng e r
4. e y e
5. m o u th
6. l e g

55

Materials
Best Friends Student Book 1 pages 54-57
Other Materials
stick puppets, index cards, Lesson 1 picture-word cards, Unit 2 alphabet letter cards, scissors, glue, old magazines

New Language
a/an
foot
Passive Vocabulary
vowels *a, e, i, o, u*

1. **Getting Started**

Review the structure *This is a...* by holding up one of your hands and saying *This is a hand.* Say the same thing, pointing to one of the stick puppet's hands. Go around the classroom and point to a few students' left or right hands and say *This is a hand.* Point to other parts of the body on the stick puppets and the students and say *This is a nose (head, mouth, hand, leg).* Then repeat the procedure by pointing to your right or left foot and saying *This is a foot.* Have students repeat with you as you go around pointing to one student's foot, then another's.

Introduce the definite article *an* by pointing to your ear, eye, and arm and saying *This is an ear (eye, arm).* Vary pointing to your left and right ear, arm, etc. Ask students to point and repeat.

Play the audio for **Exercise 1**. Go over the song, pointing to each line and tracing from left to right with a finger under the words as you read aloud. Ask students to do the same. Then play the song line by line and point to each part of the body on yourself or on one of the stick puppets as each is mentioned. Finally, play the song again and encourage students to chant along.

For **Exercise 2**, students may want to refer to the song lyrics if they are not sure which article to write.

Grammar Tips

- The indefinite article *a* goes before singular nouns or adjectives that start with a consonant letter or sound: *a book, a hand, a university, a brown eye.*
- The indefinite article *an* goes before singular nouns or adjectives that start with a vowel letter *(a, e, i, o, u)* or vowel sound: *an eye, an arm, an orange pen, an ugly monster.*

Go over the structures in the Grammar Box by contrasting *a* plus a word starting with a consonant letter/sound and *an* plus a word starting with a vowel letter/sound. Ask *What's this?* about each of the vocabulary words as you point to that part of the body on yourself or on a stick puppet. Elicit the correct article.

Then distribute two index cards to each student. Have them make word cards for *a* and *an*. Say the words in the Grammar Box in random order but without the article, for students to hold up the corresponding word card. For example, say *eye*. Students hold up the *an* card. When everyone is holding up the correct card, repeat the phrase *an eye* together.

Invite students to look at **Exercise 3**. Point to the group of letters and say *the alphabet*. Review the letters of the alphabet by chanting together the alphabet chant from a previous unit. Then write just the vowels on the board (capital *A, E, I, O, U*, then small *a, e, i, o, u*) as a reference. Ask students to pick out from their sets of alphabet letter cards the five vowels. Then tell them to match each vowel letter card to the highlighted vowel letter in Exercise 3. Finally, play the audio as students point to the vowels.

2. **Working Together**

For **Exercise 4**, students should have on hand their picture-word cards for parts of the body. Together, trace over the *a* in the example word *hand*, say the word aloud, then find that card to confirm spelling. Less capable students may want to refer to their cards at the beginning for spelling.

For **Exercise 5**, write the example on the board. Circle all the vowels. Cross out the second *a* in Natalie, then write the vowels left on the board. Students should infer that "repeat" vowels should not get listed in this activity. Pairs can check each other's work.

3. **Finishing Up**

Assign **Exercise 6**, helping as necessary with the instructions. Correct the chart together by reading aloud answers in each column, e.g., *a pencil, an eye.*

Then have students add the appropriate definite article *a* or *an* to the word side of their picture-word cards for singular parts of the body. At this point, have them make a picture-word card for *foot* and also write the definite article *a*.

Assign **Exercise 7**. Distribute old magazines to groups of four so the group members can help each other look for parts of the body to paste into their books. Members should discuss and agree before pasting their cutouts. Then groups exchange books and check their classmates' work. As they check, they can count aloud together how many items there are in each category, e.g., *three heads, eight mouths.*

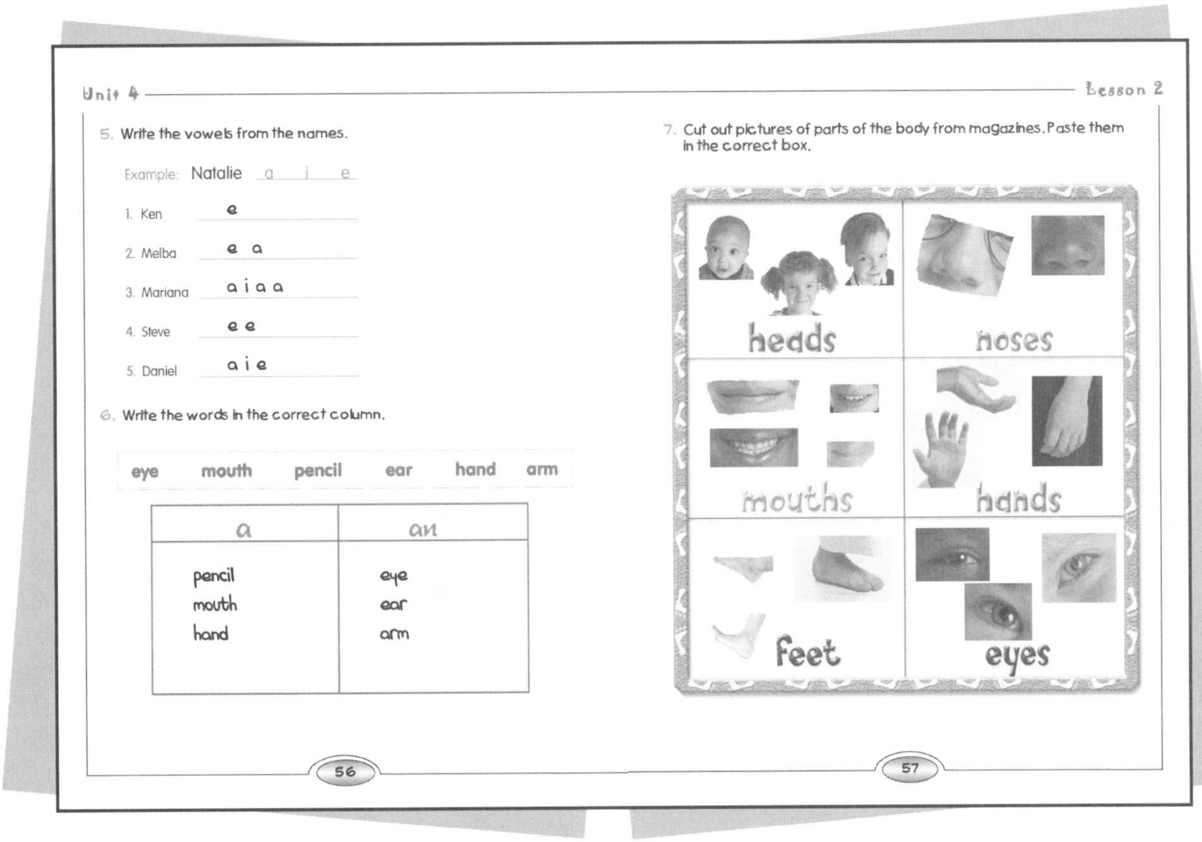
Unit 4 — Lesson 2

5. Write the vowels from the names.

Example: Natalie a i e

1. Ken e
2. Melba e a
3. Mariana a i a a
4. Steve e e
5. Daniel a i e

6. Write the words in the correct column.

eye mouth pencil ear hand arm

a	an
pencil	eye
mouth	ear
hand	arm

7. Cut out pictures of parts of the body from magazines. Paste them in the correct box.

56 57

Fun and Games

A. *A* **or** *an*? Place your *a* and *an* word cards on the chalk ledge or some other place where they are visible. Divide students into two teams. Have them stand as far as possible from the cards. Say a body-part word without the article. The object of the game is for the first student on each team to run to the cards and grab the one that goes with the word. Whoever selects the correct card wins a point for his or her team. Give every student a chance to compete. The team with the most points wins.

An alternative is to hold up the picture card for students to see. The student who gets a card first brings it to you. If the card is correctly matched, his or team wins a point. If it is the wrong card, his or team loses a point and the other team gets a point. Hold up all correct matches for student reinforcement.

B. **Make a monster.** Similar to Exercise 7 on page 57, have students cut out pictures of parts of the body of all sizes from magazines, but working alone this time. Each student will "create" a monster. First they can draw a body on a large sheet of paper in any shape they like. Then they paste onto the body their magazine cutouts. Encourage them to give their monsters names and to write a few sentences about him or her right on the picture. For example, *This is Foony. She has two noses. She is wonderful.* Help with writing as necessary. Display all artwork on the bulletin board.

C. **Dictation.** Divide the class into two teams. Use two sets of vowel letter cards, one per team. Team A sends a pair of students to the board. The first person on Team A reads a vowel aloud, and the other person on Team A writes it on the board. If it is the correct vowel, Team A gets a point; if it is wrong, Team B gets a point. The teams switch roles. Go through the cards as often as necessary to give everyone a chance to participate. The team with the most points at the end wins.

Tapescript

Unit 4 Lesson 2 Page 54

Exercise 1: Sing a song.

This is my toy. This is my toy.
This is an ear. This is an ear.
This is a hand. This is a hand.
This is a mouth. This is a mouth.
I love my toy. I love my toy.

Unit 4 Lesson 2 Page 55

Exercise 3: Listen and point to the vowels in the alphabet.

A — E — I — O — U

Lesson 3 We're all friends.

Objectives

Students will:

- describe people
- listen for a purpose

Materials

Best Friends Student Book 1 pages 58-61

Other Materials

stick puppets, index cards, scissors, glue,

New Language

It's/He's/She's/
We're/They're
am/is/are
cute
friends
funny
happy
pretty
smart

Passive Vocabulary

clown

Lesson 3 We're all friends.

1. Read, listen and repeat.

We're boys.
They're boys, and we're girls!
We're smart.
They're smart and we're smart. We're funny, too!
We're happy.
They're happy. We're happy, too.
We're all friends!

Lesson 3

Grammar

I	am	happy.
We		smart.
They	are	cute.
You		

We are = We're
They are = They're

2. Fill in the blanks with am, is or are.

1. I __am__ a girl.
2. We __are__ funny.
3. It __is__ a cute dog.
4. She __is__ my mother.
5. They __are__ happy.
6. We __are__ pretty.

58 59

1. **Getting Started**

Use the stick puppets to review the pronoun *they*. Point to the boy puppets and say *They're boys*. Point to the girl puppets and say *They're girls*. Then introduce the pronoun *we*. Hold two boy stick puppets, move them at the same time, and say in a "boy" voice *We're boys*. Repeat for the girl puppets, changing to a "girl" voice as you say *We're girls*.

Play the audio for **Exercise 1**. As each character speaks, students should trace with a finger under the words in the lines. Play the audio a second time and encourage students to repeat the dialogue. Do not try to explain the meaning of the new vocabulary for now. Students should recognize the word *friends* from previous units.

Go over the structures in the Grammar Box slowly, pointing to an appropriate person in the classroom as you combine the phrases. For example, point to yourself and say *I am happy*. Point to a student or group of students, look directly at them, and say *You are smart.*, etc. Review *he/she/it is...*, using other familiar adjectives, e.g., point to a pencil and say *It is (red)*.

You may have to translate for students the new vocabulary *smart* and *cute*. Ask them to find in their books where the word *happy* appeared (In Unit 1: on page 2 in the party banner; on page 10 in the first speech bubble; on page 13 in the card; on page 14 in the first speech bubble; on page 16 in the party banner). They should guess the meaning from the

Grammar Tips

- The verb *be* is irregular. It is conjugated as follows: *I am, you are (singular), he/she/it/is, you are (plural) we are, they are.*
- The contraction for *We are* is *We're*. The contraction for *They are* is *They're*. In this case, a contraction is formed by replacing the first letter of the third-person plural verb *are* with an apostrophe.
- The contraction for *You are* is *You're*. In this case, a contraction is formed by replacing the first letter of the second-person singular and plural verb *are* with an apostrophe.
- Remember that adjectives can come immediately before the noun it modifies or after a conjugated form of the verb *be: A happy girl/The girl is happy.*

expressions on people's faces. For *funny* (from the dialogue on page 58), point to the second scene in Exercise 2, give a big ha-ha laugh, and say *Number 2. Look. Funny. Ha, ha, ha! The clowns are funny.*

2. **Working Together**

For **Exercise 2**, write the verb forms on the board in case students have trouble identifying them in the instructions. Demonstrate the adjective *pretty* by holding up a colorful item or items and saying *Is it ugly?* (Shake your head.) *No, it isn't. It's beautiful! It's pretty!* or *Are they ugly?* (Shake your head.) *No, they aren't. They're beautiful! They're pretty!* (It may be a matter of opinion as to whether the "ladies" in number 6 are pretty or not!). Have students work in pairs to complete the activity. Circulate and check answers.

Then have students make word cards for the adjectives (*smart, funny, happy, cute, pretty*). Ask individuals to choose one of the cards randomly to pantomime, using any available props. The rest of the class guesses the adjective by holding up the card they think is being shown. Check to see how many different answers there are. If the guessers do not agree, have the volunteer hold up the card or say the adjective he or she was trying to represent.

For **Exercise 3**, demonstrate the meaning of *true* and *false* by making deliberately false statements, then true statements. For example, say *I have ten heads!* Get students' reactions, shake your head no, and say *False. False.* Write the word on the board and repeat. Then say *I have one head.* Nod your head yes and say *True. True.* Write the word on the board and repeat. Give a few more examples, using familiar vocabulary and structures, i.e., point to a ruler, say *It's a book.* then say *False*; point to a pretty animal in a magazine, say *It's pretty.* then say *True.* Play the audio several times before students mark their answers. Correct the answers together so that students can change their answers, if necessary.

3. **Finishing Up**

For **Exercise 4**, give directions for the activity. Students may want to take their books home or bring in photographs for the next time the class meets.

Unit 4 — Lesson 3

3. Listen and circle True or False.

1. They're parrots.	(True)	False
2. They're green and red.	True	(False)
3. They're happy.	(True)	False
4. They have big eyes.	True	(False)

4. Draw pictures or bring photos of your friends. Write the names.

These are my friends.

Answers will vary.

This is ________. This is ________.

This is ________. This is ________.

60 61

Fun and Games

A. **Friends.** Have students pass their Student Book around for everyone to see what they did for Exercise 4 on page 61. Classmates should check to see if their names or pictures are in someone's book. (Be sensitive to students who are not always included in the "popular" group.) If they are in someone's book, they should sign their names. If they are not in anyone's book, have them sign a sheet of paper with your name at the top and the heading *My Friends*. Display it on the bulletin board.

B. **Charades with cards.** Use your set of word cards for the adjectives *smart, funny, happy, cute, pretty*. Hold up a card or say one of these adjectives for the entire class to pantomime at the same time. They can use any available props. (Students who are not sure what to do can follow the example of others around them.) When everyone is in agreement, say together the word loudly.

C. **Dictation.** Use one set of lesson word cards. Divide the class into two teams. The first person on Team A reads a word card aloud, and the first person on Team B writes it on the board. If the word is spelled correctly, Team B gets a point; if it is wrong, Team A gets a point. Teams switch roles. Go through the cards as often as necessary to give everyone a chance to dictate and write. The team with the most points at the end wins.

Tapescript

Unit 4 Lesson 3 Page 58
Exercise 1: Read, listen and repeat.

Ken: We're boys.
Melba: They're boys, and we're girls!
Ken & Melba: We're smart.
Daniel: They're smart and we're smart.
We're funny too!
Steve: We're happy.
Mariana: They're happy. We're happy, too.
Natalie: We're all friends!

Unit 4 Lesson 3 Page 60
Exercise 3: Listen and circle True or False.

Parrot 1: We're two parrots.
Parrot 2: Look! We're green and yellow!
Parrot 1: And we're happy!
Parrot 2: We have small eyes!

Lesson 4 Review

Objectives

Students will:
- read a dialogue
- review language from Lessons 1-3
- differentiate between /h/ and /r/

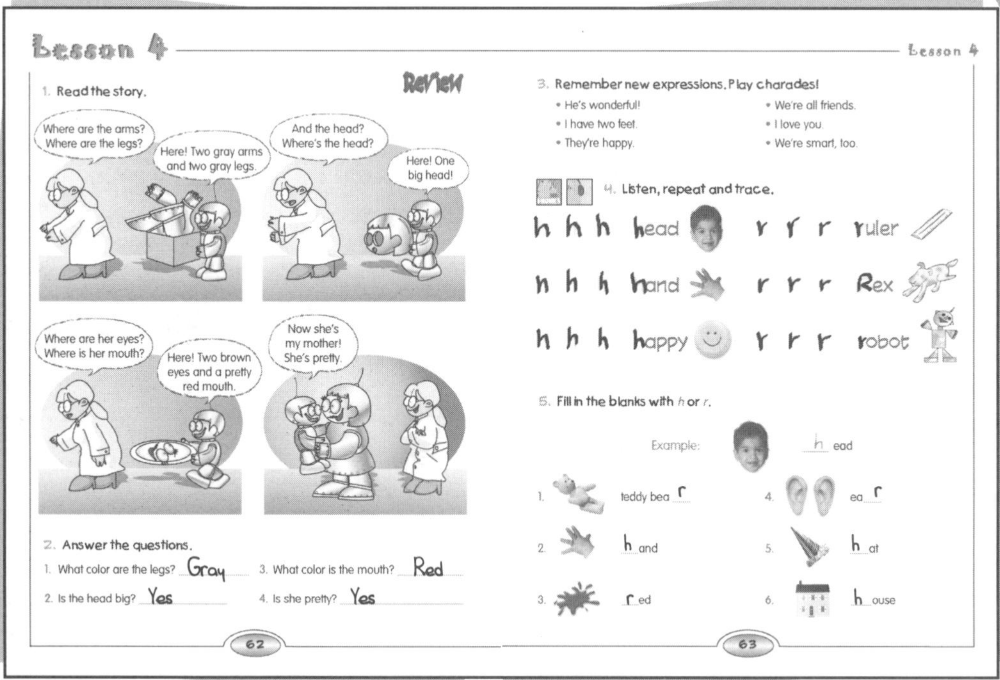

Lesson 4 Review

1. Read the story.

Where are the arms? Where are the legs?
Here! Two gray arms and two gray legs.
And the head? Where's the head?
Here! One big head!
Where are her eyes? Where is her mouth?
Here! Two brown eyes and a pretty red mouth.
Now she's my mother! She's pretty.

2. Answer the questions.

1. What color are the legs? Gray
2. Is the head big? Yes
3. What color is the mouth? Red
4. Is she pretty? Yes

3. Remember new expressions. Play charades!

- He's wonderful!
- I have two feet.
- They're happy.
- We're all friends.
- I love you.
- We're smart, too.

4. Listen, repeat and trace.

h h h head r r r ruler
h h h hand r r r Rex
h h h happy r r r robot

5. Fill in the blanks with *h* or *r*.

Example: h ead

1. teddy bea r
2. h and
3. r ed
4. ea r
5. h at
6. h ouse

62 63

Materials

Best Friends Student Book 1 pages 62-65

Other Materials

picture and word cards from Lessons 1-3, scissors

Passive Vocabulary

I love you.
knee(s)
shoulder(s)

Read

Exercise 1: Dialogue summary. A story in dialogue format tells about a girl who is asking for various parts of the body to make something. What she is making is invisible to the reader at first. The girl asks for arms, legs, a head, eyes, and a mouth. A little robot helps the girl. When she asks for specific parts of the body, the robot gives them to her. He tells her what color the parts are. The result is a pretty mother robot for the little robot. He is happy, the mother robot is happy, and the girl is happy!

Read the dialogue aloud, pointing to each speech bubble as you read. Ask students to listen and follow in their books. For fun, change voices to represent different speakers. (Hint: A typical "robot" voice has no inflection or stress. It is monotone.) Then read the dialogue again and encourage students to read aloud with you. Finally, assign the roles of the girl and the little robot to a pair of capable students, and have one student stand to represent the mother robot getting parts added to her. The speakers can use the book to read their parts or they can try to memorize and recite their parts.

Story Comprehension

Exercise 2: Do number 1 together: *What color are the legs? Gray.* Then read all the questions aloud for students, allowing time for them to look for key words in the speech bubbles and write their answers. When everyone is done, check answers as a class.

Vocabulary

Exercise 3: Read all the expressions aloud and ask students to recall in what context they are found in the unit as an aid in acting them out. Demonstrate playing charades by doing the first expression as an example. (However, charades is usually a guessing game, so the expression being acted out should not be pointed out in any way once the game starts.) Ask individuals to act out any expression, and their classmates try to guess. The guessers can read the answer aloud or point to it in their books.

Exercise 4. Play the audio for students several times so that they can practice the letter and word pronunciations. After students trace over the letters and fill in the blanks, repeat several times *Rex* and *robot*. Have students repeat. Note that the /h/ and /r/ sounds in English are quite different from how these letters are pronounced in other languages, so students need a lot of practice listening for and pronouncing these sounds.

Go over the example for **Exercise 5** together. Have students trace over the *h* in *head* as they pronounce it. After students fill in the blanks, check answers together as a class, making sure that students are pronouncing correctly. Then ask them to look in their set of cards for the /h/ and /r/ letter cards. Have them hold up the correct card as you say the letter name. Go faster and faster. Give more capable students a chance to be the caller if there is time.

Exercise 4: Start the exercise by asking students to read aloud the words or phrases in the word box. Tell them they should use them only once to fill in the blanks. Then ask them to decide which word or phrase goes best in the first blank. Tell them the first answer if necessary and ask students to write it in their books. (Have them also cross it out in the box so they know they have used it already.) Then allow students to continue on their own until all the blanks are filled. They may work in pairs if they wish.

Listening

Play the audio for **Exercise 6** several times. The first time, ask students to listen as you point to each part of the body on yourself: *head, shoulders, knees, toes, eyes, ears, mouth, nose.* Play the audio again, encouraging students to follow your gestures. Play the song as often as necessary for students to follow the song correctly. Finally, ask them to sing along as they make gestures.

Look and Read

Exercise 7: Point to the mouse with a bow in her hair and say *Dolly. This is Dolly.* Read the text aloud two or three times, then have students read silently.

Exercise 8: Read all the questions aloud before assigning students to read them silently. They may work in pairs to answer the comprehension questions, but check answers as a class.

Exercise 9: Play a game! Tell students to look at page 65 in their books. Tell them they are going to play a game. First help them with the instructions. The "blocks" they cut out at the back of the book (page 147) will be markers for the game. Similar to Bingo, the object is for students to find in their pile of blocks the one word you call out and match it on the board. As soon as they place it on the board, they call out the word. The student who calls it out first (and has it in the correct spot) is the next caller.

Unit 4

6. Sing a song.

Head, shoulders,
Knees and toes,
Knees and toes.

Head, shoulders,
Knees and toes,
Knees and toes.

Eyes and ears and mouth and nose,
Head, shoulders,
Knees and toes,
Knees and toes.

7. Look and read.

This is my friend. Her name is Dolly. She's funny. She's cute, too. She's seven years old. I love Dolly!

8. Answer the questions with *Yes* or *No*.

1. Is her name Dolly? Yes.
2. Is she cute? Yes.
3. Is she funny? Yes.
4. Is she six years old? No.

64

Lesson 4

9. Play a game! Go to page 147. Cut out the blocks.

65

Fun and Games

A. **Picture and Word Concentration.** Students should have their complete sets of Unit 4 picture and word cards. Tell them that the object of the game is to find two pictures or words that match. Pair students and have them play against each other with their sets of cards to see who gets the most cards. When they are finished playing, ask them to put their cards in order so that each student gets his or her cards back again.

B. **Draw!** Divide the class into four teams and have them stand far away from the board. Using all unit vocabulary, tell the first student in each team who/what to draw. Some ideas are: *a cute ear, a small leg, a big head, a pretty dog, a wonderful robot, an ugly foot.* The first student to finish correctly gets a point for his or her team. Give everyone a chance to draw. The team with the most points wins.

C. **Where are the arms?** Have groups of four students work together to role-play and draw a variation of the story on page 62. Assign the roles of the girl scientist, the little robot, the mother robot, and an illustrator. Give each illustrator a large sheet of paper and crayons or colored pencils. Using the speech bubbles as a model only, the girl should ask for parts of the body of her choice, e.g., *Where are the ears? Where is the nose?* The robot gives the girl what she asks for and uses familiar adjectives, e.g., *Here! Four pretty purple eyes.* The illustrator draws the mother robot as she is being "assembled." When she is finished, the student playing the mother robot greets her baby robot, saying *I love you!* Display the finished mother robots on the bulletin board.

Tapescript

Unit 4 Lesson 4 Page 63
Exercise 4: Listen and repeat. Then trace and say.

head /h/ /h/ /h/ head
hand /h/ /h/ /h/ hand
happy /h/ /h/ /h/ happy
ruler /r/ /r/ /r/ ruler
Rex /r/ /r/ /r/ Rex
robot /r/ /r/ /r/ robot

Unit 4 Lesson 4 Page 64
Exercise 6: Sing a song.

Head, shoulders,
Knees and toes,
Knees and toes.

Head, shoulders,
Knees and toes,
Knees and toes.

Eyes and ears and mouth and nose,
Head, shoulders,
Knees and toes,
Knees and toes.

Unit 4 Test

Name________________________________ Date______________

1. Draw a robot with three heads, nine ears, four hands, eight fingers, five legs, and ten feet.

2. Match.

1. They are funny.
2. He is smart.
3. She is pretty.
4. We are happy turtles.
5. They are girls.

3. Write a or an.

Example: __a__ nose

1. ________ leg
2. ________ fish
3. ________ monster
4. ________ ugly monster
5. ________ robot
6. ________ arm
7. ________ house
8. ________ eye

Unit 5 Review

Objectives

Students will:
- review language from Units 1-4
- listen for a purpose

Unit 5 Review

1. Listen and point to the dialogue.

2. Listen again and write the missing words.

Ken: Good morning! What's your name?
Tom: My name is Tom. What's your name?
Ken: I'm Ken. And this is Mariana. This is Daniel and this is Melba.
Natalie: I'm Natalie and this is my friend, Steve.
Daniel: We're all friends.
Ken: I'm seven. How old are you?
Tom: I'm seven, too.
Natalie: Look! We have a nice classroom. Come in, please!

66

3. Fill in the blanks with the words from the box. Then practice with a friend.

What's this? It's a red crayon.

What / black / bear / They're / present / purple / this

1. What's that? It's a black dog.
2. What's this? It's a pink present.
3. What are these? They're red pens.
4. What is this? It's a purple kite.
5. What is that? It's a teddy bear.

67

Materials
Best Friends Student Book 1 pages 66-73
Other Materials
picture and word cards from Units 1-4, stick puppets, crayons or colored pencils, large sheets of paper

New Language
brown
orange
white
Passive Vocabulary
Beautiful
Who...?

Review

Ask students to look at the picture on page 66 in their Student Book. Review vocabulary and structures as you talk about the scene. (Point to Steve) Say *This is Steve. He's a boy. How old is he? He's seven years old.* (Point to Melba.) *What's her name? Her name's Melba. She's a girl. They're* (point to Steve and Melba) *students. They're* (point to the other children) *students. They're* (point to all of the children) *students in a classroom* (point to the board, the vowel chart, and all around the classroom scene). Then say as you point directly at them *You are students.* Ask *Are you students?* Elicit *Yes, we are.* Repeat several times and ask students to repeat with you.

Play the tape for **Exercise 1**. Point to each line of dialogue and trace from left to right with a finger under the blanks and words. Ask students to listen the first time and trace with you.

Play the tape for **Exercise 2**. Play the dialogue several times as students try to concentrate on the missing words. Students should guess the meaning of *nice classroom* from the setting in the picture. Finally, have them write the missing words. Then read the entire dialogue aloud for students to check their answers.

For **Exercise 3**, ask *What's this?* about a classroom object that is close to you, and answer *It's a (notebook).* Then point to the same item at a distance from you and ask and answer *What's that? It's a (notebook).* Present a few more examples to contrast *this* and *that.* Be sure you only talk about singular objects. Repeat the procedure for plural nouns by asking *What are these?* about several classroom objects that are close to you, and answer *They're (notebooks).* Then point to the same items at a distance from you and ask and answer *What are those? They're (notebooks).* Present a few more examples to contrast *these* and *those.* Be sure you only talk about plural items.

Read aloud the words in the word box on page 67 and have students repeat. Then have students do the exercise individually. Check answers as a class. Finally, invite pairs to practice asking and answering about the page.

For **Exercise 4**, review the concepts of *True* and *False* by making deliberately false statements, then true statements. For example, say *I have six eyes!* Get students' reactions, shake your head no, and say *False. False.* Write the word on the board and repeat. Then say *I have two eyes.* Nod your head yes and say *True. True.* Write the word on the board and repeat. Give a few more examples, using familiar vocabulary and structures, i.e., point to a boy, say *He's a robot.*, then say *False*; point to the Mariana puppet, for example, say *Her name is Mariana*, then say *True*.

Play the audio several times before students mark their answers. You can stop the tape after each question/answer to give them time to think. Go over the answers together so that students can correct their work. Be sure students understand how to make a check (✓).

For more practice, write on the board the heading *True* and *False*. Have individuals go to the board and write a check in the appropriate column as you make true and false statements. For example, say *You are a robot.* He or she writes a check under the *False* column, then sits down for the next student. A variation on this is to make statements about picture cards, e.g., show the picture card for eyes and say *They're eyes.* (the student checks under the *True* column.)

Play the audio for **Exercise 5**. Do the first one as an example together. Point to each choice and say *two party hats, two red balls, one (red) ball and one (yellow) ball.* Play the corresponding line on the audio. Ask *Where are the two red balls?* Students point in their books, then circle their choice. Be sure all agree before continuing. Play the tape several times as students just listen. Then have them work in pairs to complete the audio activity.

For **Exercise 6**, students should be familiar enough with matching activities to do the exercise without any preview. When they are done, check answers as a class.

For **Exercise 7**, explain the directions if necessary and go over the example together. Read each word in the word box and have students repeat. Read the words again for students to then draw and label in their notebooks. A volunteer can do the same on the board as well. Finally, have students complete the activity.

For **Exercise 8**, review vocabulary for parts of the body. Point to yourself as you say *my head, my eye, my shoulder, my arm, my leg, my foot.* Then show a stick puppet, e.g., Melba, and move her so that she is walking

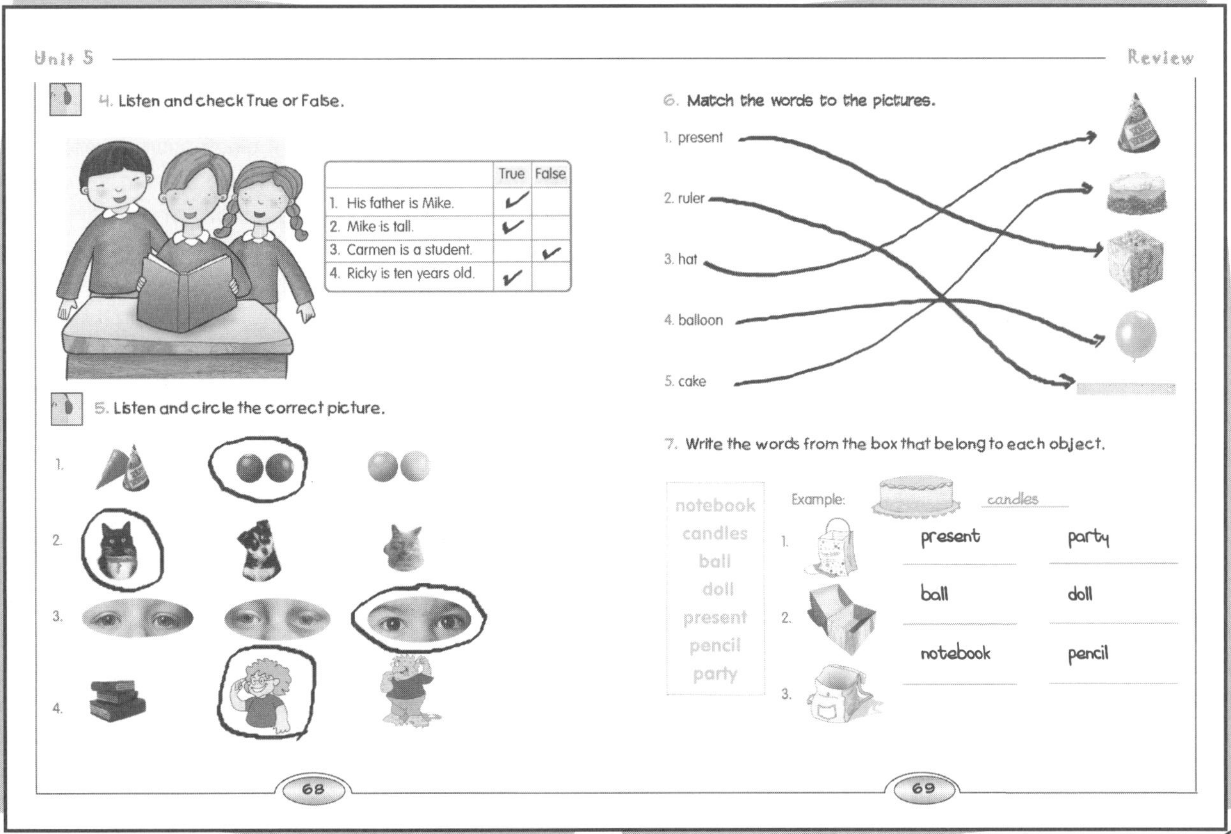
Unit 5 Review

4. Listen and check True or False.

	True	False
1. His father is Mike.	✓	
2. Mike is tall.	✓	
3. Carmen is a student.		✓
4. Ricky is ten years old.	✓	

5. Listen and circle the correct picture.

6. Match the words to the pictures.

1. present
2. ruler
3. hat
4. balloon
5. cake

7. Write the words from the box that belong to each object.

notebook, candles, ball, doll, present, pencil, party

Example: candles

1. present party
2. ball doll
3. notebook pencil

68 69

along but bangs her head into a desk and says *Ow! My head!* Do something similar to yourself, for example, bumping your shoulder into the classroom door and saying *Ow! My shoulder!* Rub your shoulder and say *Ow! My shoulder!* again.

Demonstrate the meaning of *Oh no* by doing something such as breaking a crayon into two pieces and saying in a sad voice *Oh no. My crayon.* or tipping your chair over onto the floor so you can't sit in it and saying *Oh no. My chair.* Then demonstrate the command *Come to my (place).* by pantomiming with one of the stick puppets. Hold the puppet at a distance from your desk, facing you, and say *(Natalie), come to my desk. I have a (pencil).* At the same time, make a gesture to indicate that the puppet should come toward you. Move the puppet right onto your desk and in front of you. "Give" the puppet the pencil. Then repeat the procedure, but call on a student to come to your desk. Give him or her the pencil.

Ask students to look at the picture on page 70 in their Student Book. Play the audio the first time for students to just listen. Students should understand the meaning of *Oh no* and *Ow!* from the preview activity and also the expressions on the children's faces. Play the tape again and have students point to each speech bubble, tracing from left to right. Finally, play the audio several times as student follow and repeat. Depending on students' ability, you could assign the roles of the six characters for students to read aloud and/or role-play. Encourage them to use the appropriate *Ow!, Oh no,* and *Come to...* gestures.

For extra practice with possessive adjectives and parts of the body, ask students to talk about the characters on page 70. Model the structures and gestures: *Look. This is Ken. This is his foot. Look. This is Melba. This is her shoulder.*, and so on.

For **Exercise 9**, have students look at the scene, point to the children, and ask *Where are they?* Point to Natalie and say *This is Natalie's kitchen. This is her kitchen.* Call students' attention to the list of words. Read the first one aloud (*mother*), then point to the corresponding part of the picture and say *mother* each time. Ask students to make a check next to the mother. Repeat the procedure for *dog,* saying the word several times as you look for a dog in the scene. Make it clear that you don't see one. Have students work in the same manner as they try to find (or not) a one-to-one correspondence between the words in the list and the items in the scene. Check answers as a group.

For **Exercise 10,** review the prepositions *in, on,* and *under* by moving one of the stick puppets appropriately as you say, for example, *This is Mariana. She is on my shoulder! This is Steve. He is under my desk. Look at Daniel.* (Place the Daniel puppet between two pages in a book.) *He is in my book.* Then have students look back at Natalie's kitchen on page 71 and fill in the blanks. When everyone is done, check answers by reading the sentences aloud together one at a time as you point to the items in the scene.

For **Exercise 11**, help students understand the heading *Parts of the body* by pronouncing it and pointing to the pictures of the *ear, nose, eye,* and *hand.* Then ask students to categorize the words as they did for the warm-up activity, but this time they should write the words in their Student Book in the correct columns. (Note that the picture of a doll's head represents *doll,* not *head.* However, give credit in either column, since both are technically correct.)

Play the audio for **Exercise 12** several times. The first time, ask students to listen as you point on yourself to the part of the body mentioned in each stanza: *right hand, right foot, whole body.* Play the tape again, encouraging students to pantomime all the gestures with you. Play the song as often as necessary for students to follow the song correctly. Finally, ask them to sing along as they make gestures.

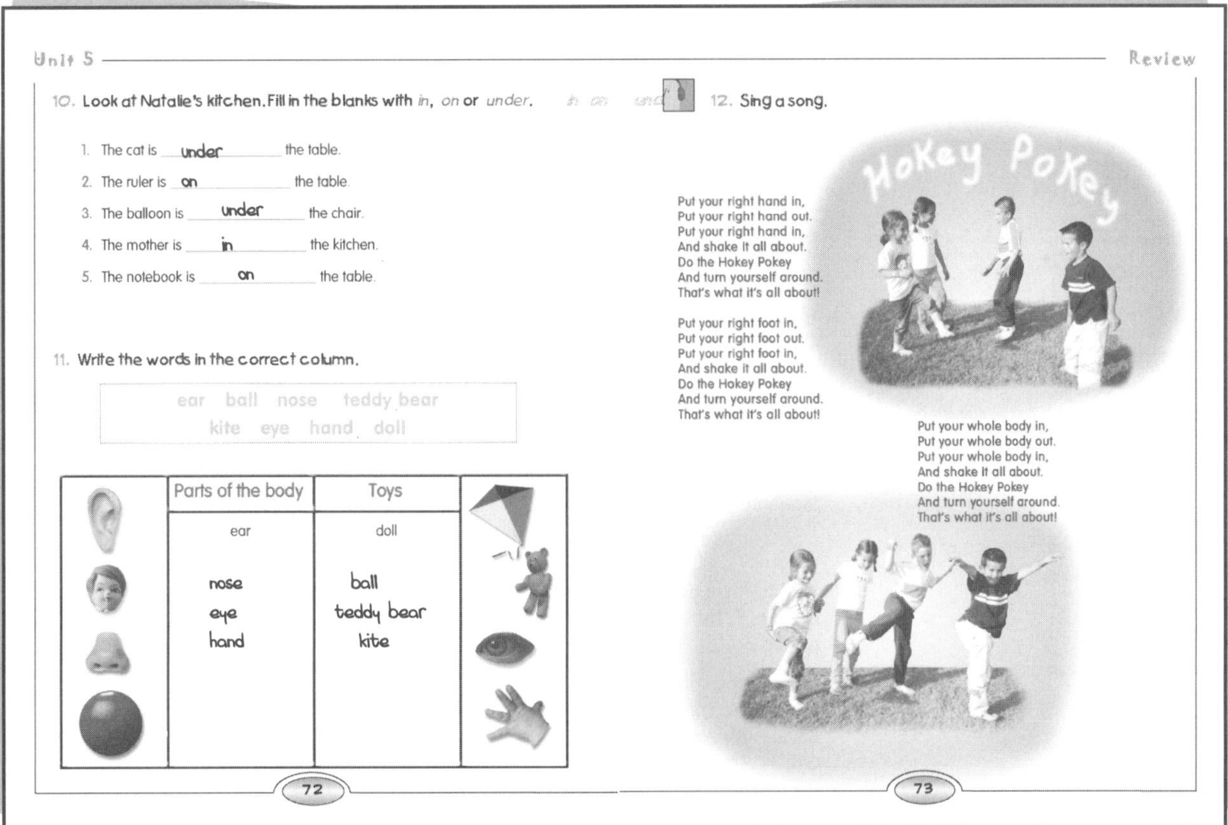
Unit 5 — Review

10. Look at Natalie's kitchen. Fill in the blanks with *in*, *on* or *under*.

1. The cat is under the table.
2. The ruler is on the table.
3. The balloon is under the chair.
4. The mother is in the kitchen.
5. The notebook is on the table.

11. Write the words in the correct column.

ear ball nose teddy bear
kite eye hand doll

Parts of the body	Toys
ear	doll
nose	ball
eye	teddy bear
hand	kite

12. Sing a song.

Put your right hand in,
Put your right hand out.
Put your right hand in,
And shake it all about.
Do the Hokey Pokey
And turn yourself around.
That's what it's all about!

Put your right foot in,
Put your right foot out.
Put your right foot in,
And shake it all about.
Do the Hokey Pokey
And turn yourself around.
That's what it's all about!

Put your whole body in,
Put your whole body out.
Put your whole body in,
And shake it all about.
Do the Hokey Pokey
And turn yourself around.
That's what it's all about!

72 73

Fun and Games

A. **Categories.** Be sure all students have their sets of picture-word cards for Units 1-4. Play the following game: Write on the board the category headings *Numbers* and *Colors.* Ask each student to take out the picture-word cards that belong to these categories. Divide the class into two teams, the *Numbers* team and the *Colors* team. When you say *Come to the board!,* the first person on each team runs to the board with one card from their assigned category and places it on the chalk ledge under the correct heading, with the word side of the card facing out. The first student who does this correctly wins a point for his or her team. Continue until all cards are properly categorized and everyone on each team has had a chance to play. (Some cards may have to be repeated.) The game can be played with other categories. Other team names and heading suggestions are: *Birthday/Toys, Colors/Classroom, House/Parts of the body, Family/Animals.*

A variation on the game is to ask team members to write the category words on the board under the correct heading. The first student to do this correctly wins a point for his or her team.

B. **Picture dictation.** Distribute crayons or colored pencils and large sheets of paper to each student. Using vocabulary from Units 1-4, dictate what to draw. If you dictate silly ideas, the students will have more fun. Students can take their time. Some ideas are: *an ear on a leg, a small head in a big red hat, a pretty friend and an ugly monster, an arm on a ruler, two fish on a cake, a pink dog, five purple turtles.* Go around the room checking that everyone is basically doing the same drawing. For extra fun, have students come up with a silly idea of their own and draw it. They should keep their drawings if they are going to do Activity C below.

C. **Label the pictures.** Students who did Activity B should label the pictures they drew, following as closely as possible your dictation from memory or based on what they see; do not repeat the dictation, but give hints with key words. Accept one-word or incomplete answers.

Tapescript

Unit 5 Page 66

Exercise 1: Listen to the dialogue.

Ken: Good morning! What's your name?
Tom: My name is Tom. What's your name?
Ken: I'm Ken. And this is Mariana. This is Daniel and this is Melba.
Natalie: I'm Natalie and this is my friend, Steve.
Daniel: We're all friends.
Ken: I'm seven. How old are you?
Tom: I'm seven, too.
Natalie: Look! We have a nice classroom. Come in, please!

Unit 5 Page 66

Exercise 2: Listen again and write the missing words.

(See Exercise 1 above.)

Unit 5 Page 68

Exercise 4: Listen and check True or False.

Mariana: Who's that man?
Tom: That's my father. His name is Mike.
Ken: He isn't very tall.
Tom: Yes, he is. He's smart, too. He's a doctor.
Ken: And who is that woman?
Tom: That's my mother. She's a teacher.
Mariana: What's her name?
Tom: Her name is Carmen. She's pretty.
Mariana: Who are those children?
Tom: That's me! And those are my brothers.
Ken: How old are your brothers?
Tom: Kevin is four years old and Ricky is ten.
Mariana: You have a nice family.
Tom: Yes, we're happy.]

Unit 5 Page 68

Exercise 5: Listen and circle the correct picture.

Girl: I have two red balls.
Man: My cat is black and white.
Boy: My eyes are brown.
Girl: I'm smart!

Unit 5 Page 70

Exercise 8: Listen, point and repeat.

Daniel: Ow! My foot! My leg!
Melba: My shoulder! My arm! Ow!
Steve: Oh no. My ball...
Tom: Oh, my eye!
Mariana: My head!
Natalie: I have toys and cake. Come to my house.

Unit 5 Page 73

Exercise 12: Sing a song.

Put your right hand in
Put your right hand out
Put your right hand in
And shake it all about
Do the Hokey Pokey
And turn yourself around
That's what it's all about!

Put your right foot in
Put your right foot out
Put your right foot in
And shake it all about
Do the Hokey Pokey
And turn yourself around
That's what it's all about!

Put your whole body in
Put your whole body out
Put your whole body in
And shake it all about
Do the Hokey Pokey
And turn yourself around
That's what it's all about!

Unit 5 Test: Review of Units 1–4

Name______________________________ Date______________

1. Draw and color a family in their favorite room in the house. Label the room, the family words, parts of the body, and colors.

2. Fill in the blanks with the correct words from the word box.

bedrooms	black	books	color	desks	
kite	legs	name	presents	three	years

1. I have ______________ dogs.
2. My ______________ is Melba.
3. What ______________ is it? It's red.
4. He is eight ______________ old.
5. My house has three ______________.
6. Happy birthday! You have five ______________.
7. The classroom has __________ and __________.
8. The __________ is blue and __________.
9. A turtle has four ______________.

3. Write about your family.

____

____

____

Unit 6

Lesson 1 It's sunny.

Objectives

Students will:

- develop vocabulary related to the classroom
- learn weather expressions

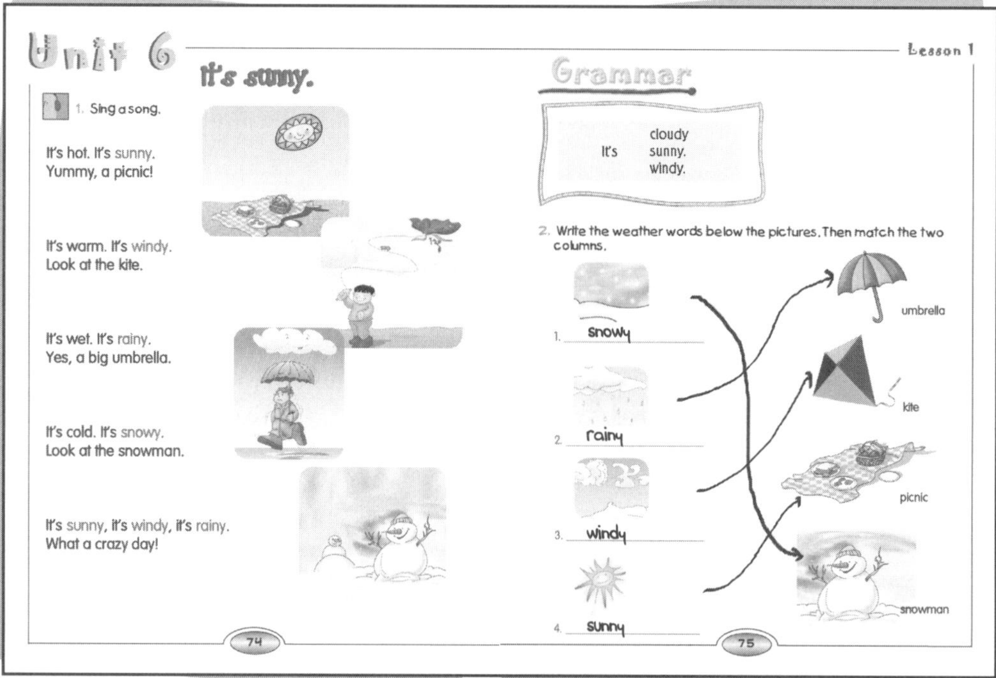
Unit 6 It's sunny. Lesson 1

1. Sing a song.

It's hot. It's sunny.
Yummy, a picnic!

It's warm. It's windy.
Look at the kite.

It's wet. It's rainy.
Yes, a big umbrella.

It's cold. It's snowy.
Look at the snowman.

It's sunny, it's windy, it's rainy.
What a crazy day!

Grammar

It's cloudy.
It's sunny.
It's windy.

2. Write the weather words below the pictures. Then match the two columns.

1. snowy
2. rainy
3. windy
4. sunny

umbrella
kite
picnic
snowman

74 75

Materials

Best Friends Student Book 1 pages 74-77

Other Materials

index cards, crayons or colored pencils, old magazines

New Language

crazy, picnic
snowman
umbrella
I'm cold/hot.
It's cloudy/cold/hot/rainy/snowy/sunny/windy.

Passive vocabulary

Yummy

1. **Getting Started**

Introduce weather expressions by presenting vocabulary from a few of the scenes on page 74 in the Student Book. First draw on the board a big blazing sun and a stick figure underneath it that is "sweating." For example, show exaggerated drops of perspiration coming out of the figure's head. Point to the sun and say *It's sunny.* Point to the sun in the first picture on page 74 and say *It's sunny.* If it is sunny outside the classroom, point to the outdoors and repeat *It's sunny.* Ask students to repeat with you. Then say *It's sunny. I'm hot!* Make gestures as if you were really warm: pretending to wipe perspiration from your forehead, taking off a jacket, or fanning yourself with your hand.

Present *It's snowy./I'm cold.* by drawing a snowman (refer to page 74, last picture, for a model), and saying *It's snowy. Look at the snowman. I'm cold* (make a shivering gesture). Have students repeat.

Play the tape for **Exercise 1**. Point to the scene on page 74 as each item or weather phenomenon is mentioned. Then repeat the audio. This time, students should point to each line in the song along with the audio. Finally, play it a few more times for students to sing along. They should guess the meanings of vocabulary and expressions from the preview activity and the scenes themselves. Pronounce *picnic, kite, umbrella,* and *snowman* as you point to each one. Have students repeat. To demonstrate *crazy day* in the context of *strange, unpredictable weather,* shake or scratch your head and show an exasperated look on your face every time the last line in the song, *What a crazy day!* is played.

Grammar Tips

- When people talk about the weather, they use impersonal expressions that start with third-person singular *It's* plus an adjective related to the weather: *It's cloudy.* = There are a lot of clouds. *It's sunny.* = The sun is shining brightly. *It's windy* = There is a lot of wind. *It's rainy* = It is raining. *It's snowy* = It is snowing.
- When people talk about how they personally feel affected by the weather, they use personal pronouns and the correct form of the verb *be*. For example, *I'm*, plus an adjective that is related to people: *I'm hot.* = I feel hot. *I'm cold.* = I feel cold. (Incorrect: *I'm cloudy/sunny/windy*, etc.)

Introduce the word *yummy* in the first stanza by pantomiming that you are eating something that you like a lot. Pretend to open your mouth, take a bite, and say *Yummy, this is good!*

Review the structures in the Grammar Box by pointing to each scene on page 74 and say *It's sunny/windy/rainy/snowy.* Point again to the first scene and say *I'm hot.* Have students repeat. Point to the last scene, shiver, and say *I'm cold.*

2. **Working Together**

Invite students to look at **Exercise 2** on page 75 in the Student Book. Relate the labels next to each picture in the right-hand column to the same word in the text on page 74. Then do the first one together as an example. Invite volunteers to give the answers or say *Number 1. It's snowy. Snowman.* Draw a connecting line from the sentence to the snowman. Pair students and have them do the exercise. Check answers as a class.

Distribute thirteen index cards per student. Each one should draw picture cards for the five weather expressions and four items in Exercise 2, as well as four word cards for the contractions *It's* and *I'm* and the adjectives *hot* and *cold.* Ask students to label each picture card clearly on the backside, using page 75 as a spelling reference. Make your own set of cards. Then point to the umbrella card and ask *What's this?* Elicit *It's an umbrella.* Repeat for the other items, eliciting *It's a kite/picnic/snowman.* Place these four cards on the chalk ledge, step away, and ask *What's that?* (Students should give the same answer as for *What's this?*) To practice the weather expressions, say, for example, *It's cloudy.* Students should hold up the appropriate word card *It's* plus either side of the *cloudy* card. Repeat for *snowy, rainy, windy, and sunny.*

Finally, pair students and encourage them to ask, answer, and point, using their picture cards in the same way.

For **Exercise 3**, students can refer to the scenes on pages 74 and 75 for inspiration, or they can use their imagination. Help students who may not be familiar with snow due to their geographic location.

For **Exercise 4**, review concepts by saying *I'm cold.* and shiver. Encourage students to hold up the appropriate word cards and to also make the *I'm cold.* gesture. Repeat the procedure for *It's hot.* Then have them complete the blanks individually and check the answers as a class.

3. **Finishing Up**

For **Exercise 5**, students can trace a snowflake from the pattern on page 77, fold it on the line patterns three times (so that it is in the shape of a triangle), and then cut out the notches. Hang everyone's snowflakes on the bulletin board.

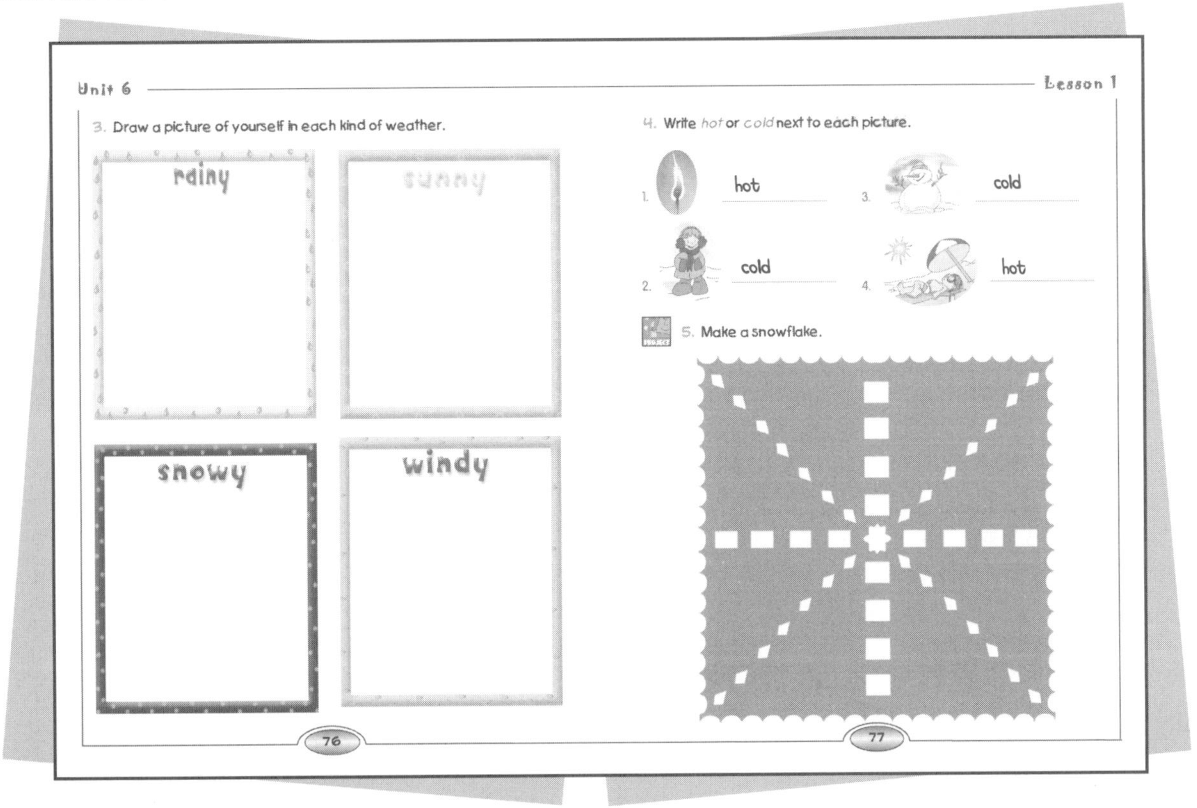
Unit 6 — Lesson 1

3. Draw a picture of yourself in each kind of weather.

rainy | sunny | snowy | windy

4. Write *hot* or *cold* next to each picture.

1. hot
2. cold
3. cold
4. hot

5. Make a snowflake.

76 | 77

Fun and Games

A. **Weather collage.** Distribute old magazines to groups of four or five students. Each group should look for scenes that show all the weather expressions from the lesson. For example, for *I'm hot.* or *It's sunny.*, they could cut out a scene of someone on a beach. Have each group make a collage of their cutouts. Check that they have enough examples before they glue their pictures onto a large piece of paper.

B. **Your favorite weather.** Have students draw a picture of themselves in their favorite kind of weather. Encourage them to label the weather represented. Then ask students to group their drawings on the bulletin board by type of weather. Count together how many students prefer which type of weather. List the results on the board under the headings *Sunny, Windy, Rainy, Snowy.*

C. **Dictation.** Use your set of Lesson 1 picture-word cards. Show the picture side of any card and ask students to write the word you dictate. Indicate a number first, for listing purposes: *Number 1: windy. Number 2: umbrella.*, and so on. Place the cards across a desk or table with the word side facing up from left to right for students to come up and check their spelling.

Tapescript

Unit 6 Lesson 1 Page 74
Exercise 1: Sing a song.

I'm hot! It's sunny.
Yummy, a picnic.

It's warm. It's windy.
Look at the kite.

It's wet. It's rainy.
Yes, a big umbrella.

I'm cold! It's snowy.
Look at the snowman.

It's sunny, it's windy, it's rainy.
What a crazy day!

Lesson 2 What a mess!

Objectives

Students will:
- listen for a purpose
- practice short-answer responses
- make negative statements

Materials
Best Friends Student Book 1 pages 78-81
Other Materials
Unit 2 picture cards (school supplies/classroom objects), stick puppets, index cards,

New Language
floor
messy
shelf
What a mess!
Is she/he/it...?
Yes, she/he/it is.
No, she/he/it isn't.
Passive Vocabulary
flag
turtle(s)

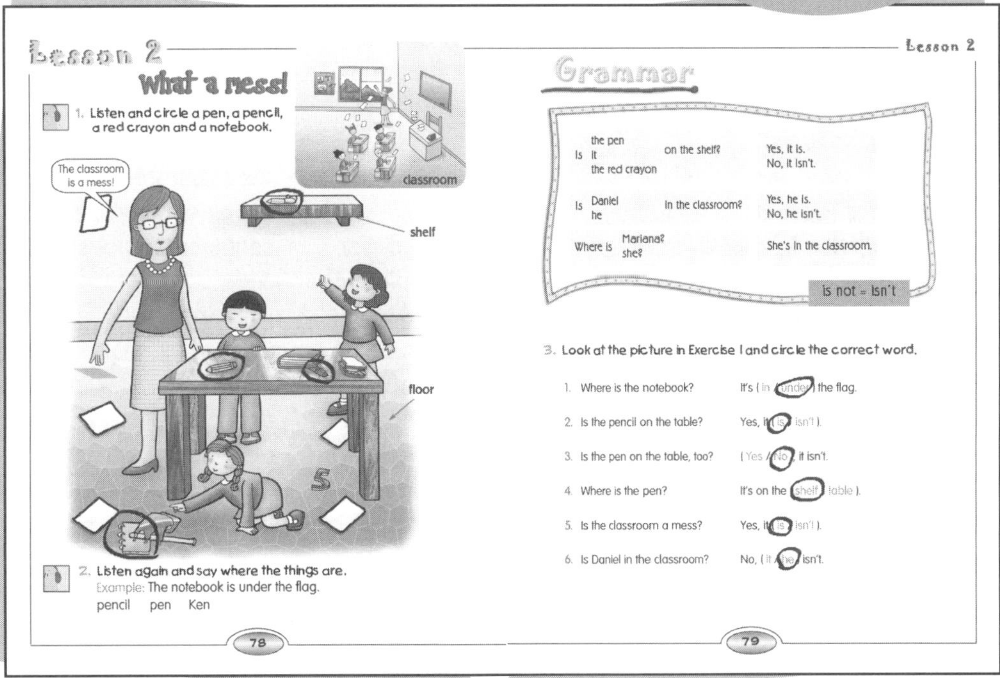
Lesson 2
What a mess!
1. Listen and circle a pen, a pencil, a red crayon and a notebook.

2. Listen again and say where the things are.
Example: The notebook is under the flag.
pencil pen Ken
78

Lesson 2
Grammar

Is	the pen / it / the red crayon	on the shelf?	Yes, it is. No, it isn't.
Is	Daniel / he	in the classroom?	Yes, he is. No, he isn't.
Where is	Mariana? / she?		She's in the classroom.

is not = isn't

3. Look at the picture in Exercise 1 and circle the correct word.
1. Where is the notebook? It's (in / under) the flag.
2. Is the pencil on the table? Yes, it (is / isn't).
3. Is the pen on the table, too? (Yes / No), it isn't.
4. Where is the pen? It's on the (shelf / table).
5. Is the classroom a mess? Yes, it (is / isn't).
6. Is Daniel in the classroom? No, (it / he) isn't.
79

1. **Getting Started**
Review vocabulary for school supplies and classroom objects with those picture cards from Unit 2. Show a card, e.g., the *table* card, place it on a desk, and say *Where is the table? It's on a desk.* Place the card on a shelf and ask *Is the table on a chair?* Shake your head and say *No, it isn't.* Then place any stick puppet on the shelf and say *Is (Natalie) on the shelf? Yes, she is.* or *Is (Steve) on the shelf? Yes, he is.*

Then point all around the classroom and say *This is a classroom.* Point to first a boy, then a girl and say *(Toni) is in the classroom. He's in the classroom. (May) is in the classroom. She's in the classroom.*

Introduce *floor, flag,* and *shelf* by pointing to these items in your classroom and repeating the words several times. Have students repeat with you. Demonstrate the concept of *a mess* by tipping over some books on a shelf, scattering your set of picture cards all over the classroom floor, and perhaps pointing to a student desk that is not very tidy. Each time, say *What a mess! The shelf/floor/desk is messy.* and shake your head in exasperation. Encourage students to repeat with you.

Before playing the tape for **Exercise 1**, tell students that they have to listen for key words so they can circle the items in the scene. Play the dialogue several times before students do the activity.

Present the structures in the Grammar Box by reading them aloud in their various combinations. Have students follow in their books by tracing along as

Grammar Tips

- *Yes/no* questions and the corresponding short answers in third-person singular require the *is* form of the verb *be: Is the boy smart? Yes, he is./No, he isn't. Is Melba under the desk? Yes, she is,/No, she isn't. Is it sunny? Yes, it is./No, it isn't.*
- The negative short answer often uses the contraction *isn't* for *is not.* However, the affirmative short answer never uses a contraction: Correct–*Is it cloudy? Yes, it is.* Incorrect–*Yes, it's.*
- Information questions start with question words such as *What* and *Where.* The answer can never be a *yes/no* answer: Correct–*Where is the red pencil? It's in the pencil box.* Incorrect–*Yes, it's in the pencil box.*

you connect the parts to make a correct question. Encourage them to read along with you as well.

Practice the structures by placing any boy stick puppet and any girl stick puppet on the floor outside the classroom. When you come back in the room, ask *Is (Daniel) in the classroom? No, he isn't. He isn't in the classroom. He's on the floor.* and *Is (Melba) in the classroom? No, she isn't. She isn't in the classroom. She's on the floor.* Repeat the pattern with other cards and puppets, changing where they are situated and using familiar vocabulary.

2. **Working Together**

For **Exercise 3**, explain the instructions and do the first one together. Be sure everyone agrees about the placement of the notebook in the scene on page 78. Students may wish to work in pairs. Check answers as a class.

Before assigning **Exercise 4**, practice word order for *yes/no* and *Where* questions by writing on the board a sentence such as *The dog is in the bedroom.* Circle *is* and "move" it in front of *The dog* by drawing an arrow from the circled *is* to in front of *The dog*. Them underneath the sentence, write the question with proper word order, capitalization, and punctuation: *Is the dog in the bedroom?* Point out how the position of *is* moved to the front, and remind students that the first word in all sentences starts with a capital letter. An alternative for this activity, is to paste sentences made with word cards on the board, move the verb card to the beginning of the sentence, add a question word where necessary and the question mark at the end of the sentence. Let several students practice making questions with the word cards.

When you are sure students have understood how to make questions, let them answer the exercise in pairs and check the answers as a class.

Before assigning **Exercise 5**, practice making negative statements by saying sentences that are true. Use props such as the stick puppets and picture cards as necessary. For example, show the Mariana puppet and say *Mariana is in the classroom.* Then place her outside the classroom, come back in, and say *Mariana isn't in the classroom.* Then, ask students to make the negative sentences in pairs and check the answers as a class.

3. **Finishing Up**

Before doing **Exercise 6**, ask students to show you what they brought for lunch. Show a sandwich to the class, and ask *What's this? Yummy! It's a sandwich.* Ask students to find a sandwich in the scene on page 81.

Tell students to look at the scene carefully and to count the number of blanks (nine) and the number of words in the box (eight). Tell them that there is one word in the box that they don't need (*table*) and that they will repeat two of the words (*it* and *is*). As a hint, remind students that the capitalized words in the word box will necessarily go in blanks at the beginning of sentences. For **Exercise 2**, go over the example so that students know what they are listening for.

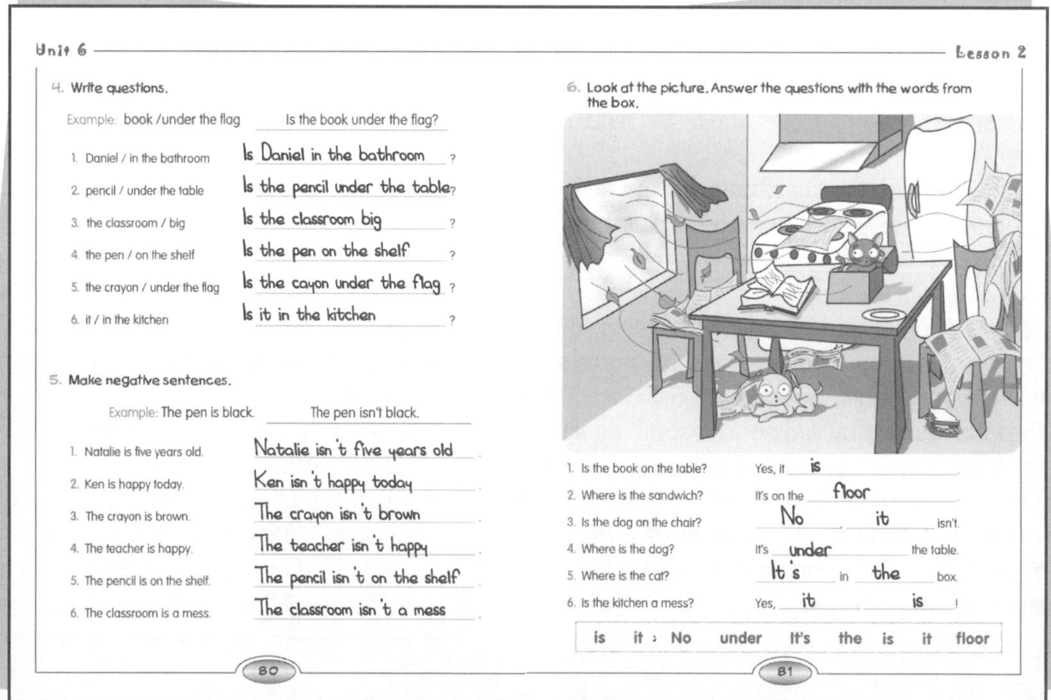

Unit 6 — Lesson 2

4. Write questions.

Example: book /under the flag — Is the book under the flag?

1. Daniel / in the bathroom — Is Daniel in the bathroom ?
2. pencil / under the table — Is the pencil under the table?
3. the classroom / big — Is the classroom big ?
4. the pen / on the shelf — Is the pen on the shelf ?
5. the crayon / under the flag — Is the cayon under the flag ?
6. it / in the kitchen — Is it in the kitchen ?

5. Make negative sentences.

Example: The pen is black. — The pen isn't black.

1. Natalie is five years old. — Natalie isn't five years old.
2. Ken is happy today. — Ken isn't happy today.
3. The crayon is brown. — The crayon isn't brown.
4. The teacher is happy. — The teacher isn't happy.
5. The pencil is on the shelf. — The pencil isn't on the shelf.
6. The classroom is a mess. — The classroom isn't a mess.

6. Look at the picture. Answer the questions with the words from the box.

1. Is the book on the table? — Yes, it is.
2. Where is the sandwich? — It's on the floor.
3. Is the dog on the chair? — No, it isn't.
4. Where is the dog? — It's under the table.
5. Where is the cat? — It's in the box.
6. Is the kitchen a mess? — Yes, it is!

is it No under It's the is it floor

80 81

Fun and Games

A. **Chain.** Have everyone stand in a circle. Ask the student to your right *Is your name (Student name)?* to elicit *Yes, it is.* Have that student ask the person to his or her right the same question, always using that child's correct name in order to elicit *Yes, it is.* Go around in a chain until the last student asks you *Is your name (name)?* An alternative chain is to ask a deliberately incorrect name to elicit *No, it isn't.*

B. **Where is he/she?** Have students close their eyes, then place a stick puppet somewhere in the classroom, face up, in a place and position that students are familiar with. Some ideas are: on the floor, in a backpack/desk/box/ (but visible), on a shelf/table/chair/desk, under a flag/table/chair/shelf/desk/umbrella. Ask *Where is (Daniel)?* Everyone must look for that puppet, stand next to it, and say *(He's)(in)(a backpack).* The first student to do this correctly gets to hide another puppet and ask *Where is (puppet name)?*

C. **Dictation.** Divide the class into four teams. The first person on each team stands at the board. Dictate short sentences with *is* and *isn't*. The first student to write it correctly wins a point for his or her team. Let every student participate. The team with the most points at the end wins. Some sample sentences are:
   1. The pen is in the box.
   2. The box isn't under the table.
   3. The kitchen is a mess.
   4. Melba isn't in the classroom.
   5. It isn't cloudy.

Tapescript

Unit 6 Lesson 2 Page 78

Exercise 1: Listen and circle a pen, a pencil, a red crayon and the notebook.

Mrs. Williams:	The classroom is a mess! Where's my notebook?
Mariana:	It's under the flag.
Mrs. Williams:	Thank you. And where's my pencil?
Ken:	Here it is! On the table.
Mrs. Williams:	Good. Is my pen on the table, too?
Melba:	No, it isn't. It's on the shelf.
Mrs. Williams:	And where's Daniel? Is he in the classroom?
Steve:	No, he isn't.
Mrs. Williams:	Where is he?
Steve:	He's in the bathroom.

Unit 6 Lesson 2 Page 78

Exercise 2: Listen and say where the things are.

(See Exercise 1 above.)

Lesson 3 It isn't messy now!

Objectives

Students will:
- learn vocabulary related to classroom objects
- recognize opposites

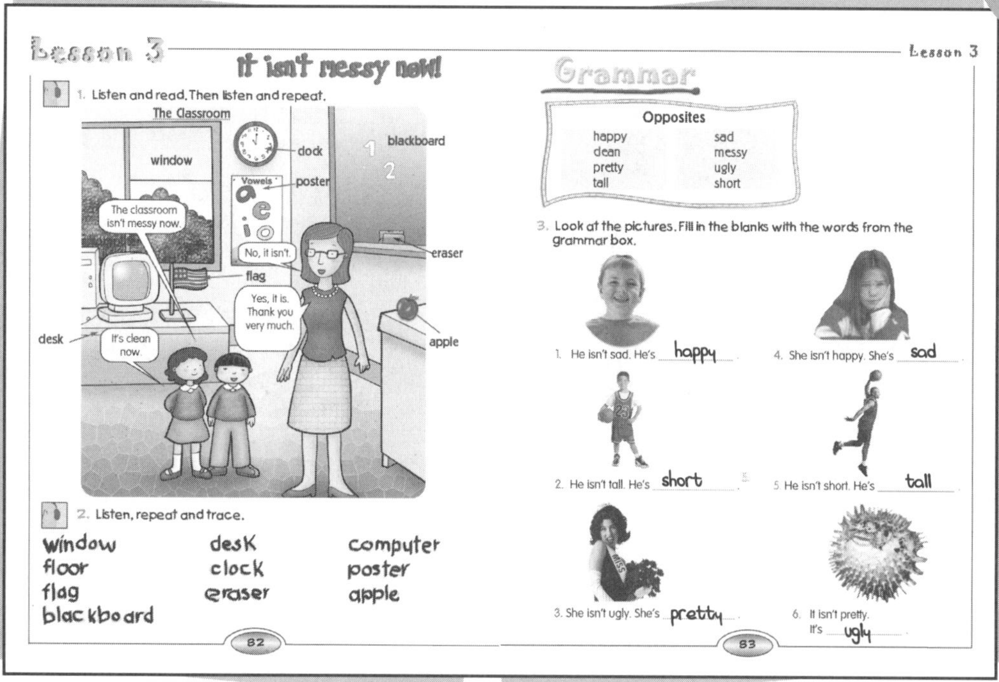

Materials
Best Friends Student Book 1 pages 82-85
Other Materials
index cards, crayons or colored pencils

New Language
clean, sad, short
Spelling
apple, board, chalkboard, clock, computer, desk, eraser, flag, floor, poster, window

1. **Getting Started**
Present or review vocabulary for the classroom by pointing to each labeled word in Student Book page 82 and pronouncing it several times. Have students point and repeat. Then distribute enough index cards per student so that they can each draw every classroom object in the scene except the classroom itself. They can use the art in the book or similar objects in their own classroom as models. Explain to students that *blackboard* and *board* are the same. Make your own set of cards. Then hold up cards and ask *yes/no* questions to elicit *Yes, it is./No, it isn't.* For example: *Is it an apple?* about the apple card (*Yes, it is.*) and *Is it a window?* about the computer card (*No, it isn't*). Drill until students are totally sure of the vocabulary.

Play the audio for **Exercise 1** for students to first listen. Play it a second time and go over the dialogue, pointing to each speech bubble and tracing from left to right with a finger under the words as you read aloud. Ask students to do the same. Then play the tape again and have students repeat.

Play the audio for **Exercise 2**. The first time, ask students to point to each object and its label in the classroom scene as it is mentioned. Stop the tape after each word and, as a group, correlate the word in Exercise 2 with the label in Exercise 1. Then play the audio for students to repeat and trace the words.

Ask students to label their picture cards on the backside, referring to page 82 for spelling. Check spelling on the cards, especially double consonants, double vowels, and final *e*'s.

Grammar Tips

- Opposites, or antonyms, are words that have the opposite meaning of another word. For example, in Unit 4, some story characters thought the monster was ugly. Others thought he was beautiful. *Ugly* and *beautiful* are opposite adjectives.
- Adjectives are not the only kind of word that have opposites, but they are the most frequent, along with verbs. Nouns don't really have opposites so much as complements, e.g., *father/mother, sister/brother, king/queen.*

Go over the adjectives in the Grammar Box and make gestures or point to pictures that show the meaning of each. For example, for *happy/sad,* smile and say *I'm happy.,* then show a sad face and say *I'm sad.* For *clean/messy,* ask students to compare scenes on pages 78 and 81 with the classroom scene on page 82. Say *messy* or *clean,* depending on which scene you are pointing to.

2. **Working Together**

For **Exercise 3**, do number 1 together as an example. When students have finished, have them exchange books and check one another's work.

Then distribute eight index cards to each student and have them create word cards for all the adjectives in the Grammar Box on page 83. (If some of these word cards were prepared in a previous lesson, students can pull them out for use.) They can refer to the box for spelling reference. Make your own set of cards as well. Using your set of cards, demonstrate the following activity: Say a word and have students either pantomime the word or hold up the card. Then have pairs practice with their cards in the same way.

Preview **Exercise 4** by writing on the board a few color words such as *red, white,* and *green* in capital letters. Read them aloud letter by letter and have students repeat with you. For example: *red...R-E-D...red.* Encourage students to write the words in their notebooks as you repeat several times. Then play the tape a few times before students do the dictation activity.

For **Exercise 5**, start students off by chanting the letters of the alphabet together. Remind them that words are formed by putting together certain letters, as they practiced in Exercise 4. Point out that the pictures represent the words they have to find in the puzzle. Read the circled example aloud letter by letter. (Have them also cross out the picture so they know they have found it already.) Then allow students to continue on their own. They may work in pairs if they wish.

3. **Finishing Up**

For **Exercise 6** students can work in groups. The object of the game is to figure out the pattern of words and fill in the blank boxes. (If students don't have enough space because their writing is large, tell them to write the words above the boxes.)

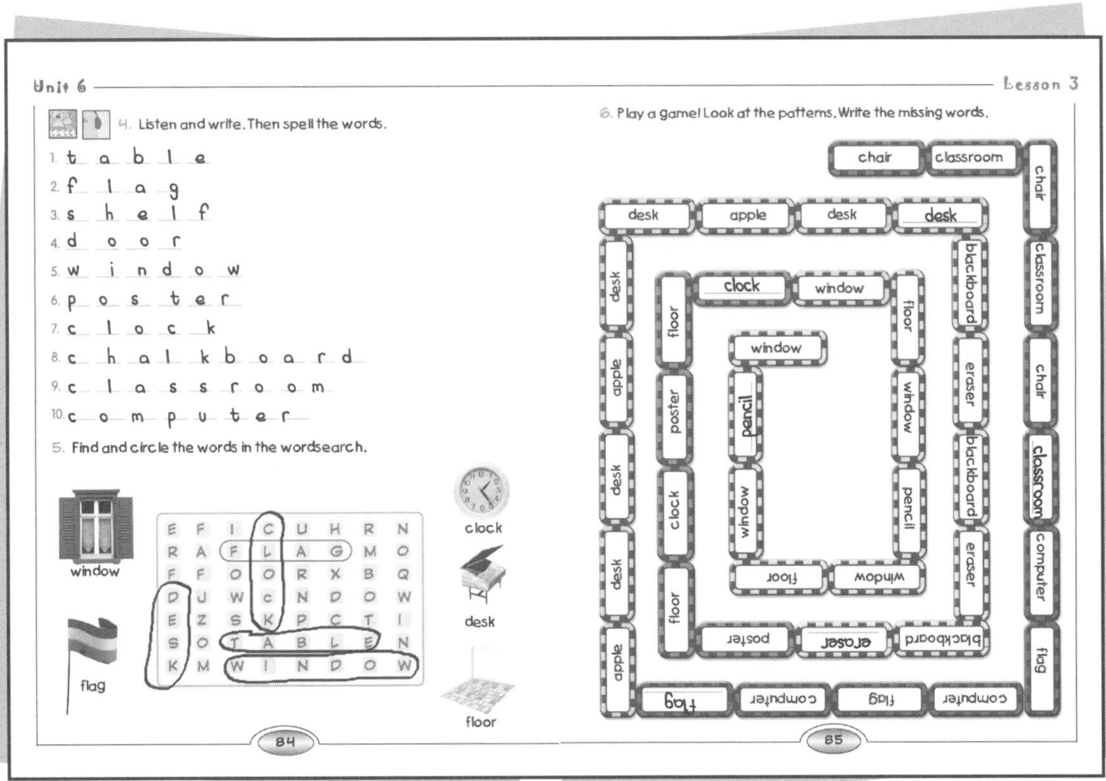

Fun and Games

A. **A clean or messy desk?** Have students draw two contrasting scenes: their desks when they are messy, and then when their desks are clean. If a student is always neat, have them draw a friend's desk. Students should label each scene *clean* or *messy* as appropriate. Put all artwork on the bulletin board and take a vote on which desk is the messiest and which is the cleanest.

B. **Say the opposite.** Be sure all students have their sets of adjective word cards. Divide the class into groups of five or six and tell them to stand up. Holding up a word card, e.g., the *happy* card, have students hold up the opposite word card as quickly as possible (*sad*). When everyone is holding up a card, say the pair of words together loudly: *happy!/sad!* Then check that everyone has the same card. Any student who isn't showing the correct card must sit down. Repeat the procedure faster and faster, alternating word cards, until only one student is left standing in each group.

C. **Dictation.** Use one set of word cards for the classroom objects. Divide the class into two teams. The first person on Team A reads a word card aloud, and the first person on Team B writes it on the board. If the word is spelled correctly, Team B gets a point; if it is wrong, Team A gets a point. However, if the "reader" on Team A doesn't pronounce the word correctly, he or she must sit down and the team loses a point. Teams switch roles. Go through the cards as often as necessary to give everyone a chance to dictate and write. The team with the most points at the end wins.

Tapescript

Unit 6 Lesson 3 Page 82

Exercise 1: Listen and read. Then listen and repeat.

Ken: The classroom isn't messy now.
Mrs. Williams: No, it isn't.
Melba: It's clean now.
Mrs. Williams: Yes, it is. Thank you very much!

Unit 6 Lesson 3 Page 82

Exercise 2: Listen, repeat and trace.

window
floor
flag
blackboard
desk
clock
eraser
computer
poster
apple

Unit 6 Lesson 3 Page 84

Exercise 4: Listen and write. Then spell the words.

Table. T-A-B-L-E. Table.
Flag. F-L-A-G. Flag.
Shelf. S-H-E-L-F. Shelf.
Door. D-O-O-R. Door.
Window. W-I-N-D-O-W. Window.
Poster. P-O-S-T-E-R. Poster.
Clock. C-L-O-C-K. Clock.
Chalkboard. B-L-A-C-K-B-O-A-R-D. Blackboard.
Classroom. C-L-A-S-S-R-O-O-M. Classroom.
Computer. C-O-M-P-U-T-E-R. Computer.

Lesson 4 Review

Objectives

Students will:
- read a dialogue
- review language from Lessons 1-3
- differentiate between /c/ and /g/

Materials
Best Friends Student Book 1 pages 86-89
Other Materials
picture and word cards from Lessons 1-3, old magazines, large sheets of paper, scissors, glue

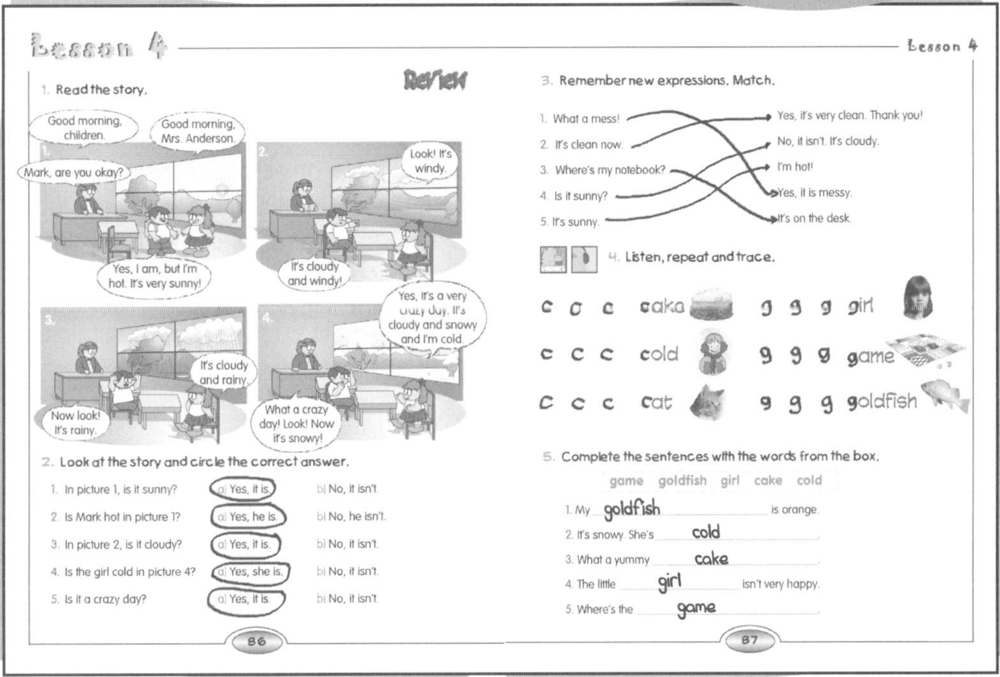
Lesson 4 Review

1. Read the story.

2. Look at the story and circle the correct answer.

1. In picture 1, is it sunny? a) Yes, it is. b) No, it isn't.
2. Is Mark hot in picture 1? a) Yes, he is. b) No, he isn't.
3. In picture 2, is it cloudy? a) Yes, it is. b) No, it isn't.
4. Is the girl cold in picture 4? a) Yes, she is. b) No, it isn't.
5. Is it a crazy day? a) Yes, it is. b) No, it isn't.

86

Lesson 4

3. Remember new expressions. Match.

1. What a mess! — Yes, it's very clean. Thank you!
2. It's clean now. — No, it isn't. It's cloudy.
3. Where's my notebook? — I'm hot!
4. Is it sunny? — Yes, it is messy.
5. It's sunny. — It's on the desk.

4. Listen, repeat and trace.

c c c cake g g g girl
c c c cold g g g game
c c c cat g g g goldfish

5. Complete the sentences with the words from the box.

game goldfish girl cake cold

1. My goldfish is orange.
2. It's snowy. She's cold.
3. What a yummy cake.
4. The little girl isn't very happy.
5. Where's the game.

87

Read

Exercise 1: Dialogue summary. A boy, a girl, and a teacher are in a classroom. The teacher says "Good morning," and they all talk about the weather. At first, the boy is hot because it is sunny. Then, through the big classroom window, the teacher, the boy, and the girl see that is it windy and cloudy. After that, it is cloudy and rainy. It's a very crazy day, because it is sunny, then, windy and cloudy, then rainy, and then--it's snowy! Now the girl is cold. She is not hot. What a crazy day!

Read the dialogue aloud, pointing to each speech bubble as you read. Ask students to listen and follow in their books. For fun, change voices to represent different speakers. Then read the dialogue again and encourage students to read aloud with you. Finally, assign the roles of the teacher, the boy, and the girl to three capable students. They can use the book to read their parts or they can try to memorize and recite their parts. If possible, have them role-play the scenes using their word cards for weather expressions.

Story Comprehension

Exercise 2: Do number 1 together as an example: *In picture 1, is it sunny? Yes, it is.* Then read all the questions aloud giving students time to circle their answers. When everyone is done, check answers as a class.

Vocabulary

Exercise 3: Read the numbered items one at a time and ask students to find the logical match for it, e.g., *What a mess! Yes, it's messy* They can read the answer aloud or point to it in their books. Give everyone a chance to answer a question.

Listen

Exercise 4: Play the tape several times so that students practice the letter pronunciation and tracing. Students may find confusing the difference in the pronunciation of /g/ in these words versus the letter name, but tell them that sometimes /g/ has the "gee" sound, just not in these words.

For **Exercise 5**, have students first match up the words in the word box with their corresponding pictures in Exercise 4. Then, tell them to complete the sentences. They may want to work in pairs. Tell students not to forget to include a question mark (*?*) after the last item. Check answers as a class.

Preview **Exercise 6** by reviewing the dialogue format with speech bubbles. Have students look at page 86 in their Student Book. Draw the first speech bubble on the board, with both the bubble and the text, but leave a blank line in place of the word *morning*. Ask students *what word is missing*? Another example is the speech bubble *What a crazy day!*, but leave out the word *crazy*. Ask again *what word is missing?* When students understand what they have to do, have them complete Exercise 6 based on the pictures and using vocabulary they are familiar with. Be sure they realize that there are four separate situations, not a continuous "story." When they finish, play the tape to check their answers.

Exercise 7: Play a game. Review vocabulary with all picture-word cards from Unit 6. Hold up either the picture side or the word side and elicit the vocabulary.

Then tell students to look at page 89 in their books. The object of the game is that all students start at the same time and circle all the items that are listed in the checklist above the mall scene. Every time they find one item, they should mark (✓) it in the checklist. When they finish, have students exchange books and correct each other's work.

Fun and Games

A. **Opposites.** Distribute several magazines, paper, scissors, and glue to groups of five students. Have them look for pictures that show the following opposites: *clean/messy, beautiful/ugly, happy/sad, tall/short.* They can make individual collages or one large group collage for the bulletin board. In either case, encourage them to label the pictures they cut out.

B. **Draw!** Divide the class into five teams and have them stand far away from the board. Using all the lesson vocabulary, tell the first student in each team what to draw, e.g., *an apple.* The first student to finish correctly gets a point for his or her team. Give everyone a chance to draw. The team with the most points wins.

C. **Teacher Says.** Play a simplified form of Simon Says. Each student should have his or her set of picture-word cards for classroom objects. Demonstrate the game as follows: Hold up a random card, e.g., the *window* card, and say *Touch the window!* Students should follow your lead as quickly as possible. Then hold up another card, e.g., the *computer* card and say *Touch the flag!* Whoever touches his or her computer card is out. Any student not holding the correct card at any time is also out. Play until a winner is declared.

Tapescript

Unit 6 Lesson 4 Page 87

Exercise 4: Listen and repeat. Then trace and say.

cake /c/ /c/ /c/ cake
cold /c/ /c/ /c/ cold
cat /c/ /c/ /c/ cat
girl /g/ /g/ /g/ girl
game /g/ /g/ /g/ game
goldfish /g/ /g/ /g/ goldfish

Unit 6 Lesson 4 Page 88

Exercise 6: What are they saying? Complete the sentences. Listen and check.

1. Mother: Where's the cat?
   Girl: The cat's on the table.

2. Boy: It's windy!

3. Man: My foot is under the television.

4. Wolf: Oh no! It's hot!

Unit 6 Test

Name________________________ Date______________

1. Draw.

1. It's rainy.
2. He's hot!
3. The umbrella is on the floor.
4. The girl isn't happy.
5. The clock is clean,

2. Write a dialogue about the weather on the board.

3. Answer the questions logically.

Example: Where is the computer? It's in the classroom.

1. Is the kitchen a mess? Yes, ______________________________.
2. Is it rainy? No, ______________________________.
3. Where is the apple? It's ______________________________.
4. Is the snowman cold? No, he ______________________________.
5. What color is the flag? It's ______________________________.

Unit 7

Lesson 1 He's a bus driver.

Objectives

Students will:
- learn vocabulary related to occupations
- listen for a purpose
- answer information questions
- recognize possessive with 's

Materials
Best Friends Student Book 1
pages 90-93
Other Materials
pictures related to occupations, index cards, old magazines, scissors, glue, stick puppets

New Language
(Mariana)'s (brother)
(Sam)'s (sister)
What/Where/Who is…?
Spelling
bus driver, dentist, doctor, homemaker, nurse, pilot, police officer, taxi driver
teacher, vet
Passive vocuabulary
big, class, good, great
student

Unit 7 He's a bus driver. Lesson 1

1. Look and listen.

2. Listen again and repeat. Circle the occupations in the dialogue.

Grammar

What			He's a doctor.
Where	is	he? she?	She's in the bathroom.
Who			He's my brother.

Mariana's brother = the brother of Mariana
Sam's sister = the sister of Sam

3. Read the sentences and circle T (True) or F (False).

1. Sam is Melba's father. T F
2. In picture one, Sam's sister is a nurse. T F
3. In picture two, Melba's brother is a pilot. T F
4. In picture three, Natalie's sister is a homemaker. T F

4. Circle the correct question.

1. Who's that? / Where is she? — That's my mother
2. What is he? / Where is he? — He's a teacher
3. What is she? / Who is she? — She's a doctor.
4. What is he? / Who is he? — He's a vet.
5. Where is your sister? / What is she? — She's a student.

90 91

1. **Getting Started**
Introduce new vocabulary related to occupations by showing pictures of *bus driver, nurse, pilot, police officer,* and *homemaker.* Point to a picture and first say the word, e.g., *bus driver* and then, depending on the person in the picture, say *He/She is a bus driver.* Repeat for all professions mentioned in the dialogue on page 90.

Then ask students to turn to page 71 in their book for another example of *homemaker* and to introduce *What/Where/Who* questions. Ask and answer as you point to Natalie's mother *Who is she? She's Natalie's mother. Where is she? She is in her kitchen. What is Natalie's mother? She is a homemaker.* Repeat the sequence several times. Then point to Natalie and ask and answer *Where is Natalie? She's in her kitchen. What is she? She's a girl.* Finally, ask about the rest of the characters on page 71, eliciting the answer *He's/She's in Natalie's kitchen. He's/She's a boy/girl.*

Play the tape for **Exercise 1**. As each character speaks, students should trace with a finger under the words in the speech bubbles. Play the audio a second time and point to the appropriate picture as occupations are mentioned. Encourage students to do the same as they listen to the dialogue.

Play the audio for **Exercise 2** and ask students to repeat. Then play the tape again, encouraging them to circle the occupation words in the speech bubbles as each is mentioned. Check answers as a class.

Grammar Tips

- Information questions with *What* ask what someone or something is or does: *What is your sister?/She's a student. What is that?/It's a pen. What has two heads?/The monster has two heads.*
- Information questions with *Who* ask about the identity of someone: *Who is she?/She's my teacher. Who has beautiful fish?/Daniel has beautiful fish.*
- Information questions with *Where* ask for the location of someone or something: *Where is Melba?/She's in the classroom. Where is the computer?/It's on my desk.*

❖ We can say *Daniel has fish* to talk about a person that has something (or someone), or we can show a relationship of possession by adding an apostrophe plus an *s ('s)* to the person that is the "*possessor*" or "*owner*": *Daniel's fish* = the fish that Daniel has; *Ken's family* = the family that Ken has.

Review the structures in the Grammar Box by pointing to the characters on page 90 and asking and answering questions. Have students repeat the answers with you.

2. **Working Together**
For **Exercise 3**, be sure students understand the numbering sequence of the pictures on page 90. If they have problems, help them to write the correct numbers next to each speech bubble. Then, do the first one as an example: *Sam is Melba's father. False. Circle F.* (Sam is Melba's brother). Students can work in pairs or by themselves. Check the answers as a class.

Before students complete **Exercise 4**, read aloud the statements in the right-hand column, point to the pictures, and repeat several times the occupation words (*mother, teacher, doctor, vet, student*). Then say directly to individual students *We are in a classroom. I am the teacher. You are a student.* Then do number 1 as an example together to show how the answer goes with *Who's that?* Point out that even though the pictures may show these people in certain places, the answers give information about their identities, not where they are. Tell students to match the statements to the pictures. Check answers as a class.

For **Exercise 5,** pair students and have them work together following the example. They can refer to Exercise 4 if necessary. When students are done, check answers together. Then distribute index cards for students to create the following picture cards: *bus driver, dentist, doctor, homemaker, nurse, pilot, police officer, taxi driver, student, teacher, vet.* Ask them to draw representative symbols of these occupations, e.g., a bus for a bus driver, a tooth for a dentist, etc. Make a set for yourself. Then write on the board the occupation words for students to copy onto the backside of their cards. Then check comprehension by saying an occupation and having students hold up the appropriate picture card.

For **Exercise 6**, preview by pointing to the people and say *Look! This is Steve's family. This is Steve's father. His name is Mark. This is Steve's mother. Her name is Tina.* Then play the audio a few times for students to just listen before they actually fill in the chart. When they are done, check the answers together.

3. **Finishing Up**
For **Exercise 7**, review family-member vocabulary to help students see the relationships in the family tree: *This is Steve's family. It is a big family. Jack is four years old. He is Steve's brother. Laurie is seven years old. She is Jack's sister and She is Steve's sister.*, etc. Introduce the word *baby* by showing a picture of a baby. Show the picture and say *This is a baby. Greg is a baby.* Then ask students to make their *baby* card and add it to their set of cards for Unit 7. When you are sure they have understood the family tree, ask students to fill in the blanks by copying the correct word from the two alternatives in parenthesis. Ask students to exchange books and check each other's answers, then check answers as a class.

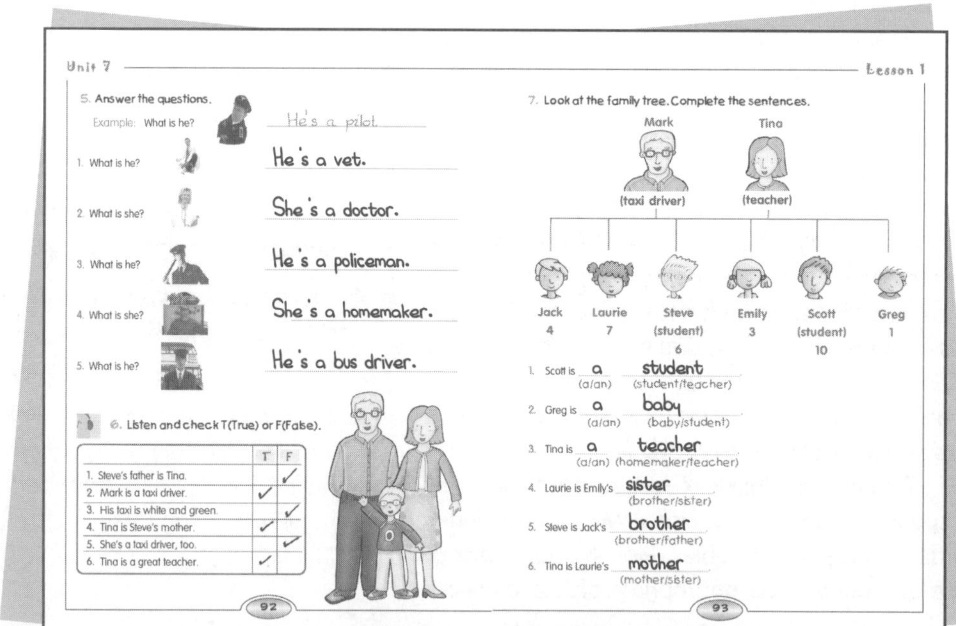
Unit 7 — Lesson 1

5. Answer the questions.

Example: What is he? He's a pilot.

1. What is he? He's a vet.
2. What is she? She's a doctor.
3. What is he? He's a policeman.
4. What is she? She's a homemaker.
5. What is he? He's a bus driver.

6. Listen and check T (True) or F (False).

	T	F
1. Steve's father is Tina.		✓
2. Mark is a taxi driver.	✓	
3. His taxi is white and green.		✓
4. Tina is Steve's mother.	✓	
5. She's a taxi driver, too.		✓
6. Tina is a great teacher.	✓	

7. Look at the family tree. Complete the sentences.

1. Scott is a (a/an) student (student/teacher)
2. Greg is a (a/an) baby (baby/student)
3. Tina is a (a/an) teacher (homemaker/teacher)
4. Laurie is Emily's sister (brother/sister)
5. Steve is Jack's brother (brother/father)
6. Tina is Laurie's mother (mother/sister)

92 93

Fun and Games

A. **Draw!** Divide the class into small teams and have them stand far away from the board. Using all the lesson vocabulary, tell the first student in each team who or what to draw on the board, e.g., *Draw a vet. Draw Steve's mother and father.* The first student to finish correctly gets a point for his or her team. Give everyone a chance to draw. The team with the most points wins.

B. **What is he/she?** Distribute old magazines to each group of five. Have groups look for people who practice the occupations learned in the lesson. Encourage them to make appropriate statements such as *He's a police officer.* or *She's a vet.* Students can cut out their pictures and make one large display per group for the bulletin board under the heading *Occupations.*

C. **Who/What/Where...?** Use the stick puppets and your set of occupation picture cards. Pair students and demonstrate the game as follows with a volunteer: Hold up a random puppet and a random card, e.g., Melba/pilot card, and ask *Who is she?* Elicit from your partner *She's Melba.* Ask *What is she?* and elicit *She's a pilot.* Finally, place the puppet somewhere in the classroom and ask *Where is she?* Elicit *She is in/on/under (place).* Have each pair do the routine for the rest of the class until everyone has had a chance.

Tapescript

Unit 7 Lesson 1 Page 90
Exercise 1: Look and listen.

Natalie: Is that your brother, Sam?
Melba: Yes. And that's me.
Natalie: What is he?
Melba: He's a bus driver and I'm a nurse.

Natalie: What are you here?
Melba: I'm a pilot.
Natalie: And what is he? Is he a pilot, too?
Melba: No, he's a police officer.

Natalie: What are you in this picture?
Melba: I'm a homemaker.
Natalie: Where is your brother?
Melba: He isn't here. He's at home!

Unit 7 Lesson 1 Page 90
Exercise 2: Listen again and repeat. Circle the occupations in the dialogue.

(See Exercise 1 above.)

Unit 7 Lesson 1 Page 92
Exercise 6: Listen and check T (True) or F (False).

Hi! I'm Steve. This is my father. His name is Mark. He's a taxi driver. His taxi is white and blue. He's a good taxi driver. This is my mother. Her name is Tina. She's a teacher. Her class is big. She's a great teacher.

Lesson 2 I'm on a bike.

Objectives

Students will:
- learn vocabulary related to transportation
- use prepositions of place correctly
- listen for a purpose

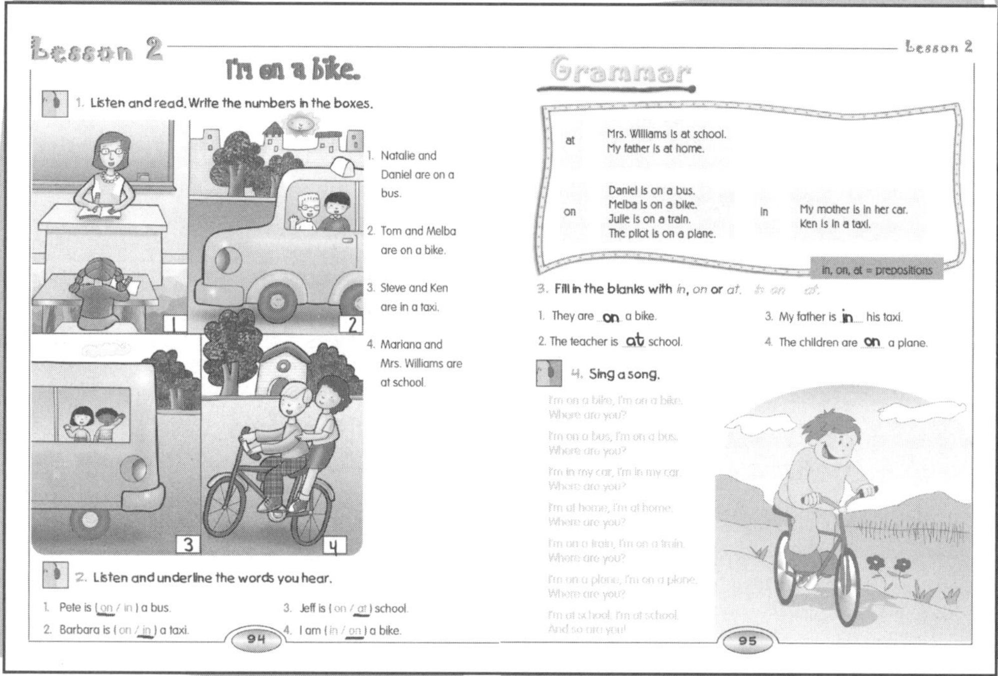
Lesson 2

I'm on a bike.

1. Listen and read. Write the numbers in the boxes.

1. Natalie and Daniel are on a bus.
2. Tom and Melba are on a bike.
3. Steve and Ken are in a taxi.
4. Mariana and Mrs. Williams are at school.

2. Listen and underline the words you hear.

1. Pete is (on / in) a bus.
2. Barbara is (on / in) a taxi.
3. Jeff is (on / at) school.
4. I am (in / on) a bike.

94

Lesson 2

Grammar

at	Mrs. Williams is at school. My father is at home.		
on	Daniel is on a bus. Melba is on a bike. Julie is on a train. The pilot is on a plane.	in	My mother is in her car. Ken is in a taxi.

in, on, at = prepositions

3. Fill in the blanks with *in*, *on* or *at*.

1. They are on a bike.
2. The teacher is at school.
3. My father is in his taxi.
4. The children are on a plane.

4. Sing a song.

I'm on a bike, I'm on a bike.
Where are you?
I'm on a bus, I'm on a bus.
Where are you?
I'm in my car, I'm in my car.
Where are you?
I'm at home, I'm at home.
Where are you?
I'm on a train, I'm on a train.
Where are you?
I'm on a plane, I'm on a plane.
Where are you?
I'm at school, I'm at school.
And so are you!

95

Materials

Best Friends Student Book 1 pages 94-97

Other Materials

index cards, stick puppets

New Language

bike
bus
car
plane
taxi
train
at home/school
in a car/taxi
on a bike/bus/plane/train

1. **Getting Started**

Review the prepositions of place *in* and *on* by making true statements, e.g., *The pencil is in a pencil box.* and *The pencil box is on a desk.* Point to other classroom objects and ask students to point and repeat. Introduce the preposition *at* by drawing on the board a school building and a typical house or apartment. Point to the appropriate picture as you say to the class *You are at school. Your family is not at school. Your pets are not at school. They are at home.*

Then ask students to look at page 94 in their Student Book. Preview vocabulary by saying *school, taxi, bus, bike,* as you point to the pictures from left to right. Then read the sentences and stress the prepositions loudly.

Play the tape for **Exercise 1**. Tell students to associate the audio statements with the corresponding picture, listening for key words, but not to write anything. Point out to them that key words can be the names of the characters they are familiar with or the new words drilled previously. Then play the audio to do the activity.

Before playing the audio for **Exercise 2**, be sure students know the meaning of *underline*. Depending on students' ability level, you may want to point out that the names mentioned are new names, not the main *Best Friends* characters' names. In this exercise, the key words to listen for are the prepositions *on, in,* or *at*. If possible, stop the audio after each statement to give students time to do each one, or play it a number of times to ensure comprehension.

Grammar Tips

- The expressions *at school* and *at home* are used to talk about people or things when they are in their usual, expected places:

  at school

  The teacher is at school = The teacher always works in a particular school building.

  The student is at school = The student always attends class at the same school.

  at home

  My father (or pet) is at home = That family member (or pet) habitually lives with the speaker in his or her house (or other dwelling).

- The prepositions of place *in* and *on* are paired with certain modes of transportation and must be learned by heart. They are not interchangeable: *The police officer is in a car/taxi. I am on a bike/bus/plane/train.*

Invite students to refer to the Grammar Box on page 95 to do **Exercise 3**. Then distribute three index cards to each student and have them make word cards for the prepositions. Make your own set of cards.

Play the audio for **Exercise 4**. Go over the song, pointing to each line and tracing from left to right with a finger under the words as you read aloud. Ask students to do the same. Play the song again, this time holding up the appropriate preposition cards at the same time *at, in,* and *on* are mentioned. Finally, play the song again and encourage students to chant along.

2. **Working Together**

For **Exercise 5**, go over the vocabulary together as you point to the pictures: *bike, plane, bus, school, train, home, taxi.* Play the audio several times for students to just listen. Have them check each other's work when they do the circling activity.

Then practice the structures in the Grammar Box on page 95 by first having student make picture cards for the places and modes of transportation mentioned. Distribute eight index cards per student. They can refer to the art on pages 94 and 96 for inspiration. Help as necessary. Accept for *school* a picture of a classroom or a building. Have students take out their *at, in, on* words cards, too. Say the vocabulary in the Grammar Box in random order, e.g., *a train,* for students to hold up the corresponding picture card. Have them repeat. Then elicit the correct preposition word card for that particular picture card. Students hold up the *on* card. When everyone is holding up the correct cards, repeat the phrase *on a train* together. Finally, have students label their picture cards on the backside, referring to pages 94 and 95 for spelling.

3. **Finishing Up**

Assign **Exercise 6,** helping as necessary with the instructions. Go over the example together and point out that there may be more than one possible question to ask. For example, *Where is the doctor?* or *What is he?* (pointing to the taxi and answering *He's in a taxi* or *He's a taxi driver.*)

Play the audio for **Exercise 7** as many times as necessary for students to trace over the words with precision.

For **Exercise 8**, remind students that they have done other word searches in previous units. (Hint: These words all go left to right.)

Fun and Games

A. ***At, in,* or *on*?** Place your *at, in,* and *on* word cards on the chalk ledge or some other place where they are visible. Divide students into two teams. Each team should have a set of lesson picture cards, placed face up in front of the team. Have them stand as far as possible from the chalk ledge. The object of the game is for the first student on each team to run to the chalk ledge with a picture card that goes with the preposition word you say. For example, say *in*, and students run up with the *car* picture card. Any student who establishes a correct match wins a point for his or her team. Have them hold up all correct matches for reinforcement. Give every student a chance to compete. The team with the most points wins.

B. **Sing with cards.** Students should have on hand their preposition word cards and their picture-word cards from the lesson. Chant together the song in Exercise 4 on page 95. As you chant, hold up the appropriate word card and picture card as they are mentioned and encourage student to follow your lead. Repeat the procedure a few times, each time chanting faster and faster until no one can keep up the pace.

C. **Draw!** Divide the class into small teams and have them stand far away from the board. Using all the lesson vocabulary, tell the first student in each team to draw and where, e.g., *Draw a pilot in a taxi. Draw three students at school. Draw Natalie's mother in a kitchen.* The first student to finish correctly gets a point for his or her team. Give everyone a chance to draw. The team with the most points wins.

Tapescript

Unit 7 Lesson 2 Page 94

Exercise 1: Listen and read. Write the numbers in the boxes.

Natalie and Daniel are on a bus.
Tom and Melba are on a bike.
Steve and Ken are in a taxi.
Mariana and Mrs. Williams are at school.

Unit 7 Lesson 2 Page 94

Exercise 2: Listen and circle the words you hear.

Pete is <u>on</u> a bus.
Barbara is <u>in</u> a taxi.
Jeff is <u>at</u> school.
I am <u>on</u> a bike.

Unit 7 Lesson 2 Page 95

Exercise 4: Sing a song.

I'm on a bike, I'm on a bike,
Where are you?

I'm on a bus, I'm on a bus,
Where are you?

I'm in my car, I'm in my car,
Where are you?

I'm at home, I'm at home,
Where are you?

I'm on a train, I'm on a train,
Where are you?

I'm on a plane, I'm on a plane,
Where are you?

I'm at school, I'm at school,
And so are you!

Unit 7 Lesson 2 Page 96

Exercise 5: Listen and circle.

1. The pilots are on the plane.
2. My brother is on his bike.
3. Where are the nurses? They're at home.
4. Where are the police officers? They're on the bus.

Unit 7 Lesson 2 Page 97

Exercise 7: Listen, repeat and trace.

1. teacher
2. vet
3. doctor
4. nurse
5. pilot
6. dentist
7. bus driver
8. taxi driver
9. police officer
10. homemaker

Lesson 3 Are the dogs sick?

Objectives

Students will:

- listen for a purpose
- practice short-answer responses
- make negative statements

Materials

Best Friends Student Book 1 pages 98-101

Other Materials

stick puppets, Lesson 1 and 2 picture cards, old magazines, scissors, glue

New Language

Are they…?

Yes, they are…/No, they aren't…

sick

fine

Lesson 3 Are the dogs sick?

1. Look at the picture. Choose words from the box to complete the paragraph.

white vets three animals fine

These men are vets. They are Dr. Smith and Dr. Taylor. They're happy and they love animals. The dogs are Tilly and Fifi. They are three years old. Tilly is black and Fifi is white. They are not sick. They are fine.

2. Listen to the conversation. Check T (True) or F (False).

	T	F
1. Tilly and Fifi are babies.		✓
2. Tilly and Fifi are not sick.	✓	
3. Tilly and Fifi are happy.	✓	
4. Tilly and Fifi are fine.	✓	

98

Lesson 3

Grammar

Are the dogs fine? Yes, they are.

Are the dogs sick? No, they aren't.

aren't = are not

3. Write questions.

Example: the dogs / sick Are the dogs sick?

1. they / happy Are they happy?
2. they / at home Are they at home?
3. Tilly and Fifi / students Are Tilly and Fifi students?
4. Melba and Steve / dentists Are Melba and Steve dentists?
5. the vets / at school Are the vets at school?

4. Make negative sentences.

Example: Natalie and Steve are funny. Natalie and Steve aren't funny.

1. The dogs are ugly. The dogs aren't ugly.
2. Steve's sisters are teachers. Steve's sisters aren't teachers.
3. Mariana's cats are Tilly and Fifi. Mariana's cats aren't Tilly and Fifi.
4. The doctors are at school. The doctors aren't at school.
5. The students are happy. The students aren't happy.

99

1. **Getting Started**

For **Exercise 1**, even though students should recognize the words in the word box from previous units, review pronunciation and demonstrate the new words in some way such as: something that is white; picture cards that represent vets; hold up three fingers; picture cards of various animals; say *How are you? I'm fine.* and smile. Then convey *sick* by holding your forehead and saying *Oh, my head! I'm not fine. I'm sick.* Have students do the exercise. Then check together.

Preview **Exercise 2** by asking and answering questions about the picture and the text in Exercise 1. Point as necessary: (pointing to the men) *What are they? They are vets. Are they sad? No, they are not. They are happy.* (pointing to the dogs) *What are they? They are dogs. Are they green? No, they are not. Are they sick? No, they are not. They are fine. Who are they? They are Tillie and Fifi.* Then play the audio a few times as students listen and look at the picture in their books. Play the tape again and have them decide *True* or *False*. Finally, play the audio again and check answers as a group.

Grammar Tips

- *Yes/no* questions and the corresponding short answers in third-person plural require the *are* form of the verb *be* : *Are the vets sad? No, they aren't. Are the dogs fine? Yes, they are.*
- The negative short answer often uses the contraction *aren't* for *are not*. However, the affirmative short answer never uses a contraction: Correct–*Are the teachers nice? Yes, they are.* Incorrect–*Yes, they're.*
- Remember: Information questions start with question words such as *What, Where,* and *Who*. The answer can never be a *yes/no* answer: Correct–*Where are the bus drivers? They're in the buses.* Incorrect–*Yes, they're in the buses.*
- In questions, adjectives come immediately after the nouns they modify: Correct–*Are the dogs ugly?* Incorrect–*Are ugly the dogs?*

Practice the structures in the Grammar Box, using the stick puppets as you ask questions such as *Are they on the shelf?* Answer as appropriate, e.g., *Yes, they are. (Melba) and (Ken) are on the shelf./No, they aren't. (Melba) and (Ken) aren't on the shelf.)* Have students repeat. Repeat the pattern with different puppets, changing where they are situated and using familiar vocabulary.

Then practice with Lesson 1 and 2 picture cards for occupations and modes of transportation. Demonstrate asking and answering with a volunteer and his or her set of cards. For example, pick the nurse card from each set, place them next to one taxi card, and ask *Are they nurses? Are they in a bus?* Elicit the corresponding answers *Yes they are.* or *No, they aren't.* from your partner. Combine the cards as many ways as possible while making sense and practice with students.

2. **Working Together**

Before assigning **Exercise 3**, practice word order for *yes/no* questions by writing on the chalkboard a sentence such as *The dogs are in the bedroom.* Circle *are* and "move" it in front of *The dogs* by drawing an arrow from the circled *are* to in front of *The dogs.* Then underneath the sentence, write the question with proper word order, capitalization, and punctuation: *Are the dogs in the bedroom?* Point out how the position of *are* moved to the front, and remind students that the first word in all sentences starts with a capital letter. Another alternative is to do this with word cards.

Before assigning **Exercise 4**, practice making negative statements by saying sentences that are true. Use props such as the stick puppets as necessary. For example, show the Mariana and Natalie puppets and say *Mariana and Natalie are girls. They aren't dentists. They are happy. They aren't sad.*

3. **Finishing Up**

For **Exercise 5**, give directions to find page 153 at the back of the Student Book. Then encourage students to add people to the drawing in an appropriate setting or vehicle, e.g., a teacher in the school building, a pilot in a plane in the sky.

For **Exercise 6**, divide students into small groups to share scissors, glue, and magazines. If someone can't find pictures related to the occupation they chose, suggest that they draw something.

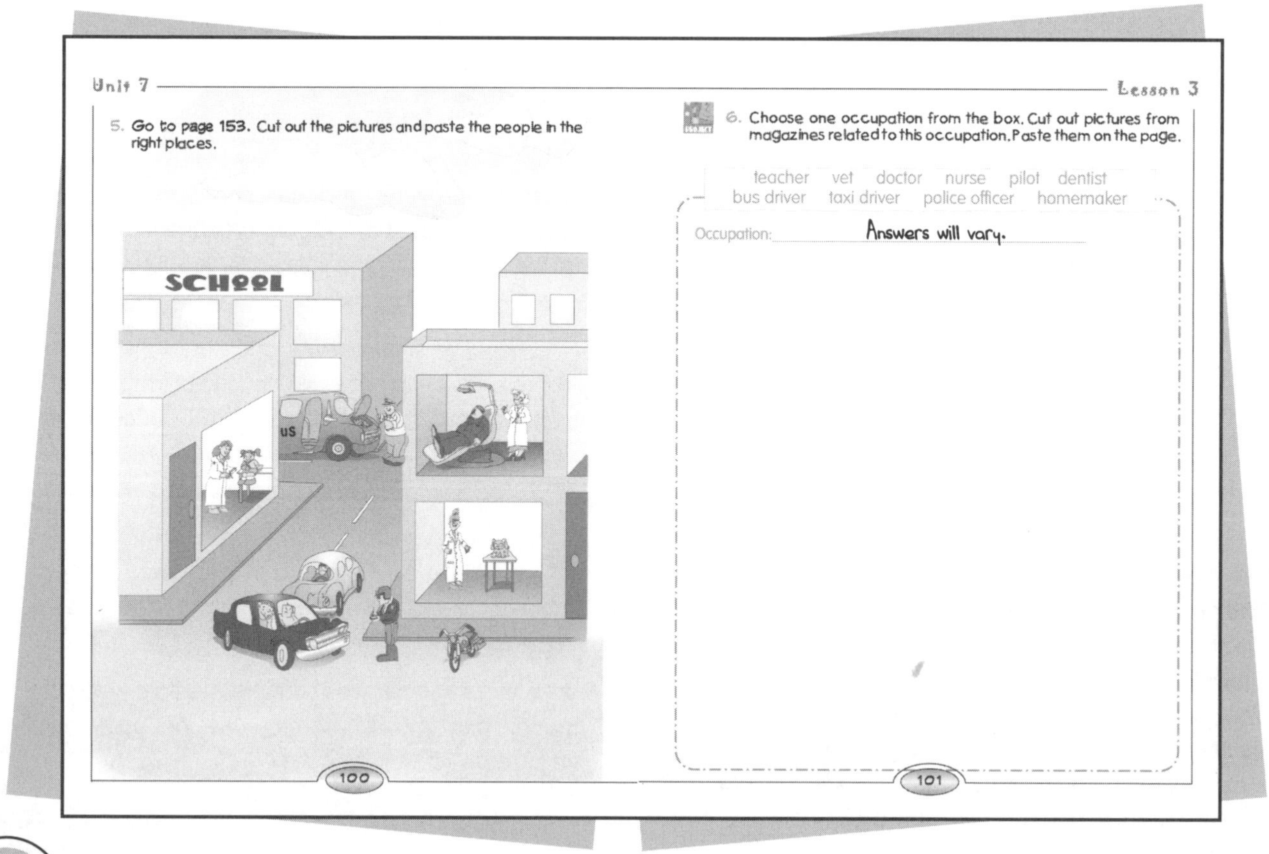
Unit 7 — Lesson 3

5. **Go to page 153.** Cut out the pictures and paste the people in the right places.

6. Choose one occupation from the box. Cut out pictures from magazines related to this occupation. Paste them on the page.

teacher vet doctor nurse pilot dentist
bus driver taxi driver police officer homemaker

Occupation: Answers will vary.

100 101

Fun and Games

A. **Occupations.** Have students draw two people who have one of the occupations listed on page 101 in the Student Book. The people can be people they know or imagined. Ask them to identify the occupation by writing at the top, for example *They are dentists.* Display all artwork on the bulletin board, grouping pictures by occupation category.

B. **Charades with cards**. Each student should have their Lesson 1 and 2 picture cards for occupations and modes of transportation. Pair students and demonstrate with a volunteer and his or her set of cards. The student picks either two of the same occupation cards or two of the same modes of transportation cards, places them face down so no one sees them, and then pantomimes actions related to them. You guess the cards by asking *Are they (nurses)? Are they (buses)?* Elicit the corresponding answers *Yes, they are.* or *No, they aren't.* from your partner. Once cards have been used, place them in a separate pile. Partners switch roles.

C. **Dictation.** Divide the class into four teams. The first person on each team stands at the board. Dictate short sentences with *are* and *aren't.* The first student to write the sentence correctly wins a point for his or her team. Give every student a chance to participate. The team with the most points at the end wins. Some sample sentences are:

1. The dolls aren't in the box..
2. My friends are at school.
3. The students aren't happy.
4. Melba's dogs are black.
5. The animals aren't funny.

Tapescript

Unit 7 Lesson 3 Page 98

Exercise 2: Listen to the conversation. Check True or False.

Woman:	How are Fifi and Tilli? How are my babies?
Dr. Smith:	Your <u>dogs</u> are fine.
Woman:	Are they sick?
Dr. Smith:	No, they aren't sick.
Woman:	Are they happy?
Dr. Taylor:	Yes, they are. They're fine.
Woman:	Thank you, thank you. Come on, my babies....

Lesson 4 Review

Objectives

Students will:

- read a dialogue
- review language from lessons 1-3
- differentiate between /h/ and /sh/

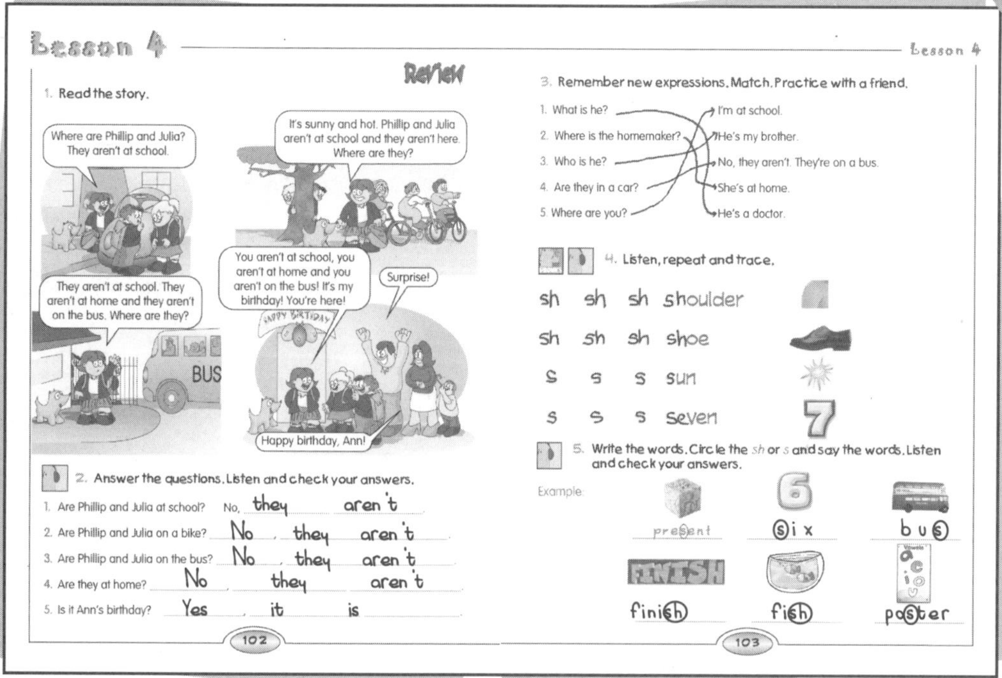

Lesson 4 — Lesson 4

Review

1. Read the story.

2. Answer the questions. Listen and check your answers.

1. Are Phillip and Julia at school? No, they aren't
2. Are Phillip and Julia on a bike? No, they aren't
3. Are Phillip and Julia on the bus? No, they aren't
4. Are they at home? No, they aren't
5. Is it Ann's birthday? Yes, it is

3. Remember new expressions. Match. Practice with a friend.

1. What is he? — He's a doctor.
2. Where is the homemaker? — She's at home.
3. Who is he? — He's my brother.
4. Are they in a car? — No, they aren't. They're on a bus.
5. Where are you? — I'm at school.

4. Listen, repeat and trace.

sh sh sh shoulder

sh sh sh shoe

s s s sun

s s s seven

5. Write the words. Circle the *sh* or *s* and say the words. Listen and check your answers.

Example: present, six, bus, finish, fish, poster

102 — 103

Materials

Best Friends Student Book 1 pages 102-105

Other Materials

index cards, picture and word cards from Lessons 1-3, scissors, glue, bits of paper for game markers

New Language

surprise

Read

Exercise 1: Dialogue summary. A story in dialogue format tells about a girl named Ann who is looking for her friends Phillip and Julia. She is at school and thinks they are not at school because she doesn't see them. Ann then goes out into the sunny, hot weather looking for them, but she only sees three children on bikes. She doesn't see Philip and Julia. Ann then looks on the bus, but they aren't on the bus. They aren't at school, they aren't at home, and they aren't on the bus. Where are they? They are at Ann's house for her birthday party. It is a surprise. Happy birthday, Ann!

Read the dialogue aloud, pointing to each speech bubble as you read. Ask students to listen and follow in their book. For fun, change voices to represent different speakers. Then read the dialogue again and encourage students to read aloud with you. Students should infer the meaning of *surprise* from the story line and the expression on Ann's face. Finally, assign the roles of the Phillip, Julia, Ann, Ann's father and mother, to capable students, and have other students pantomime the dog, the children on bikes, and Ann's little brother. The speakers can use the book to read their parts or they can try to memorize and recite their parts.

Story Comprehension

Exercise 2: Do number 1 together: *Are Phillip and Julia at school? No, they aren't.* Then read all the questions aloud for students, allowing time so that they look for key words in the speech bubbles and write their answers. When everyone is done, play the tape for students to check answers.

Vocabulary

Exercise 3: Read the numbered items one at a time and ask students to find the logical match to it, e.g., *What is he? He's a doctor.* They can read the answer aloud or point to it in their book. Give everyone a chance to answer a question and be sure everyone draws a line to match the columns.

Then have students practice the structures. Encourage them to role-play the situations by pantomiming actions related to the answers, e.g., *He's a doctor.* = pantomime using a stethoscope on a patient. Students can make use of their classmates and other props imaginatively, such as a volunteer's necklace for a stethoscope and a classmate as the patient.

Exercise 4: Start the exercise by asking students to read aloud the words or phrases in the word box. Tell them they should use them only once to fill in the blanks. Then ask them to decide which word or phrase goes best in the first blank. Tell them the first answer if necessary and ask students to write it in their books. (Have them also cross it out in the box so they know they have used it already.) Then allow students to continue on their own until all the blanks are filled. They may work in pairs if they wish.

Listening

Exercise 4: Play the audio for students several times for them to practice the letter and word pronunciations. Students may find the /sh/ sound difficult to pronounce if it is not in their native language's phonetic system. In addition, the pronunciation of the letter *s* varies depending on its position in a word. Sometimes it is pronounced as voiced /z/, as in *present,* and other times it is pronounced as voiceless /s/, as in *bus*. Students will need a lot of practice listening for and pronouncing these sounds.

Exercise 5: Similar to Exercise 2, students write their answers and then check by listening to the audio. Then ask students to search in their set of alphabet cards for the /s/ letter card. Distribute one index card per student and ask them to make a letter card for */sh/*. Be sure they write the letters *s* and *h* closely together to show that they make one sound. Then practice by having them hold up the correct card as you say the letter name. Go faster and faster. Give more capable students a chance to be the caller if time allows.

Exercise 6: Before playing the audio, help students go to page 153 and cut out the pictures. Then play the tape once for them to just listen. On the second listening, they should place the cutouts where they think they should go but not paste them. Finally, play the audio again for students to check their work before they paste the cutouts to the page.

Exercise 7: Play a game. Tell students to look at page 105 in their book. Tell them they are going to play a game. Ask them to make themselves game markers out of small bits of paper. Give directions to play. The object is for students to move from the start line to the scene that matches a question or statement that you make. For example, say *The dog is under the table.* (Students move two steps.) Check where players landed. If someone is in the wrong place he or she must go back to the start line. Play until someone gets to the finish line.

Then allow groups of three students to play the game, with one as the caller and the other two as the players. The first student who follows the caller's commands correctly and gets to the finish line wins.

A variation on the game is for students to move the number of scenes you say and make a logical statement about the scene. For example, say *Go three steps.* Go around the classroom and have each student say something. Accept any reasonable statement. Some examples are: *I have a chalkboard. It's a chalkboard. It isn't a computer.*

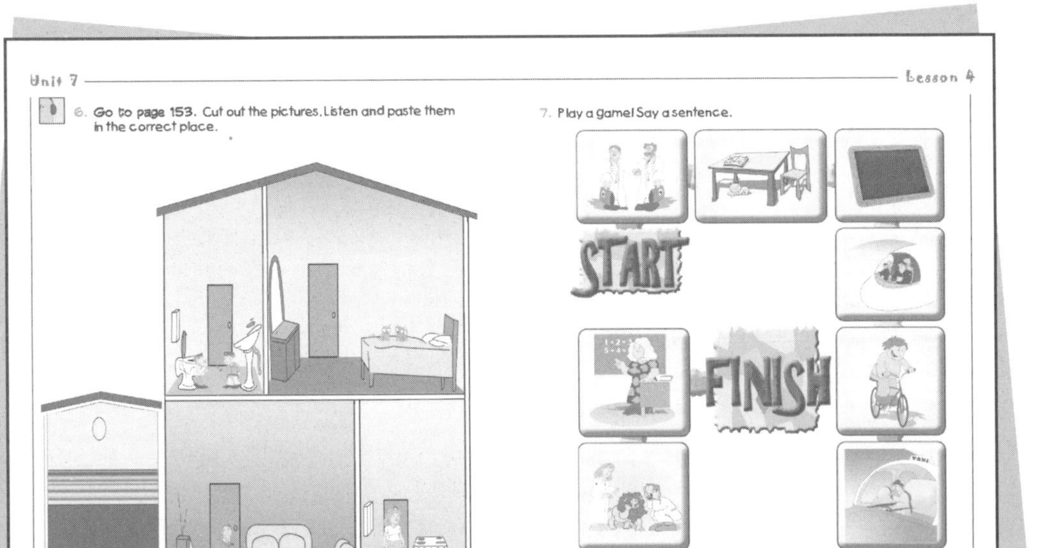

Fun and Games

A. **Picture and Word Concentration.** Students should have their complete sets of Unit 7 picture and word cards. Remind them that the object of the game is to find two pictures or words that match. Pair students and have them play against each other with their sets of cards to see who gets the most cards. When they are finished playing, ask them to put their cards in order so that each student gets his or her cards back again.

B. **Draw!** Divide the class into four teams and have them stand far away from the board. Using all unit vocabulary, tell the first student in each team who/what to draw. Some ideas are: *He's a pilot on a bike, He's Melba's brother Sam, She's a taxi driver. Mrs. Williams and a student are at school. The vets aren't sad. The teachers are on a train.* The student who finishes drawing a correct picture first gets a point for his or her team. Give everyone a chance to draw. The team with the most points wins.

C. **His or her car?** Use your set of modes of transportation picture cards. Hold up a random vehicle, name a familiar character in the book, and elicit whose vehicle it is. For example, hold up the car card and say *Melba* to elicit *Melba's car.* Be sure to name only one character at a time for students to react to.

Tapescript

Unit 7 Lesson 4 Page 102

Exercise 2: Listen and check your answers.

Are Phillip and Julia at school?	No, they aren't.
Are Phillip and Julia on a bike?	No, they aren't.
Are Phillip and Julia on the bus?	No, they aren't.
Are they at home?	Yes, they are.
Is it Ann's birthday?	Yes, it is.

Unit 7 Lesson 4 Page 103

Exercise 4: Listen and repeat. Then trace and say.

shoulder /sh/ /sh/ /sh/ shoulder
shoe /sh/ /sh/ /sh/ shoe
sun /s/ /s/ /s/ sun
seven /s/ /s/ /s/ seven

Unit 7 Lesson 4 Page 103

Exercise 5: Write the words. Circle the *sh* or *s* and say the words. Listen and check your answers:

present
six
bus
finish
fish tank
poster

Unit 7 Lesson 4 Page 104

Exercise 6: Cut out the pictures. Listen and glue in the correct place.

It's a crazy day! Look at my house. The cats are in the bedroom. The police officers are in the bathroom and the doctors are in the garage. I'm a homemaker and I'm in the kitchen. And there is a teacher in the living room!

Unit 7 Test

Name________________________________ Date______________

1. Draw a doctor and a teacher at a surprise birthday party for their friend, the vet. Draw the friends at the party. Don't forget the animals!

2. Fill in the blanks with the correct words from the word box.

sick	cats	Where	aren't	Ken's

1. They aren't dogs. They are ______________.
2. ______________ father is happy.
3. Sam's brother and sister ______________ Tillie and Fifi.
4. Are the bus drivers ______________? No, they are fine.
5. ____________ are the homemakers? They are at home.

3. Write *in*, *on* or *at*.

1. The students are ________ school.
2. The homemaker is ________ a taxi.
3. The teacher's family is ________ a plane.
4. Ann's birthday party is ________ home.
5. Where is the doctor? She's _______ a train.

Unit 8

Lesson 1 You aren't a monkey!

Objectives

Students will:
- learn vocabulary related to zoo animals
- recognize a command
- listen for a purpose
- answer yes/no questions

Materials
Best Friends Student Book 1 pages 106-107
Other Materials
Pictures related to animals, index cards, stick puppets, crayons or colored pencils

New Language
Am I…?
Yes, you are./No, you aren't
Are you…?
Yes, I am./No, I'm not.
Sit down.
Spelling
bear, elephant, giraffe, lion, monkey, seal, tiger, zebra

1. **Getting Started**
Introduce new vocabulary related to animals by showing available pictures of *monkey, lion, bear, giraffe,* and *elephant.* Point to a picture and first say the word, e.g., *a monkey* and then, look directly at the picture and say *You are a monkey. You aren't a dog.* Repeat for all animals mentioned in the dialogue on page 106, alternating "telling" the animal *You are…/You aren't…* statements. For the *You aren't…* sentences, use familiar vocabulary from previous units and shake your head no each time. For fun you can make silly statements such as *You aren't an arm.* or *You aren't an eraser.*

Then ask students to turn to page 106 in their Student Book. Point to the Steve character and say *Look! A monkey. A monkey on the blackboard.* Then ask *Is Steve really a monkey?* Elicit *No, he isn't monkey.* Then say *Look at Natalie. She's a lion. Look at Daniel. He's a bear.*, and so on for all the characters on the page. (Students should infer from the scene that the characters are only acting like animals.)

Play the audio for **Exercise 1**. As each character speaks, students should trace with a finger under the words in the speech bubbles.

Play the audio for **Exercise 2** and point to the appropriate words as animals are mentioned. Encourage students to do the same as they listen to the

Grammar Tips

- *Yes/no* questions and the corresponding short answers in first-person singular and second-person singular or plural, *you*, respectively, require the *am* and *are* forms of the verb *be.* These forms are used for a direct exchange between two speakers, or between one speaker and more than one speaker: *Am I an elephant? Yes, you are./No, you aren't.* or *Are you a student? Yes, I am./No, I'm not.*
- The negative short answer often uses the contraction *aren't* for *are not.* Note that the affirmative short answer when the speaker is *I* never uses a contraction: Correct–*Are you a lion? Yes, I am,* Incorrect–*Yes, I'm.*
- In questions with the verb *be,* adjectives come immediately after the nouns they modify: Correct–*Are you funny? Am I happy?* Incorrect–*Are ugly you? Am happy I?*

dialogue. They should infer the meaning of the teacher's command *Sit down.* from her tone of voice on the audio, her impatient posture in the picture, and the general craziness happening in her classroom.

Review the structures in the Grammar Box by using the stick puppets. Intentionally have the puppets ask *I/you* questions that require a negative answer, e.g., have the Melba puppet ask the Ken puppet *Am I Steve?* The Ken puppet says *No, you aren't.* Make the Ken puppet ask the Melba puppet *Are you a lion?* She says *No, I'm not.* Have students repeat with you.

2. Working Together

For **Exercise 3**, be sure students understand that there are four different dialogues on page 107. Do the first one as example: *Am I a monkey? Yes, you are.* Make sure students understand that they can repeat the words in the box. Students can work in pairs or by themselves. Then distribute five index cards per student and have them make picture cards for *monkey, lion, bear, giraffe,* and *elephant.* Help with labeling on the backside as necessary.

For **Exercise 4**, on page 108, review or introduce new vocabulary by reading aloud the words in the word box and pointing to the corresponding pictures on the Information sign. Repeat the words several times, allowing students to make the proper associations. Then do number 1 as an example together to show how the letter *e* completes *bear.* Have students complete the exercise alone or in pairs and then check the answers as a class.

Then distribute three index cards per student for them to make picture cards in the singular for *seal, tiger,* and *zebra* and label them accordingly. Check comprehension for all lesson picture cards by saying an animal and having students hold up the appropriate card. They can either show the picture side or the word side.

3. Finishing Up

For **Exercise 5**, help students with the directions, as this is a two-part activity. Circulate to check that the written answers start with *You are….,* not *It is…* or *He/She is…*

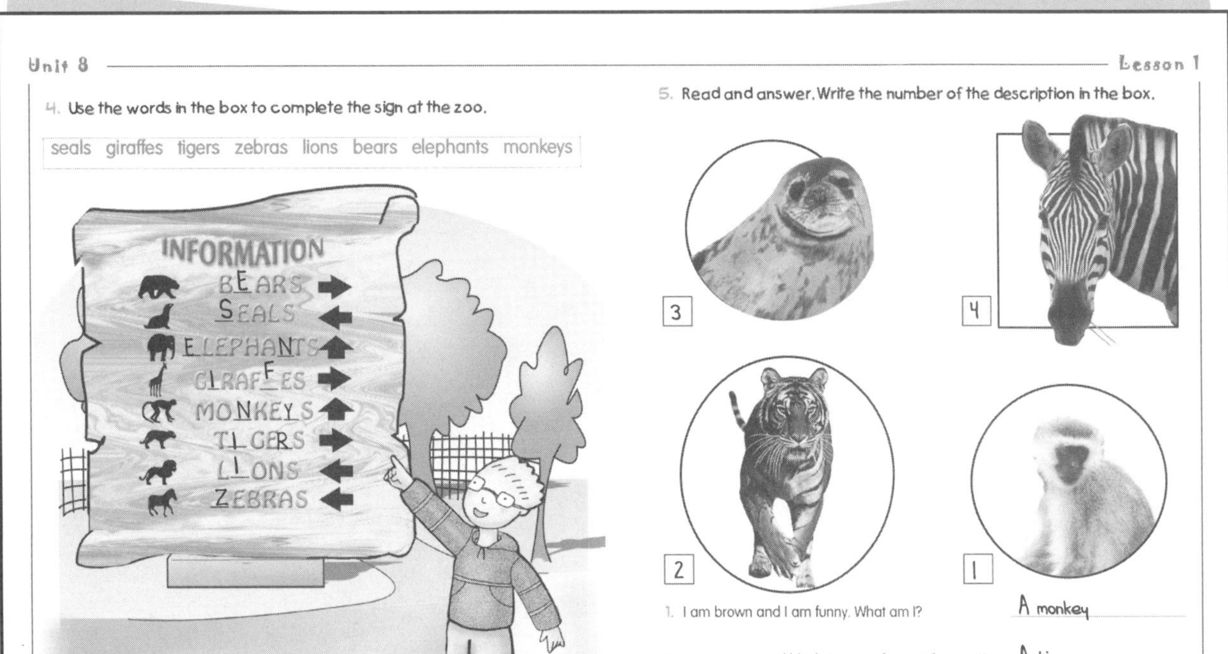
Unit 8 — Lesson 1

4. Use the words in the box to complete the sign at the zoo.

seals giraffes tigers zebras lions bears elephants monkeys

5. Read and answer. Write the number of the description in the box.

1. I am brown and I am funny. What am I? A monkey
2. I am orange and black. I am not funny. What am I? A tiger
3. I am brown. I have no legs. What am I? A seal
4. I am black and white. I am beautiful. What am I? A zebra

108 109

Fun and Games

A. **Information.** Have students design an information board following the example on page 108. However, they should only draw and label the five animals they like the best. Then encourage them to write the heading *(Name)'s Favorite Animals* at the top of their pictures, filling in their first names as appropriate.

B. **What am I?** Play a guessing game similar to Exercise 5 on page 109 using your set of lesson picture cards. Place two random cards on the chalk ledge facing students, e.g., the seal card and the giraffe card, and give a description for students to guess which one you are talking about. Use the first-person singular: *I am yellow. I am beautiful. I am orange and brown. What am I?* Students should shout out *You're a giraffe!*

A variation on the game is to place one random card face down and give a description. Students make guesses, but do not turn the card face up until someone guesses correctly.

C. **Animal conversations.** Have students draw any two animals from the lesson having a conversation. The setting is not important, but they should draw speech balloons and a meaningful dialogue. They can refer to pages 106 and 107 for ideas, but should invent their own dialogues. Depending on students' level of ability, they might describe their work to the class, e.g., *This is a bear and a monkey. The bear is white and beautiful. The monkey is brown and funny.* Accept incomplete sentences as long as they make sense with the drawing. Display the drawings on the bulletin board under the heading *Animals Are Friends.*

Tapescript

Unit 8 Lesson 1 Page 106
Exercise 1: Listen and read.

Steve:	Look at me! I'm a monkey!
Natalie:	You're a monkey and I'm a lion.
Daniel:	Look at me! I'm a bear!
Melba:	What am I?
Tom:	Are you a giraffe?
Melba:	No, I'm not!
Ken:	You're an elephant!
Mrs. Williams:	You aren't a monkey! You aren't a lion! You aren't an elephant! You aren't a bear! You're students! Sit down. Now!

Unit 8 Lesson 1 Page 106
Exercise 2: Listen again and point to the words.

(See Exercise 1 above.)

Lesson 2 There are three monkeys.

Objectives

Students will:
- learn the number words eleven through twenty
- listen for a purpose
- use prepositions of place correctly
- learn vocabulary related to shapes

Materials
Best Friends Student Book 1 pages 110-113
Other Materials
index cards, crayons or colored pencils

New Language
eleven, twelve,
thirteen, fourteen
fifteen, sixteen
seventeen, eighteen
nineteen, twenty
There is.../There are...
at the zoo
circle, rectangle
square, triangle

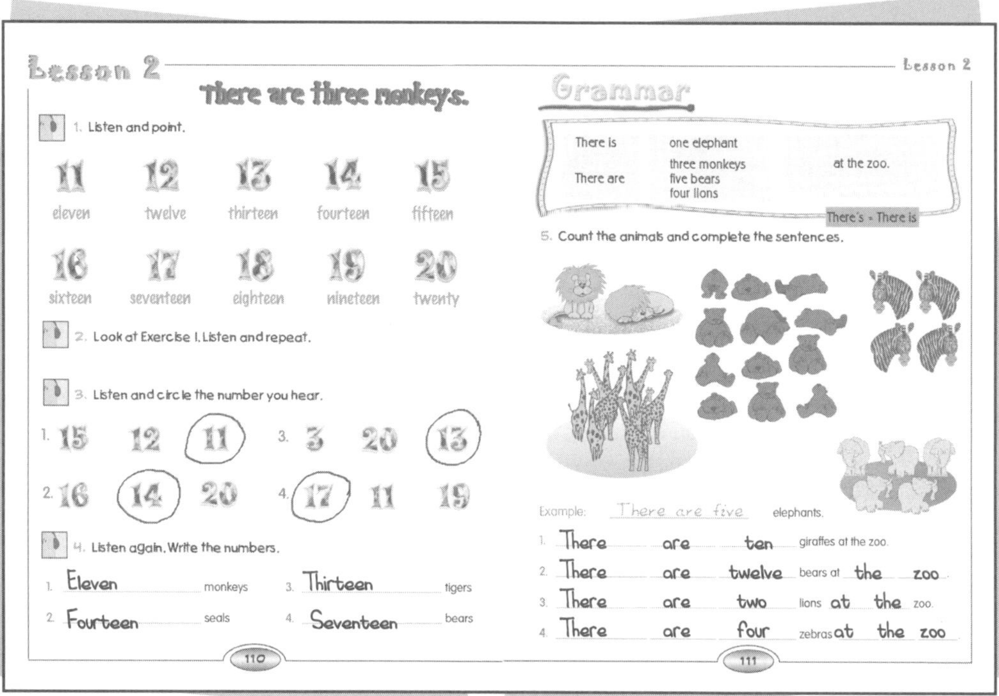

Lesson 2
There are three monkeys.

1. Listen and point.

11	12	13	14	15
eleven	twelve	thirteen	fourteen	fifteen
16	17	18	19	20
sixteen	seventeen	eighteen	nineteen	twenty

2. Look at Exercise 1. Listen and repeat.

3. Listen and circle the number you hear.

1. 15 12 (11)
2. 16 (14) 20
3. 3 20 (13)
4. (17) 11 19

4. Listen again. Write the numbers.

1. Eleven monkeys
2. Fourteen seals
3. Thirteen tigers
4. Seventeen bears

110

Lesson 2

Grammar

There is	one elephant	
There are	three monkeys five bears four lions	at the zoo.

There's = There is

5. Count the animals and complete the sentences.

Example: There are five elephants.

1. There are ten giraffes at the zoo.
2. There are twelve bears at the zoo.
3. There are two lions at the zoo.
4. There are four zebras at the zoo

111

1. **Getting Started**

Play the audio for **Exercise 1** to introduce the numbers *eleven* through *twenty*. Tell students not to concentrate on the number words below the numerals for now.

Play the audio for **Exercise 2** a few times for students to practice pronunciation. Then distribute ten index cards to each student and have them write the numerals 11 through 20 on one side and the corresponding number words on the other side, as large as possible. They can refer to page 110 in their book as necessary for spelling reference. Make your own set of cards as well. Circulate to check the spelling and that the handwriting is clear so all cards can be easily read. Using your set of cards with the numeral side showing, demonstrate the following activity: Point to a numeral randomly and ask questions such as *Is it a fourteen?* or *Is it an eighteen?* Answer as appropriate *Yes, it is.* or *No, it isn't.* Then have pairs practice with their cards. Circulate and encourage the use of *an* for number words that start with a vowel (*eleven* and *eighteen*).

Before playing the audio for **Exercise 3**, be sure students know they are listening for one of the three numbers in each row, and that they shouldn't worry about understanding the whole sentence that they will hear. Do a trial run by writing on the chalkboard the row 20 15 7, and saying *There are fifteen zebras at the zoo.* Ask which number they heard, repeating the sentence until someone can give a correct answer. Circle the answer. Then play the tape. If possible, stop it after each statement to give students time to answer, or play it a number of times to make sure they understand. Check answers as a group.

For Exercise 4, allow students to refer to Exercise 1 or their picture-word cards in order to write the number words correctly.

Grammar Tips

- Similar to the expressions *at school* and *at home,* which are used to talk about people or things when they are in their usual, expected places, *at the zoo* is used to talk about animals being at their expected place, i.e., the zoo is their home. However, the article *the* means that this expression can also be used with anyone or anything that is not necessarily always at the zoo: *The teacher and the students are at the zoo.* = They are visiting the zoo only; they do not live there.
- The impersonal expression *There is* is used for singular, and *There are* is used for plural: *There is one bus at school. There is one bear at the zoo. There are seven monkeys at the zoo.* These expressions are used when you want to talk about the existence of something.
- *There is* and *There are* often indicate the number of objects that are being talked about, but not always: *There are beautiful fish at home.*

Introduce the structures in the Grammar Box on page 111 by making true statements about the classroom. For example: *There is one flag in the classroom. There are two pencil sharpeners. There are fifteen students. There are twenty books.* Then review the preposition of place *at* by making true statements, e.g., *You are at school. Your family is not at school. Your pets are not at school. They are at home.*

2. **Working Together**

Invite students to refer to the Grammar Box to do **Exercise 5**. Allow them to refer to Exercise 1 or their picture-word cards in order to write the number words correctly. Check answers as a class. Then distribute two index cards to each student and have them make word cards for *There is* and *There are.* (Be sure they capitalize the *t* in *there* each time.) Make your own set of cards. For extra practice, say phrases using familiar vocabulary to elicit either *There is* or *There are* as appropriate: ____ *four students at school;* ___ *a dentist in a taxi.*, etc. Students can either hold up the card or say the phrase.

Play the tape for **Exercise 6** a few times to introduce the four shape words and their pronunciation. Then distribute four index cards to each student and have them make picture-word cards for the shapes. Make your own set as well. Using your set of cards with the picture side showing, demonstrate the following activity: Point to a shape randomly and ask questions such as *Is it a circle?* Elicit the appropriate answer *Yes, it is.* or *No, it isn't.* Then have pairs practice with their cards.

3. **Finishing Up**

For **Exercise 7**, allow students to work in pairs. Check answers as a group.

For **Exercise 8**, help as necessary with the instructions. Have students label the picture with the name of their animal, e.g. *This is Bernie. It is a bear.* When students have finished, display all the pictures in the bulletin board.

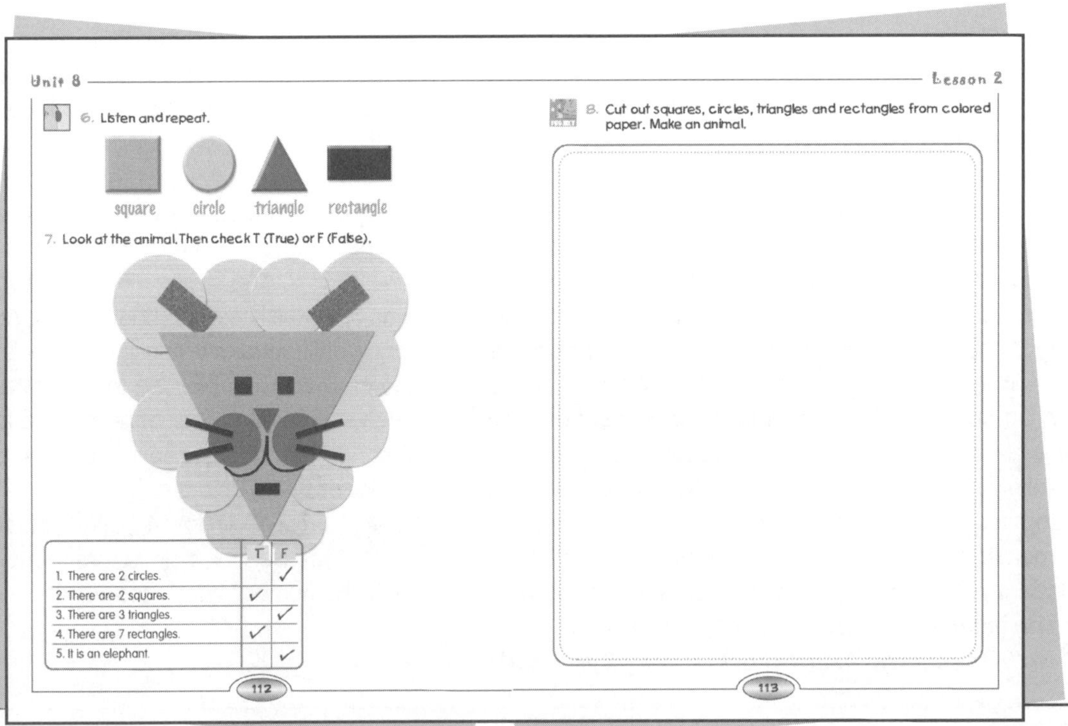
Unit 8 — Lesson 2

6. Listen and repeat.

square circle triangle rectangle

7. Look at the animal. Then check T (True) or F (False).

	T	F
1. There are 2 circles.		✓
2. There are 2 squares.	✓	
3. There are 3 triangles.		✓
4. There are 7 rectangles.	✓	
5. It is an elephant.		✓

112

8. Cut out squares, circles, triangles and rectangles from colored paper. Make an animal.

113

Fun and Games

A. *At the zoo.* Have students draw a zoo showing animals from Lessons 1 and 2. When they are done, encourage them to label the animals and how many there are. They can write the numeral or number word next to the animal word. Ask them to describe their pictures, e.g., *There are twelve bears. There is one girl.*

B. **Say the number.** Be sure all students have their sets of picture-word cards for numbers eleven through twenty. Divide the class into groups of five or six and ask them to stand up. Alternate holding up any numeral, then any number-word, and have students hold up the exact same card as quickly as possible. When everyone is holding up a card, name the number together loudly. Then check that everyone has the same card. Any student who isn't showing the correct card must sit down. Repeat the procedure faster and faster until only one student is left standing in each group.

C. **Number Concentration.** Demonstrate the following Concentration game with a volunteer: Combine your set of picture-word cards for numbers with your partner's cards. Place in random order on a flat surface one set of cards with the picture side face down, and the other set with the word side down. In this case, the numerals are the "picture side." The object of the game is to play Concentration matching one picture card with its corresponding word card, or vice versa. Then pair students and have them play against each other with their sets of number cards to see who gets the most cards. When they are finished playing, ask them to put their cards in order so that each student gets his or her cards back again.

Tapescript

Unit 8 Lesson 2 Page 110
Exercise 1: Listen and point.

Eleven — Twelve — Thirteen — Fourteen — Fifteen — Sixteen — Seventeen — Eighteen — Nineteen - Twenty

Unit 8 Lesson 2 Page 110
Exercise 2: Look at Exercise 1. Listen and repeat.

(See Exercise 1 above.)

Unit 8 Lesson 2 Page 110
Exercise 3: Listen and circle the number you hear.

There are eleven monkeys at the zoo.
There are fourteen seals at the zoo.
There are thirteen tigers at the zoo.
There are seventeen bears at the zoo.

Unit 8 Lesson 2 Page 110
Exercise 4: Listen again. Write the numbers.

(See Exercise 3 above)

Unit 8 Lesson 2 Page 112
Exercise 6: Listen and repeat.

It's a square.
It's a circle.
It's a triangle.
It's a rectangle.

Lesson 3 There's a duck on the farm.

Objectives

Students will:
- learn vocabulary related to farm animals
- use classifying skills
- review prepositions of place
- listen for a purpose
- express preferences

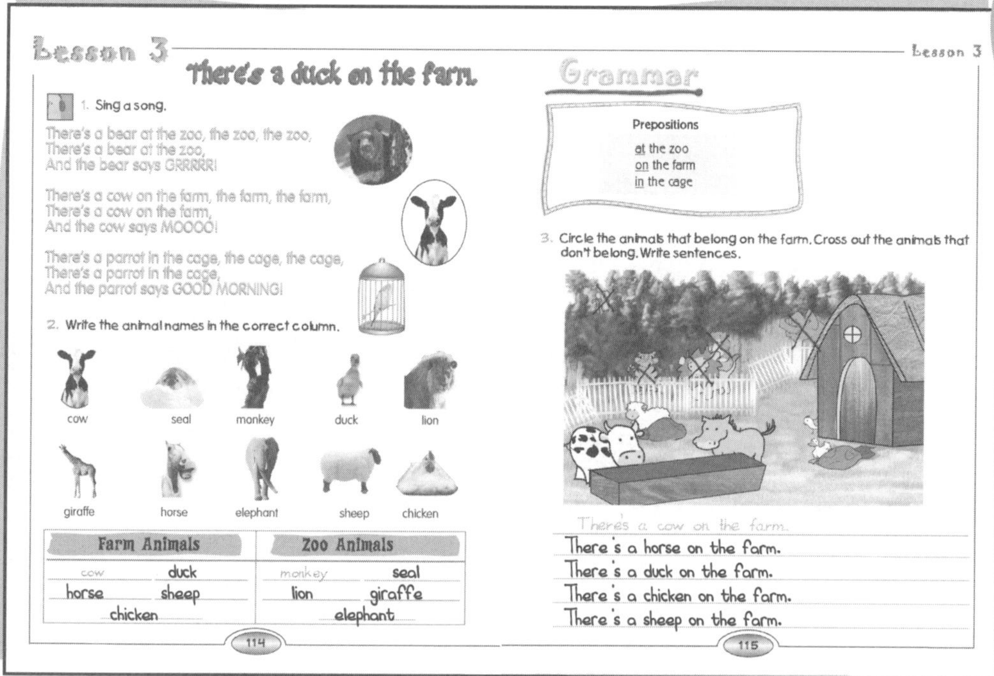
Lesson 3

There's a duck on the farm.

1. Sing a song.

There's a bear at the zoo, the zoo, the zoo,
There's a bear at the zoo,
And the bear says GRRRRR!

There's a cow on the farm, the farm, the farm,
There's a cow on the farm,
And the cow says MOOOO!

There's a parrot in the cage, the cage, the cage,
There's a parrot in the cage,
And the parrot says GOOD MORNING!

2. Write the animal names in the correct column.

cow, seal, monkey, duck, lion, giraffe, horse, elephant, sheep, chicken

Farm Animals		Zoo Animals	
cow	duck	monkey	seal
horse	sheep	lion	giraffe
chicken		elephant	

114

Lesson 3

Grammar

Prepositions
at the zoo
on the farm
in the cage

3. Circle the animals that belong on the farm. Cross out the animals that don't belong. Write sentences.

There's a cow on the farm.
There's a horse on the farm.
There's a duck on the farm.
There's a chicken on the farm.
There's a sheep on the farm.

115

Materials
Best Friends Student Book 1 pages 114-117
Other Materials
Picture cards from Lesson 1 (zoo animals), index cards, large sheets of paper, crayons or colored pencils
New Language
on the farm
Spelling
chicken, cow, duck, horse, sheep

1. Getting Started

Play the audio for **Exercise 1**. Go over the song, pointing to each line and tracing from left to right with a finger under the words as you read aloud. Ask students to do the same. At the end of each stanza, point to the corresponding picture to the right as the animal sounds *Grrrrr!, Moooo!* and *Good Morning!* are mentioned. Then play the tape again and have students point to the picture of the animal as it is mentioned. Finally, play the song a few more times and encourage students to chant along. Students should infer the meaning of *cage* from the picture of the parrot, but if there is a cage of some type in the classroom, point to it and say *It's a cage.* or *There is a cage in the classroom.*

For **Exercise 2,** review zoo animals and introduce the farm animals *cow, duck, horse, sheep,* and *chicken.* Point to and name each one, being very careful to differentiate between the soft /sh/ sound in *sheep* and the stronger /ch/ sound in *chicken.* Students should associate *farm* with *cow* from the song lyrics as well as from examples shown for each category. Check answers as a group.

Practice the structures in the Grammar Box with the lyrics of the song on page 114 and zoo animal picture cards from Lesson 1. For the first stanza, use your lion card; for the second stanza, use the duck card; and for the third stanza, use the seal card. Hold up the appropriate card for each stanza and sing or chant the stanza, substituting the animal words and sounds or greeting for new ones: *There's a lion...And the lion says Rooar! There's a duck...And the duck says Quaaack!* and *There's a seal...And the seal says Good afternoon!* Repeat the stanzas several times, encouraging students to chant along.

Grammar Tips

- Remember that the expression *at the zoo* is used for animals that live there and also for anyone or anything that is not necessarily always at the zoo: *The monkey is at the zoo.* = The monkey lives there. *The bus is at the zoo. The boys and girls are at the zoo.* = The bus and the children are visiting the zoo only; they do not live there or stay there for any great length of time.
- The prepositions of place *in* and *on* are paired with certain places and must be learned by heart. They are not interchangeable: *The parrot is in the cage. The animals are on the farm.*

Then distribute seven index cards to each student to make picture-word cards for the five farm animals *cow, duck, horse, sheep,* and *chicken.* and word cards for *farm* and *zoo.* (They could write each word on both sides or attempt to draw a scene representing the places.) Make a set for yourself as well.

2. **Working Together**

Before assigning the classifying activity in **Exercise 3,** be sure students understand how to cross something out. Remind them that the first word in all sentences should start with a capital letter, as seen in the example sentence. Circulate round the class giving help as necessary, then check the answers as a class.

Before assigning **Exercise 4,** practice using the possessive with *'s* by saying sentences that are true using familiar vocabulary such as Daniel's fish are beautiful. Melba's brother is four years old. Then play the tape several times until students feel comfortable drawing. You might want to point out that that this form for possessive is not used only with people's names. For example, ask them to look at page 114 in their book. Point to the animal pictures in Exercise 1 and say *The bear's nose is big. The cow's ears are black. The parrot's cage is pretty.* Have students repeat with you.

For **Exercise 5,** give directions to do the survey. Encourage students to ask classmates their preferences being careful that nobody gathers information about the same three students.

3. **Finishing Up**

For Exercise 6, have students write the animal names on the blanks using their word cards for reference if necessary. Then play the tape several times so that they can check their answers.

For **Exercise 7,** have students work in pairs. Point out that the first letter of each word in already given in the puzzle. Have students exchange books to check each other's answers.

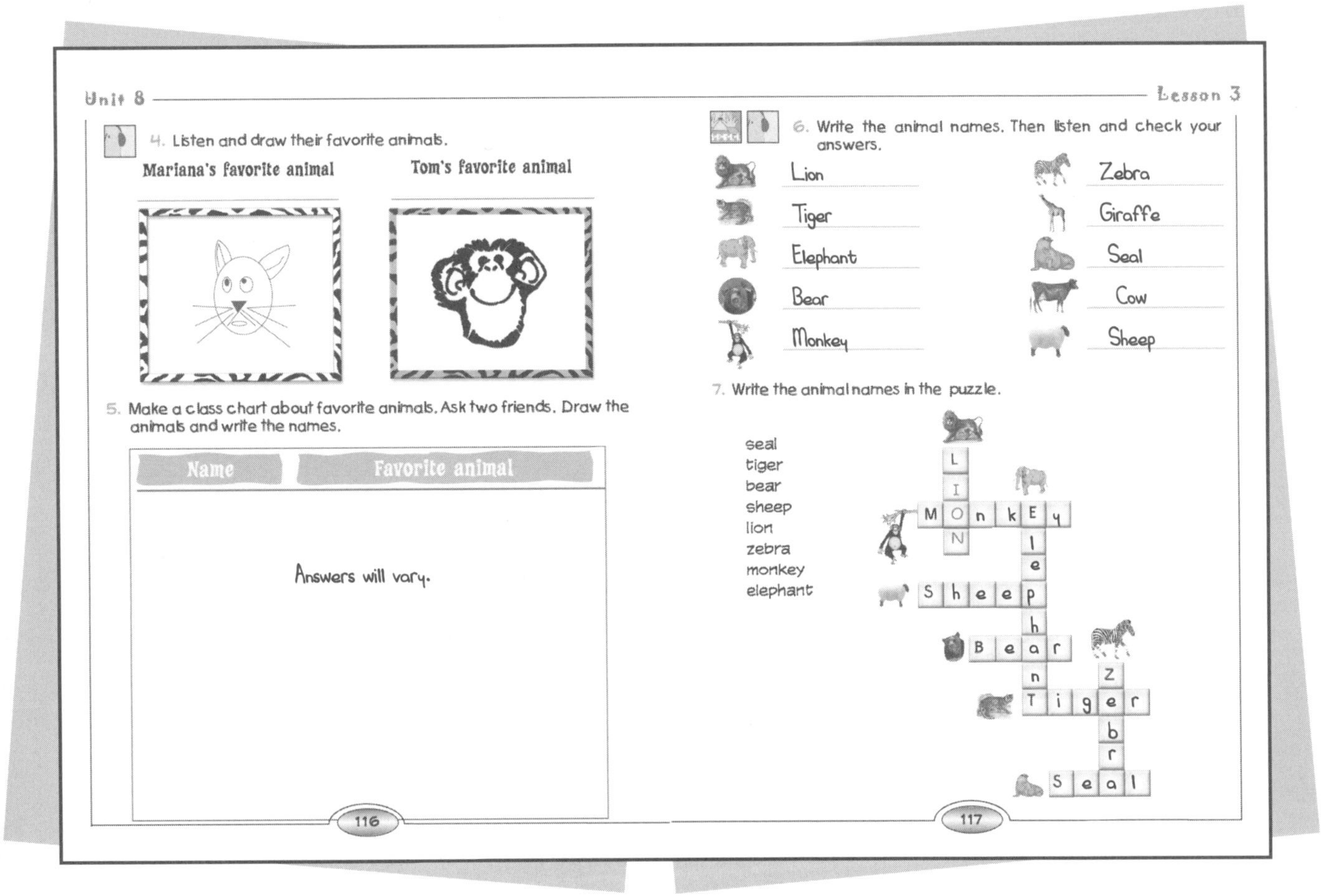

Unit 8 — Lesson 3

4. Listen and draw their favorite animals.

Mariana's favorite animal — Tom's favorite animal

5. Make a class chart about favorite animals. Ask two friends. Draw the animals and write the names.

Name	Favorite animal
Answers will vary.	

6. Write the animal names. Then listen and check your answers.

Lion, Tiger, Elephant, Bear, Monkey, Zebra, Giraffe, Seal, Cow, Sheep

7. Write the animal names in the puzzle.

seal
tiger
bear
sheep
lion
zebra
monkey
elephant

116 117

Fun and Games

A. **Design a zoo.** Distribute large sheets of paper and crayons or colored pencils. Have students plan the layout of a zoo using the shapes circle, square, triangle, and rectangle as much as possible. They should also decide which animals don't need to be in cages, which can be together in the same cage, and which should be in their own cage. Ask students to write the heading *My Zoo* at the top and to sign their names on their design. Take a poll on which designs work the best and discuss why.

B. **At the zoo or on the farm?** Use your set of picture cards from Lesson 1 (zoo animals) and Lesson 3 picture cards for farm animals. To indicate places, divide the blackboard in half and write at the top the headings *Zoo* and *Farm*. Demonstrate the game as follows with a volunteer: Place a random card, e.g., the *elephant* card, on the chalk ledge under *either* of the headings and have your partner make a correct statement using *There is a/an (animal) at the zoo/on the farm*. For example, *There is an elephant at the zoo*. or *There is an elephant on the farm*. After everyone has had a chance, for fun, have students share which animals they really have seen in both places. e.g., they may have seen ducks at a zoo and an elephant on a farm.

C. **Draw!** Distribute large pieces of paper and crayons or colored pencils. Have students work individually. They should divide the paper into four areas and draw as large as possible the outline of a circle, rectangle, square, and triangle. Inside the shapes, they should draw what you suggest, labeling all the animals they can. Then ask them to compare their work with a partner's. Some sample scenes to draw are:
1. The tigers are on the farm.
2. My friends are at the zoo.
3. There are two giraffes in a cage.
4. Melba's bears are black.

Tapescript

Unit 8 Lesson 3 Page 114

Exercise 1: Sing a song.

There's a bear at the zoo, the zoo, the zoo,
There's a bear at the zoo,
And the bear says GRRRRR!

There's a cow on the farm, the farm, the farm
There's a cow on the farm,
And the cow says MOOOO!

There's a parrot in the cage, the cage, the cage
There's a parrot in the cage,
And the parrot says GOOD MORNING!

Unit 8 Lesson 3 Page 116

Exercise 4: Listen and draw their favorite animals.

Tom: Mariana, what's your favorite animal?
Mariana: It's a cat. I love cats. What's your favorite animal?
Tom: It's a monkey. I love monkeys.

Unit 8 Lesson 3 Page 117

Exercise 6: Write the animal names. Then listen and check your answers.

Lion. L-I-O-N. Lion.
Tiger. T-I-G-E-R. Tiger.
Elephant. E-L-E-P-H-A-N-T. Elephant.
Bear. B-E-A-R. Bear.
Monkey. M-O-N-K-E-Y. Monkey.
Zebra. Z-E-B-R-A. Zebra.
Giraffe. G-I-R-A-F-F-E. Giraffe.
Seal. S-E-A-L. Seal.
Cow. C-O-W. Cow.
Sheep. S-H-E-E-P. Sheep.

Lesson 4 Review

Objectives

Students will:
- read a dialogue
- review language from lessons 1-3
- differentiate between /ch/ and /sh/

Materials
Best Friends Student Book 1 pages 118-121
Other Materials
index cards, picture and word cards from Lessons 1-3, scissors

New Language
Passive Language
Good night

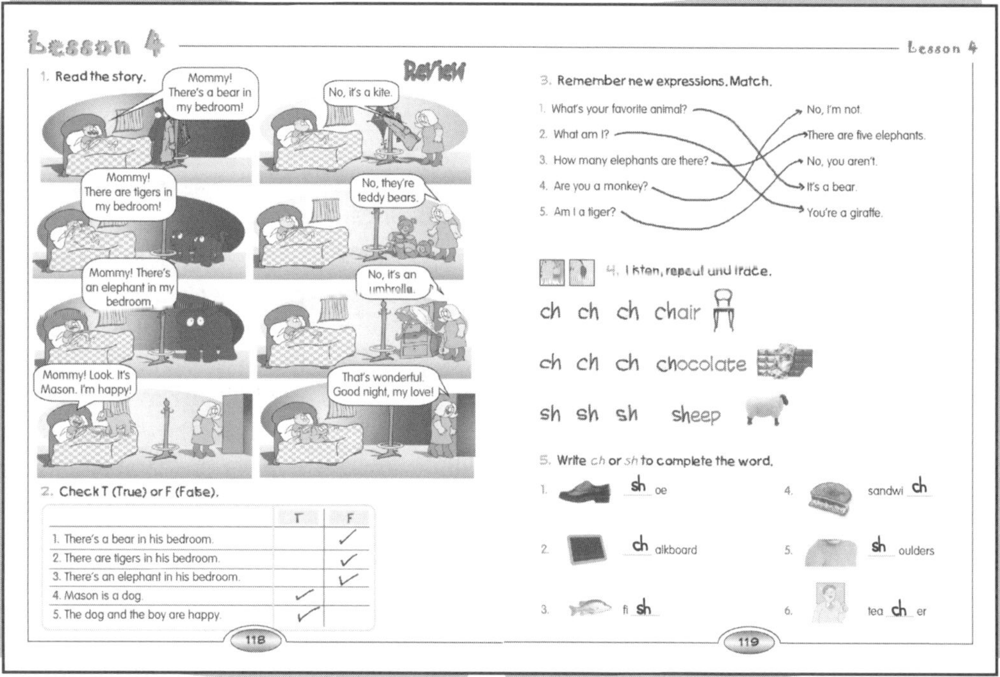

Read

Exercise 1: Dialogue summary. A story in dialogue format tells about a boy who is having trouble getting to sleep. He calls his mother because it is dark in his bedroom and he thinks there is a bear. She comes to his bedroom, turns on the light, and tells him that it isn't a bear, it is a kite. Then he thinks there are tigers in his bedroom. His mother says that they are teddy bears, not tigers. Then the boy "sees" an elephant. Is it an elephant? No, it isn't. It is an umbrella! Finally, his dog, Mason, comes to his bedroom. The boy is very happy because now he has a friend. His mother is also happy and tells him "Good night."

Read the dialogue aloud, pointing to each speech bubble as you read. Ask students to listen and follow in their book. For fun, change voices to represent different speakers. At the end of the dialogue, wave good-bye or blow a kiss as you read the last speech bubble. Then read the dialogue again and encourage students to read aloud with you. Students should infer the meaning of *Good night* from *Good morning* and *Good afternoon* and from the story line. Finally, assign the roles of the boy and Mommy to capable students, and have other students pantomime Mason the dog and the animals that the boy imagines. The speakers can use the book to read their parts or they can try to memorize and recite their parts.

Story Comprehension

Exercise 2: Do number 1 together: *There's a bear in his bedroom.* Checkmark the *F* column. Then read all the questions aloud for students, allowing time for them to look for key words in the speech bubbles and write their answers. Check answers as a class.

Vocabulary

Exercise 3: Read the numbered items one at a time and ask students to find the logical match to it, e.g., *What's your favorite animal? It's a bear.* They can read the answers aloud or point to them in their book. Give everyone a chance to answer a question and be sure everyone draws a line to match the columns.

Then have students practice the structures. Encourage them to role-play the situations by pantomiming actions related to the answers, e.g., *It's a bear.* = pantomime roaring and standing on two legs with arms up high. Students can make use of their classmates and other props imaginatively, such as rounding up five classmates for number 3 and having them make an elephant's trunk with their arms coming off of their noses.

Listening

Exercise 4: Play the audio for students several times for them to practice the letter and word pronunciations. In general, students will need a lot of practice listening for and pronouncing these sounds. They may find it difficult to hear the difference between the stronger /ch/ sound and the softer /sh/ sound. Some students may find it difficult to pronounce them correctly.

Exercise 5: Have students do the exercise. Then ask them to search in their set of alphabet cards for the /sh/ letter card. Distribute one index card per student and ask them to make a letter card for */ch/.* Be sure they write the letters *c* and *h* closely together to show that they make one sound. Then practice by having them hold up the correct card as you say words randomly from Exercise 5. Go faster and faster. Give more capable students a chance to be the caller if time allows.

Exercise 6: Help students follow the directions as necessary. Do the first one together as an example: *(Mother) There are three triangles.* After correcting the exercise as a group, ask students to count the total number of each shape for the whole family, or decide which family member has the most triangles, circles, and so on.

Exercise 7: Play a game. Tell students to look at page 121 in their book. Tell them they are going to play a game of Concentration, but they won't use this page as a game board. Help them find the correct page at the back of their book (page 151). Since students have been playing Concentration with their own picture cards and word cards, they shouldn't require a lot of direction. Allow groups of three students to play the game, with one as monitor and the other two as the players.

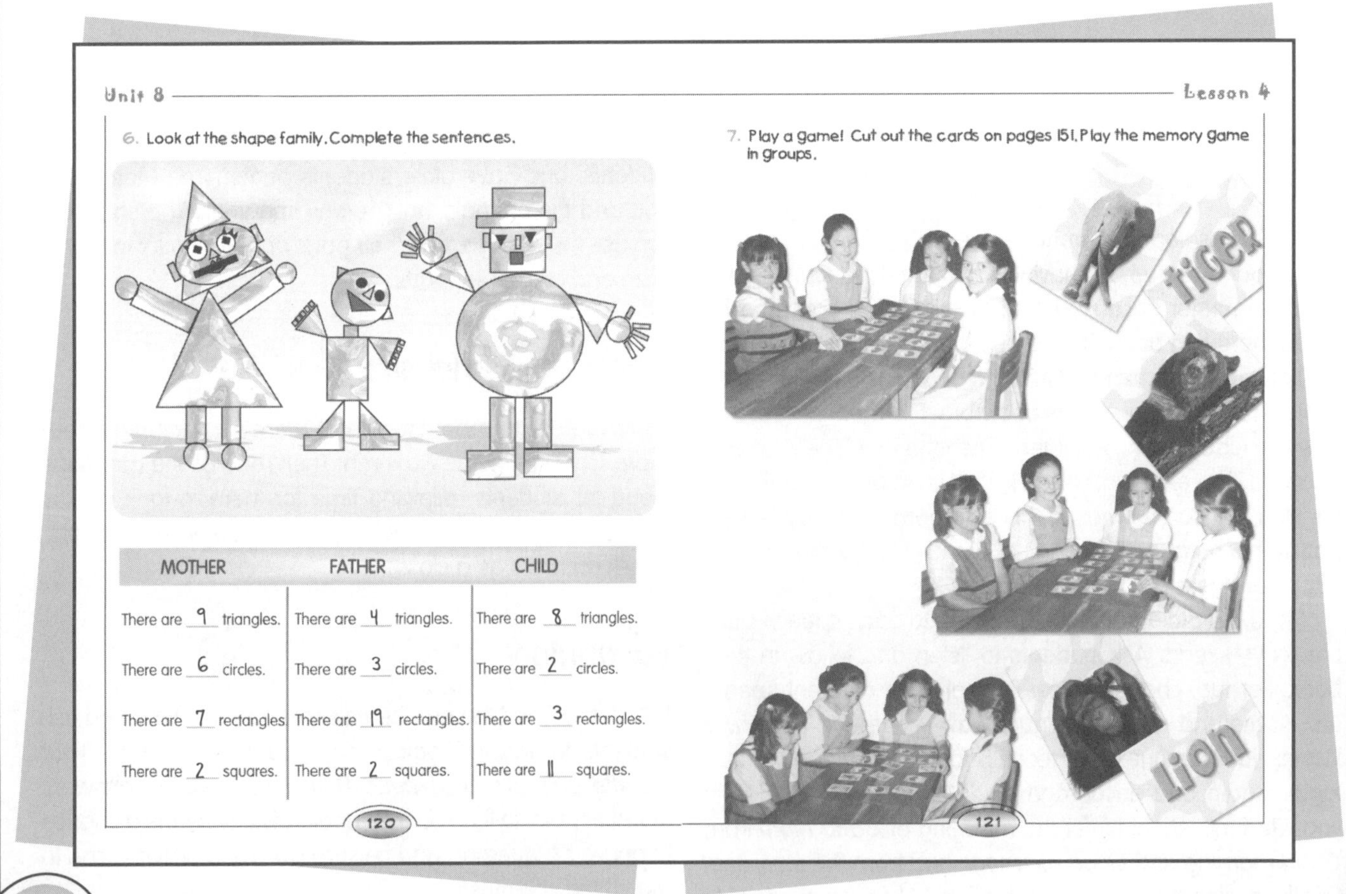
Unit 8 — Lesson 4

6. Look at the shape family. Complete the sentences.

MOTHER	FATHER	CHILD
There are 9 triangles.	There are 4 triangles.	There are 8 triangles.
There are 6 circles.	There are 3 circles.	There are 2 circles.
There are 7 rectangles	There are 19 rectangles.	There are 3 rectangles.
There are 2 squares.	There are 2 squares.	There are 11 squares.

7. Play a game! Cut out the cards on pages 151. Play the memory game in groups.

120 121

Fun and Games

A. **Draw a shape animal family.** Have students draw an animal family totally made up of shapes, similar to the shape family on page 120 in the Student Book. They can choose either a farm animal family or a zoo animal family. Encourage them to use all four shapes in their drawings.

B. **Charades with cards.** Each student should have their Lesson 1 and 3 picture cards for zoo and farm animals. Pair students and demonstrate with a volunteer and his or her set of cards. The student picks either one of the animal cards, places it face down so no one sees it, and then pantomimes actions related to it. You guess the cards by asking *Are you a (tiger)?* Elicit the corresponding answer *Yes, I am.* or *No, I'm not.* from your partner. Once cards have been used, place them in a separate pile. Partners switch roles.

C. **Dictation.** Dictate the following sentences and have students sign their names and hand in their papers. Check their spelling and use of numerals for making lists versus spelling out number words. Return the lists for feedback:

Number 1. There are thirteen giraffes at the zoo.
Number 2. You aren't a bear. You are a student.
Number 3. Am I nineteen years old? No, I'm not.
Number 4. There are twelve zebras on the farm.
Number 5. There are eighteen squares and fifteen rectangles.

Tapescript

Unit 8 Lesson 4 Page 119
Exercise 4: Listen, repeat and trace.

chair.../ch/ /ch/ /ch/ chair
chocolate.../ch/ /ch/ /ch/ chocolate
sheep.../sh/ /sh/ /sh/ sheep

Unit 8 Test

Name____ Date__________________

1. Draw twelve animals using shapes. Label the animals and the shapes.

2. Fill in the blanks with the correct words from the word box.

seventeen	zoo	sheep	circle	elephant	are	There	Am	is	farm

1. There ______________ thirteen giraffes at the ______________.
2. ______________ I a triangle? No, you aren't. You are a ______________.
3. There ____________ an ________________ in the cage.
4. ______________ ________________ three tigers at the zoo.
5. Where is the ______________? It's on the _____________.

3. Write.

Example: 19  nineteen ducks

1. 16  ____
2. 20  ____
3. 11  ____
4. 18  ____

Unit 9

Lesson 1 Don't eat in the classroom!

Objectives

Students will:
- recognize affirmative and negative command forms
- listen for a purpose

Materials
Best Friends Student Book 1
pages 122-125
Other Materials
picture-word cards from Unit 8 (zoo and farm animals)

New Language
candy
Don't talk... Talk...
Don't eat... Eat...
Don't stand up. Stand up.
Don't sit down. Sit down.
Open, Run
Passive vocabulary
banana, ice cream, lollipop

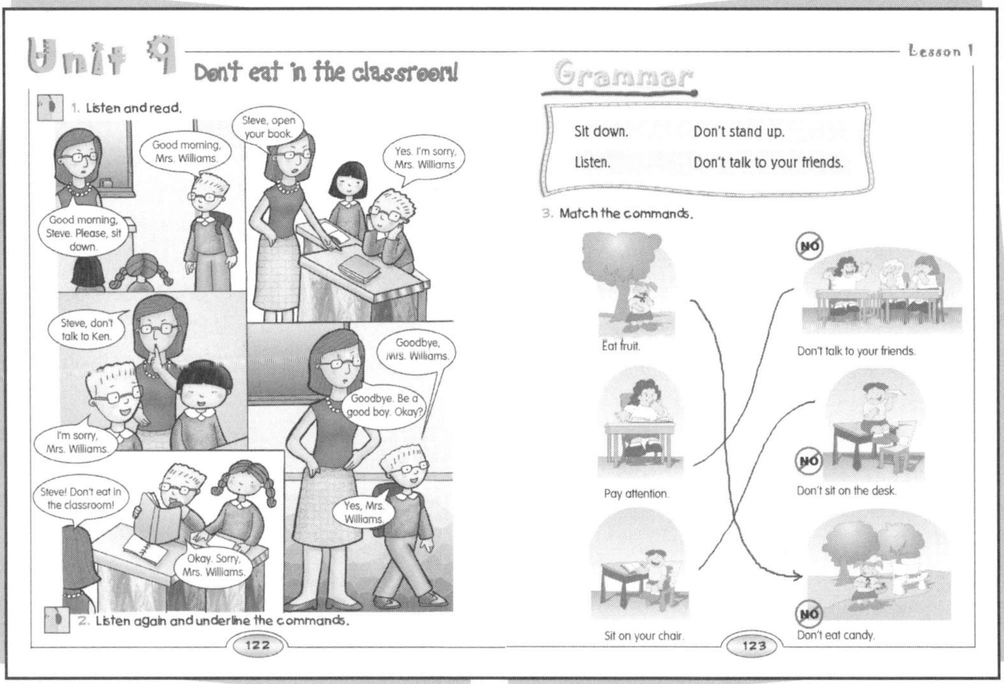

1. **Getting Started**
Review with students the commands *Look!, Look at..., Come...,* and *Sit down,* which were presented informally in previous units. Ask a student who does not get frustrated easily to follow your commands. Point and help with gestures: *Look! This book is big./ Look at that flag./ Come to my desk./ Sit down.* Then introduce negative commands by repeating the commands in negative form and shaking your head no as you make gestures to the student to follow your commands: *Don't look at that flag. Look at the chalkboard./ Don't come to my desk. Sit down./ Don't sit down. Stand up!*
Play the audio for **Exercise 1**. As each character speaks, students should trace with a finger under the words in the speech bubbles. Be sure they follow the order of the dialogue between the Mrs. Williams and Steve characters.
Play the tape for **Exercise 2** and point to the appropriate words as commands are mentioned. Encourage students to do the same as they listen to the dialogue. They should guess the tone of command in the teacher's voice on the audio and by the impatient expression on her face. Then play the audio again and have students follow the directions. Be sure they use a pencil that can be erased in case they need to correct their underlining. Check answers as a group.

Grammar Tips

- Affirmative commands come from the base form (or infinitive without *to*) of a verb: *Sit down. Listen. Look at the animals on the farm.*
- Negative commands come from the base form of a verb and are preceded by *Don't: Don't sit down. Don't listen. Don't look at the animals on the farm.*
- Affirmative and negative commands can be directed at just one person or at more than one person. The form is the same.
- Affirmative and negative commands may be preceded by the word *Please*. This makes the command more polite or makes it a kind of request: *Please come to my birthday party. Please don't open my presents.*
- *Don't* is the contraction for *Do not*. *Don't* is more usual, especially in spoken English.

Practice the structures in the Grammar Box first with individuals, then with small groups, to make students aware that the command form is the same no matter how many people are being addressed. Try to have them follow your commands in each case.

2. **Working Together**
   For **Exercise 3**, point out the "prohibited" icon next to the negative commands. Do the first one as example: *Don't talk to your friends./Pay attention.* Students should be able to find the matches even if they don't know every single word in the statements.

   Play the tape for **Exercise 4** several times before students start to circle their choices. Tell them that they don't have to understand every word in the statements in order to select the correct answer.

3. **Finishing Up**
   Before starting **Exercise 5**, demonstrate the meaning of *run* by pantomiming the action. Then ask a capable student to come to the front and give him or her the command *Run!* while he or she follows your instructions. When you are sure students understand the meaning of *run,* help students with the directions, telling them to cross out the commands in the boxes when they have used them. Circulate to check that the written answers start with a capital letter. Check answers as a group.

   Then point out to students that throughout the course, they have been responding to affirmative commands every time they do an exercise in the Student Book. Refer them to the directions for Exercise 5 as an example. Have them circle the commands (*Look at* and *write*).

   For **Exercise 6,** go through the process with students, pointing to and naming the ingredients. If available, share with students a recipe with the exact amounts of ingredients needed to make the dough. Have students copy the recipe in their notebooks and do the project at home under the supervision of an adult. They can bring in the results for a session of Show and Tell.

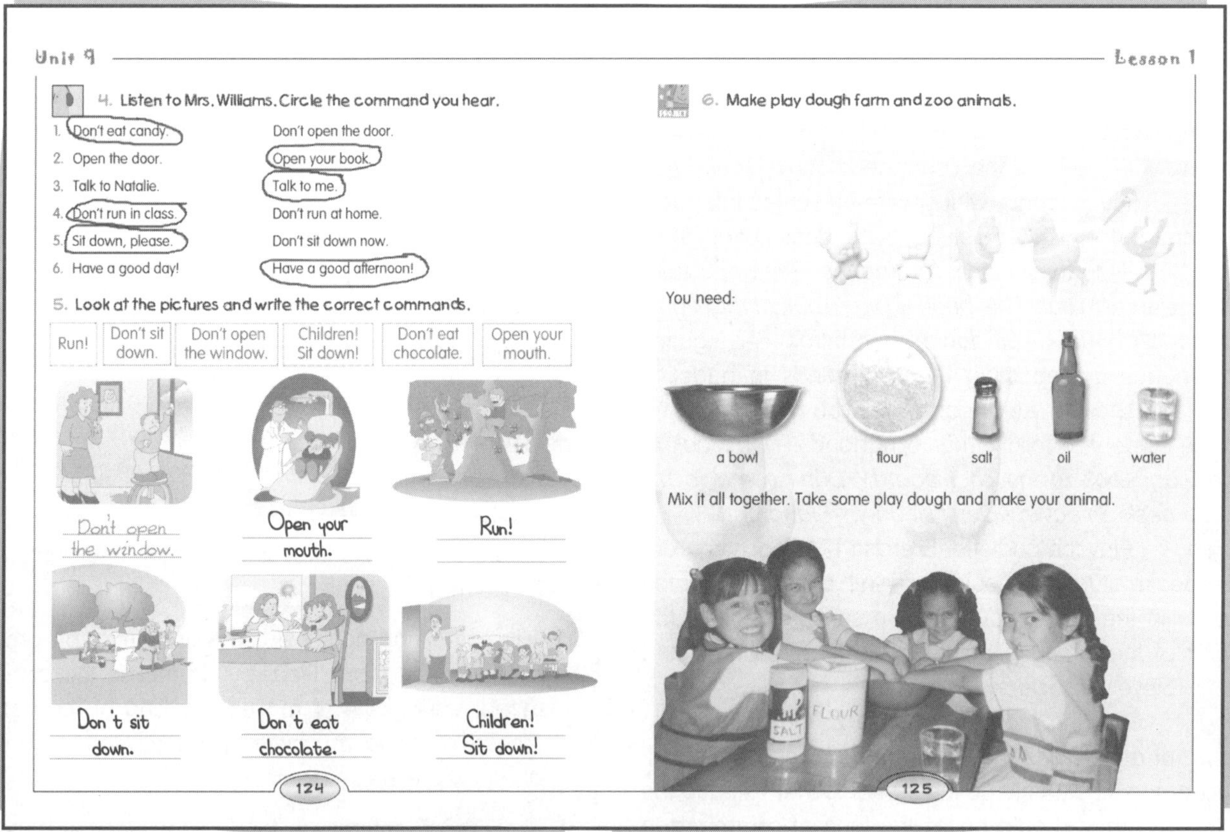
Unit 9 — Lesson 1

4. Listen to Mrs. Williams. Circle the command you hear.

1. Don't eat candy. — Don't open the door.
2. Open the door. — Open your book.
3. Talk to Natalie. — Talk to me.
4. Don't run in class. — Don't run at home.
5. Sit down, please. — Don't sit down now.
6. Have a good day! — Have a good afternoon!

5. Look at the pictures and write the correct commands.

Run!	Don't sit down.	Don't open the window.	Children! Sit down!	Don't eat chocolate.	Open your mouth.

Don't open the window. — Open your mouth. — Run!

Don't sit down. — Don't eat chocolate. — Children! Sit down!

124

6. Make play dough farm and zoo animals.

You need:

a bowl — flour — salt — oil — water

Mix it all together. Take some play dough and make your animal.

125

Fun and Games

A. **Teacher Says.** Play a simplified form of Simon Says. Give the *command stand up!* Each student should have his or her set of picture-word cards for zoo and farm animals. Demonstrate the game as follows: Hold up a random card, e.g., the lion card, and say *Sit on the lion!* Students should follow your command as quickly as possible. Then hold up another card, e.g., the monkey card and say *Don't sit on the monkey!* Any student who sits on the monkey card must sit down. Any student not holding the correct card at any time is also out and must sit down. Use language from the lesson and practice both affirmative and negative commands. Play until a winner is declared.

B. **Don't do that!** Pair students and demonstrate the following activity with a volunteer: He or she pantomimes any action from the lesson, e.g., eating something. Identify the action by telling the student *not* to do it, e.g., *Don't eat.* If you guessed correctly, then you switch roles. If you guessed incorrectly, he or she should say *Please repeat.* An alternative is to have students form small groups. One student pantomimes, and the others guess. The first student to guess pantomimes another action.

C. **Teacher and student conversations.** Have students draw a teacher and a student having a conversation in a classroom. They should draw speech balloons and a dialogue that makes sense with the details in their scenes. For example, there should be a flag in the picture if a flag is mentioned. Students can refer to pages 122 and 123 for ideas but should invent their own pictures and dialogues. Encourage them to write complete sentences in the speech bubbles. Display the drawings on the bulletin board under the heading *Please listen to the teacher.*

Tapescript

Unit 9 Lesson 1 Page 122

Exercise 1: Listen and read.

Steve:	Good morning, Mrs. Williams.
Mrs. Williams:	Good morning, Steve. Please, sit down.
Mrs. Williams:	Steve, open your book.
Steve:	Yes. I'm sorry, Mrs. Williams.
Mrs. Williams:	Steve, don't talk to Ken.
Steve:	I'm sorry, Mrs. Williams.
Mrs. Williams:	Steve! Don't eat in the classroom!
Steve:	OK. Sorry, Mrs. Williams.
Steve:	Goodbye, Mrs. Williams.
Mrs. Williams:	Goodbye. Be a good boy. Okay?.
Steve:	Yes, Mrs. Williams.

Unit 9 Lesson 1 Page 122

Exercise 2: Listen again and underline the commands.

(See Exercise 1 above.)

Unit 9 Lesson 1 Page 124

Exercise 2: Listen to Mrs. Williams. Circle the command you hear.

1. Don't eat candy!
2. Open your book.
3. Talk to me.
4. Don't run in class.
5. Sit down, please.
6. Have a good afternoon!

Lesson 2 I want that boat.

Objectives

Students will:

- learn vocabulary related to stores and food
- listen for a purpose

Lesson 2 I want that boat.

1. Listen, point and read.

Daniel: I want that boat, Mommy. Please, Mommy, please.
Mother: Hurry up, Daniel.
Daniel: I want that book. Please, Mommy, please!
Mother: Not now, Daniel. Let's hurry.
Daniel: Look. There's a restaurant. Look at those hot dogs and hamburgers. I want a hot dog.
Mother: Not now, Daniel. Hurry up!

Doctor: Very good, Daniel. You're a brave boy.
Mother: Yes, he is. Now he wants his surprise. It's his favorite.
Daniel: I want my surprise!

2. Listen again. What is Daniel's surprise?

126

Lesson 2

Grammar

I	want	this	book.
		that	boat.
He	wants	these	hot dogs.
She		those	hamburgers.

3. Listen and circle the words you hear.

1. I want — that boat. — that ball.
2. Sit on — that chair. — this chair.
3. Don't eat — those hot dogs. — these hot dogs.
4. Don't talk to — that boy. — that girl.
5. She wants — these posters. — those posters.

4. Play *Simon Says*.

127

Materials

Best Friends Student Book 1 pages 126-129

Other Materials

word cards for *There is* and *There are*, index cards, scissors, glue, crayons or colored pencils

New Language

boat
brave
bookstore
restaurant
toy store
Hurry up.
I want…

1. **Getting Started**

Tell students *Open your books to Lesson 2,* helping as necessary to locate page 126. Review and introduce new language by pointing to the scene and saying *Who is that boy? It's Daniel, and that is Daniel's mother. She is pretty. Where is Daniel? He's not at home.* (Point to the toy store.) *What is this? It's a toy store.* Repeat for *bookstore* and *restaurant.* (Point to the man.) *What is he? He's a doctor.* Then point to items in each establishment in the order the characters "pass by" and have students repeat: *A boat. There is a boat in the toy store. A book. There is a book in the bookstore. Hot dogs and hamburgers. There are hot dogs and hamburgers in the restaurant.*

Play the audio for **Exercise 1**. As each character speaks, students should trace with a finger under the words in the lines. Students should guess the meaning of *I want…*, *Hurry up,* and *brave* from the context of the picture and the characters' tone of voice. (The verb *want* will be formally introduced in the Grammar Box.)

Play the tape for **Exercise 2** a few times for students to just listen as they look at the scene of Daniel, his mother, and the doctor. Be sure students realize that this is a continuation of the dialogue in Exercise 1, but it is not printed in the Student Book.

Grammar Tips

- The verb *want* has the same present tense form for the following pronouns: *I, You (singular), We, You (plural),* and *They.*
- The form for third-person singular pronouns *He, She, and It* is *wants.*
- The verb *want* means "to have a desire for." The desired thing can be abstract or concrete: *I want more time to study English. My mother wants a red car.*
- This verb always requires an object: *(In a bookstore) I want these magazines. (In a restaurant) He wants those hot dogs, please.*

Introduce the structures in the Grammar Box on page 127 by pointing to Daniel's obvious interest in the toy store window display on page 126 and making true statements about the scene. For example: *Look! A boat in the toy store. Daniel wants that boat. Look! A monster book in the bookstore. He wants that monster book. Look at those hot dogs in the restaurant. He wants those hot dogs.*

Then distribute eight index cards for students to make picture-word cards for *boat, hot dog, hamburger, restaurant, bookstore, toy store* and word cards for *want,* and *wants.* Be sure students write *hot dog* and *toy store* as two words. Then place one hot dog card nearby and saying *I want this hot dog.* Place it further away and say *I want that hot dog.* Pronounce each sentence several times and have students repeat. Give a plural example using two toy store cards to practice *these* and *those.* Then have partners practice placing and "wanting" cards.

2. **Working Together**

Play the entire tape for **Exercise 3.** Then play each sentence individually for students to answer or play the audio several times for students to be comfortable making choices. Do the first one together as an example. Check answers by playing the audio a final time. See if everyone agrees. Be sure students understand why their answers are (or aren't) correct.

Before playing the audio for **Exercise 4,** you may want to remind students about the basic rules for playing Simon Says.

Preview **Exercise 5** on page 128. Hold up your word cards for *There is* and *There are* as appropriate as you make true statements about available classroom objects: *There are eight boys and seven girls in the classroom. There is one teacher.* etc. Then point to and name the objects on the page, asking students to repeat: *CDs, a lollipop, an apple, a banana, an ice cream, lollipops, apples, bananas, hot dogs, kites.* Distribute three index per student to make picture-word cards for new vocabulary *lollipop, banana, ice cream.* Then read together the example on the page and count the hot dogs. together: *One, two, three hot dogs.* Finally, have students work individually, but check answers as a class by having everyone hold up the *There is* or *There are* card. Note that answers will vary because there are more objects to write about than blanks provided.

3. **Finishing Up**

For **Exercise 8,** help as necessary with the instructions. Students should be able to do the exercise following the pictures and using background knowledge.

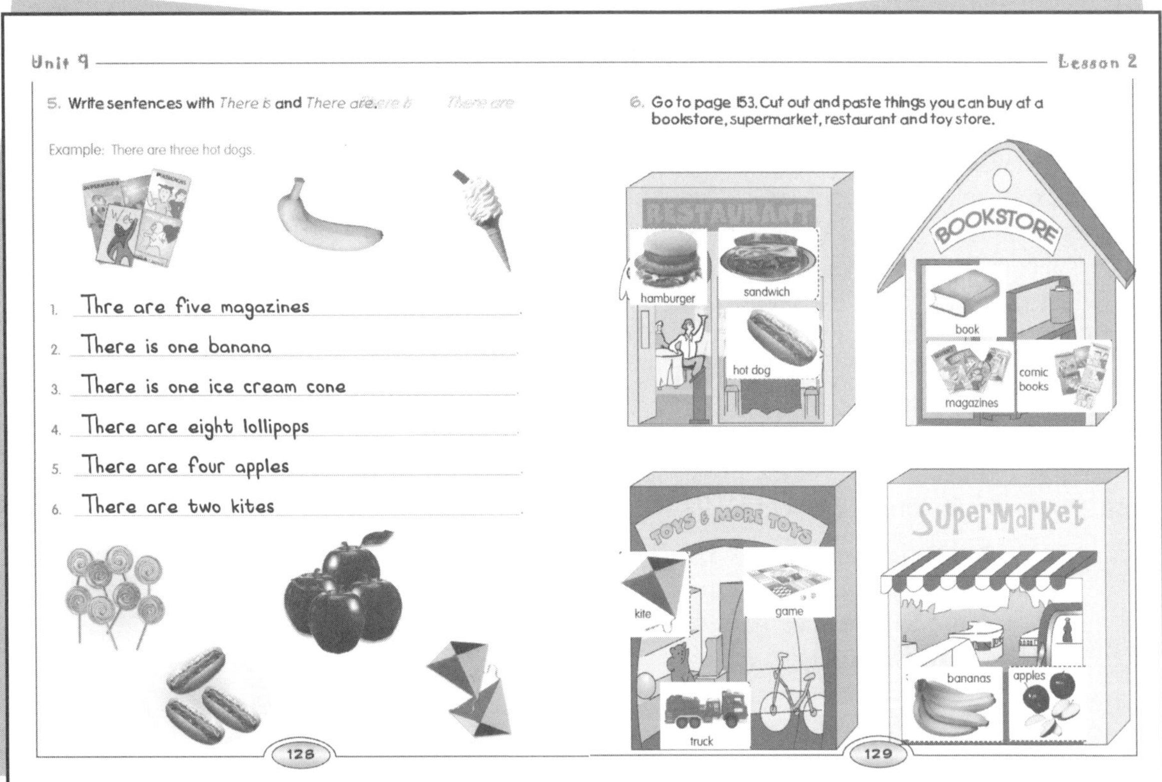

Fun and Games

A. *Favorite Places.* Have students choose one of the following places as their favorite: a toy store, a bookstore, or a restaurant. Encourage them to add as many pertinent details to the place and label it. Ask them to describe their pictures, e.g., *This is a toy store. There are three boats and two teddy bears. There is one boy and there are two girls.* Gather all artwork on the bulletin board under the heading *Our Favorite Places.*

B. **I want...He/She wants...** Be sure all students have their sets of picture-word cards for Lesson 2. Arrange students in groups of three and have them play a card game. Demonstrate as person 1 with two volunteers: Person 1 asks person 2 for any card, saying, for example, *I want a hot dog.* Before giving him or her the card, person 2 says to person 3, as appropriate, *He/She wants this hot dog.* When person 1 has the two hot dog cards, person 3 says *I want those hot dogs!* . (For fun, emphasize *I* as you demonstrate.) Person 1 then says *He/She wants these hot dogs!* If person 1 says the sentence correctly, he or she keeps the cards; if not, persons 3 gets the cards. Then group members switch roles by one, and person 1 becomes person 2, etc. Check to see who has the most cards after four rounds of the game.

C. **Dictation.** Give students five minutes to study the last part of the dialogue on page 126, where the speakers are Doctor, Mother, and Daniel. Dictate the lines and collect for evaluation. Check for use of capitalization, commas, and apostrophes in contractions, and give an extra point for writing a colon after the speakers' names.

Tapescript

Unit 9 Lesson 2 Page 126

Exercise 1: Listen, point and read.

Daniel: I want that boat, Mommy. Please, Mommy, please.
Mother: Hurry up, Daniel.
Daniel: I want that book. Please, Mommy, please!
Mother: Not now, Daniel. Let's hurry.
Daniel: Look. There's a restaurant. Look at those hot dogs and hamburgers. I want a hot dog.
Mother: Not now, Daniel. Hurry up!
Doctor: Very good, Daniel. You're a brave boy.
Mother: Yes, he is. Now he wants his surprise. It's his favorite.
Daniel: I want my surprise!

Unit 9 Lesson 2 Page 126

Exercise 2: Listen again. What is Daniel's surprise?

Mother: Daniel, You're a brave boy. Look, I have a surprise for you!
Daniel: Give it to me! Give it to me!
Mother: Stand up, please. Look. Here you are.
Daniel: Wow! A toy car. Thanks, Mom!
Mother: And it's red — your favorite color.

Unit 9 Lesson 2 Page 127

Exercise 3: Listen and circle the words you hear.

1. I want that ball.
2. Sit on this chair.
3. Don't eat those hot dogs.
4. Don't talk to that girl.
5. She wants these posters.

Unit 9 Lesson 2 Page 127

Exercise 4: Play *Simon Says.*

Simon Says:
Touch your nose.
Sit down.
Simon says:
Stand up.
Open your book.
Simon Says:
Sit down.

Lesson 3 Please give me one!

Materials
Best Friends Student Book 1 pages 130-133
Other Materials
index cards, large sheets of paper, crayons or colored pencils
New Language
box/boxes
bus/buses
sandwich/sandwiches
baby/babies
candy/candies
family/families
child/children
foot/feet
man/men
woman/women
Spelling
apple, banana, candy
chocolate, hamburger
hot dog, ice cream
lollipop, sandwich, little

Objectives
Students will:
- learn vocabulary related to food
- learn irregular plurals
- express preferences

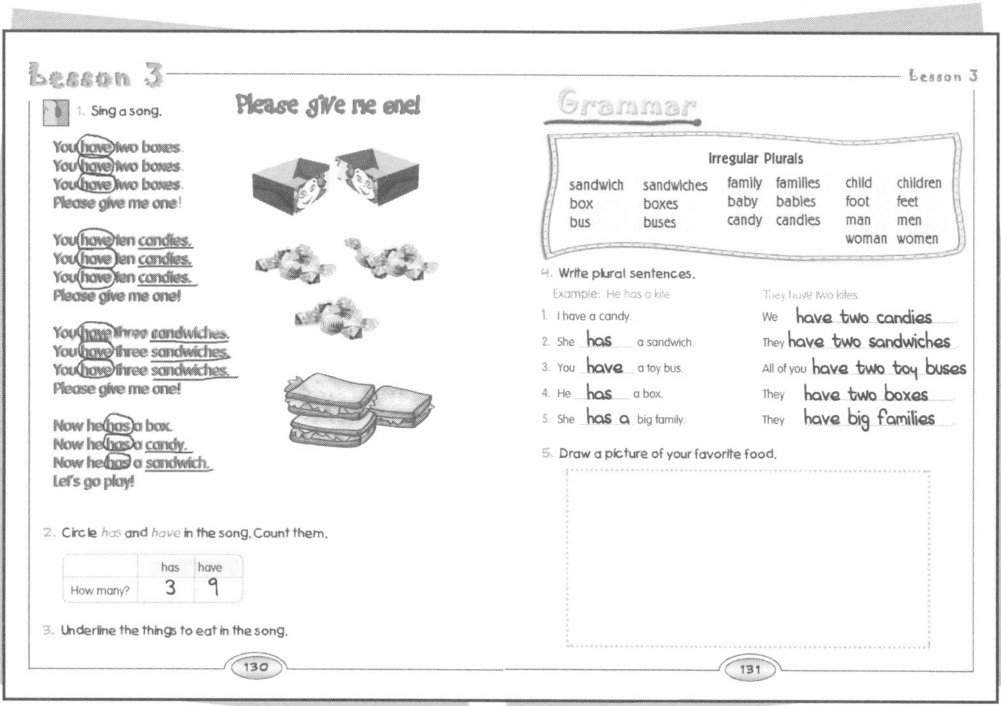
Lesson 3 — Lesson 3

Please give me one!

1. Sing a song.

You have two boxes.
You have two boxes.
You have two boxes.
Please give me one!

You have ten candies.
You have ten candies.
You have ten candies.
Please give me one!

You have three sandwiches.
You have three sandwiches.
You have three sandwiches.
Please give me one!

Now he has a box.
Now he has a candy.
Now he has a sandwich.
Let's go play!

2. Circle *has* and *have* in the song. Count them.

	has	have
How many?	3	9

3. Underline the things to eat in the song.

Grammar

Irregular Plurals

sandwich	sandwiches	family	families	child	children
box	boxes	baby	babies	foot	feet
bus	buses	candy	candies	man	men
				woman	women

4. Write plural sentences.
Example: He has a kite. They have two kites.
1. I have a candy. We have two candies.
2. She has a sandwich. They have two sandwiches
3. You have a toy bus. All of you have two toy buses
4. He has a box. They have two boxes
5. She has a big family. They have big families

5. Draw a picture of your favorite food.

130 131

1. **Getting Started**

Play the audio for **Exercise 1**. Go over the song, pointing to each line and tracing from left to right with a finger under the words as you read aloud. Ask students to do the same. Point to the corresponding picture to the right as they are mentioned. Then play the tape again and have students point to the pictures. Finally, play the song a few more times and encourage students to chant along.

For **Exercise 2**, review *have* and *has* by making true statements about yourself, the students, and your surroundings. Point as necessary: *I have a notebook. You have a backpack. He has a big crayon. She has a red book. We have a flag. All of you have pencils. They have sandwiches.* Then have students do the exercise. Check answers as a group.

For **Exercise 3**, students should underline each example of a food word.

Practice the pronunciation of the structures in the Grammar Box, contrasting the singular with the plural. Have students repeat with you. In the case of adding *es*, students may notice that there is an extra syllable. This can help with spelling. Then go back to the pictures for the song on page 130, point, and say *One box, two boxes. Ten candies, one candy. Three sandwiches, one sandwich.*

Grammar Tips

- Not all nouns become plural by adding an *s*. Those that don't are called *irregular plurals*.
- Nouns that end in voiceless consonants or consonant sounds such as /ch/, /sh/, /s/ and /x/ add *es* to become plural: *watch/watches, dish/dishes, gas/gases, six/sixes.*
- Nouns that end in a consonant plus *y* drop the *y* and add *ies: baby/babies, candy/candies, family/families.* Note that *monkey* ends in a vowel plus *y*, so it is regular*: monkey/monkeys.*
- Some plural nouns do not end with any kind of s. They are a variant form of the singular*: child/children, foot/feet, man/men, woman/women.* Note that the *o* in *women* is pronounced like the *i* in *fish, in, it, is.*

Present new vocabulary *child/children, man/men,* and *woman/women* by drawing on the board generic male, female, and child stick figures and saying the singular forms. Have students repeat. Add another of each to the group and say as you point *two children, two men, two women*. Then distribute ten index cards to each student to make picture-word cards for the words in the Grammar Box. On one side, students should draw the item in the singular and write the singular word. On the backside they should draw the item in the plural (two sandwiches, two small families, etc.) and the plural word. Make a set for yourself as well. Practice the following activity: Hold up the plural side of a random card, e.g., *buses,* and say *I have buses*. Place the card on a student's desk and say *You have my buses*. That student passes it to a random classmate, and you say *He/She has my buses*. That student comes to stand next to you, and you say *We have my buses*. Encourage the rest of the class to hold up their own cards on the same side as you and say to them *You have buses*. Finally, touch two random students on the head and say *They have buses*.

2. **Working Together**

For **Exercise 4**, do the first column first, in which students have to write either *have* or *has*. Notice that in number five they also have to write *a (She has a big family.)* Go over the first column together, and do the first sentence in the second column as an example. Remind students to refer to the structures in the Grammar Box if they are not sure how to write the plural noun forms.

After students are done with **Exercise 5**, encourage them to form groups having the same favorite food. Count group members together to see which group has the most people. Announce the results loudly by saying, for example, *Favorite food: sandwiches!*

For **Exercise 6**, do number one as an example together *(hot dog)*, then have students work in pairs at unscrambling the words. They can use the pictures on the left side as a guide. Then play the audio several times for students to check their answers.

3. **Finishing Up**

For **Exercise 7**, have students work in pairs. Have them compare this crossword puzzle with the one they did on page 117. (Similarities: The clues are icons. Differences: There is no word bank to get words from; the first letter of each word is not given.) Point out that most of the words are in Exercise 6 if they need a "word box" to spell from.

For **Exercise 8**, introduce the word *tall* by drawing stick figures of two boys on the board. One of them should be tall, the other one short. Tell students *This boy is short* while you point to the tall figure. Say *This boy is tall* as you point to the tall boy. Say *Giraffes are tall*. Then ask *Who is tall in the classroom?* Then, help students with directions as necessary and check answers as a group.

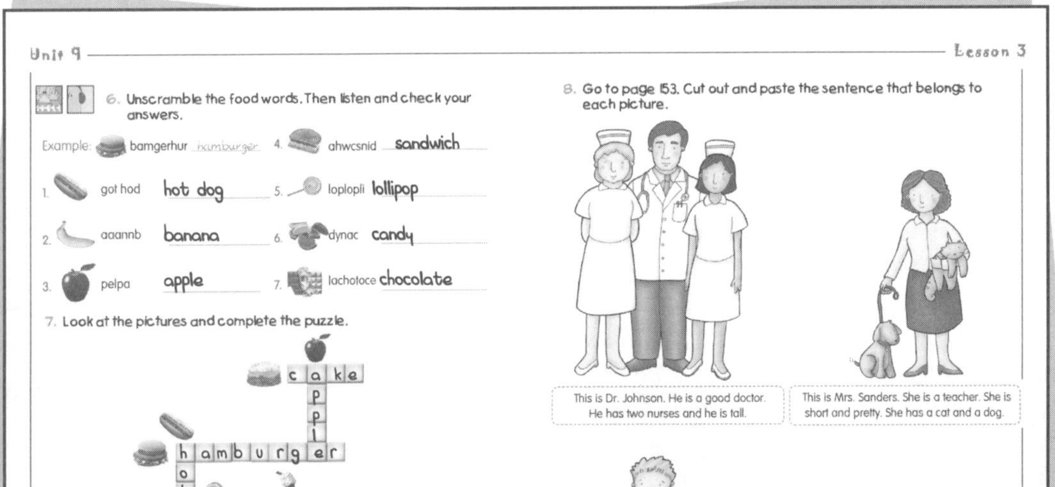

Unit 9 — Lesson 3

6. Unscramble the food words. Then listen and check your answers.

Example: bamgerhur hamburger — 4. ahwcsnid sandwich
1. got hod hot dog — 5. loplopli lollipop
2. aaannb banana — 6. dynac candy
3. pelpa apple — 7. lachotoce chocolate

7. Look at the pictures and complete the puzzle.

8. Go to page 153. Cut out and paste the sentence that belongs to each picture.

This is Dr. Johnson. He is a good doctor. He has two nurses and he is tall.

This is Mrs. Sanders. She is a teacher. She is short and pretty. She has a cat and a dog.

This is Pete. He is nine years old. He is short. He has a red kite. He is not very happy today.

132 — 133

Fun and Games

A. **My favorite things.** Distribute large sheets of paper and crayons or colored pencils. Have students draw themselves and their best friend and draw their favorite things around them. Ask students to write the heading *My favorite things* at the top and to sign their names on their design. Then collect all drawings and display them on the bulletin board. Encourage students to speak about their pictures, saying, for example *This is my friend (name). These are his/her favorite things: a teddy bear, a red ball, etc. I am this boy/girl. My favorite things are: a monster book, a yellow tiger, etc.*

B. **Chain.** Form a circle and do a trial run of this activity. Using your set of lesson cards, hold up a random card, e.g., *family,* and say *I have a family.* Pass the card to the student to your right and say *You have a family.* Elicit from him or her *I have a family.* That student then passes the card to the student on his or her right and says *You have a family.* The correct side of the card (the plural side) must be showing at each passing. Repeat the chain until the card comes back to you. Do the chain with other cards, encouraging players to go faster and faster as the card is passed around the circle. If a student doesn't make the correct statement at any given time, he or she is out. Play until there are only three students left. Announce *We have three winners!* and hold their wrists up in the air, or make some other gesture to indicate victory.

C. **Draw!** Distribute large pieces of paper and crayons or colored pencils. Have students work individually. They should draw what you suggest, labeling all the items they can. Then ask them to compare their work with a partner's. Some sample drawings are:
1. The man has two children.
2. My two friends have four feet.
3. Three babies and three apples
4. Chocolate ice cream

Tapescript

Unit 9 Lesson 3 Page 130

Exercise 1: Sing a song.

You have two boxes.
You have two boxes.
You have two boxes.
Please give me one!

You have ten candies.
You have ten candies.
You have ten candies.
Please give me one!

You have three sandwiches.
You have three sandwiches.
You have three sandwiches.
Please give me one!

Now he has a box.
Now he has a candy.
Now he has a sandwich.
Let's go play!

Unit 9 Lesson 3 Page 132

Exercise 6: Unscramble the food words. Then listen and check your answers.

1. Hot dog. H-O-T D-O-G. Hot dog.
2. Banana. B-A-N-A-N-A. Banana.
3. Apple. A-P-P-L-E. Apple.
4. Sandwich. S-A-N-D-W-I-C-H. Sandwich.
5. Lollipop. L-O-L-L-I-P-O-P. Lollipop.
6. Candy. C-A-N-D-Y. Candy.
7. Chocolate. C-H-O-C-O-L-A-T-E. Chocolate.

Lesson 4 Review

Objectives
- read a dialogue
- review language from Lessons 1-3
- differentiate between /b/ and /v/

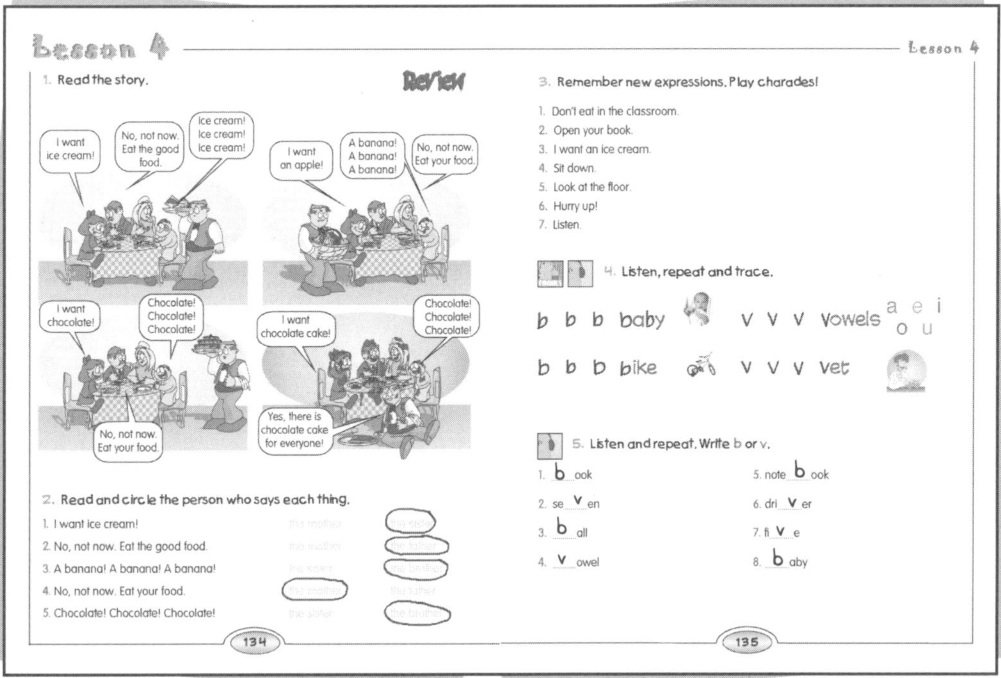
Lesson 4

1. Read the story.

Review

2. Read and circle the person who says each thing.

1. I want ice cream!
2. No, not now. Eat the good food.
3. A banana! A banana! A banana!
4. No, not now. Eat your food.
5. Chocolate! Chocolate! Chocolate!

134

Lesson 4

3. Remember new expressions. Play charades!

1. Don't eat in the classroom.
2. Open your book.
3. I want an ice cream.
4. Sit down.
5. Look at the floor.
6. Hurry up!
7. Listen.

4. Listen, repeat and trace.

b b b baby v v v vowels a e i o u

b b b bike v v v vet

5. Listen and repeat. Write b or v.

1. b ook
2. se v en
3. b all
4. v owel
5. note b ook
6. dri v er
7. fi v e
8. b aby

135

Materials
Best Friends Student Book 1 pages 134-137
Other Materials
picture and word cards from Lessons 1-3, scissors, glue, stick puppets

New Language
Passive Language
everyone
food

Read

Exercise 1: Dialogue summary. A story in dialogue format tells about two children at a restaurant with their mother and father. One child is a boy, and the other child is a girl. The girl wants ice cream, and her small brother wants ice cream, too. Their father says "No, not now. Eat your food." The sister then wants an apple, and the brother wants a banana. But their father repeats "No, not now. Eat your food." When the sister wants chocolate, and her brother does too, the poor father repeats the same thing--"No, not now. Eat your food." Finally, everyone is happy because there is a big chocolate cake.

Read the dialogue aloud, pointing to each speech bubble as you read. Ask students to listen and follow in their books. For fun, change voices to represent different speakers. Each time the father speaks, shake your head no and use an exasperated tone of voice. Then read the dialogue again and encourage students to read aloud with you. Students should infer the meaning of *Give me* and *No, not now. Eat your food.* from the story line and the expressions on people's faces. Finally, assign the roles of all the characters to capable students. The speakers can use the book to read their parts or they can try to memorize and recite their parts. Have everyone but the waiter pantomime as much as possible as they speak their parts. The waiter can sit on a chair to act out falling on the floor.

Story Comprehension

Exercise 2: Do number 1 together: *I want ice cream! (the sister).* Then read all the questions aloud for students, allowing time for them to look for key words in the speech bubbles and write their answers. Then check by asking several students to read their answers.

Vocabulary

Exercise 3: Read all the expressions aloud and ask students to recall what context they are found in the unit as an aid in acting them out. Demonstrate playing charades by doing the first expression as an example. (However, charades is usually a guessing game, so the expression being acted out should not be pointed out in any way once the game starts.) Ask individuals to act out any expression, and their classmates try to guess. The guessers can read the answer aloud or point to it in their books.

Listening

Exercise 4: Play the audio for students several times for them to practice the letter and word pronunciations. Help students differentiate between the letters by doing a "pronunciation demonstration." For *b*, close your lips completely, whereas for *v*, your top teeth should touch your bottom lip without actually closing your lips. Play the tape one more time for students to fill in the blanks, then check their answers.

Exercise 5: Have students do the exercise. Even if students can't tell the difference between the two sounds, they should be able to fill in the blanks correctly because they are familiar with the spelling of all these words. Play the tape several times for students to check their answers and to repeat for correct pronunciation. Then ask them to search in their set of cards for all the words from Exercise 5. (Students probably don't have a card for vowels or baby. They can make them at this time, using the art in Exercise 4 as a model). Then practice by having students hold up the correct card as you say words randomly. Go faster and faster. Give more capable students a chance to be the caller if time allows.

Write

Exercise 6: Help students follow the directions as necessary. Look at the example together. Ask why *There* is the first word in the unscrambled sentence and not *bear*, for example (because *There* is capitalized, and it makes no sense anywhere else in the sentence). Note that the end punctuation, in this case a period, is between slashes as a separate unit, so that students have to make an extra effort to place it correctly. When students are done, ask seven of them to stand up and write the unscrambled sentence on the board to check the answers.

Exercise 7: Before students do the exercise, review the meaning of the more difficult words in the word box, such as *Open* and *Hurry* by pantomiming as you pronounce them. Have students exchange books to check each other's answers.

Exercise 8: Play a game. Help with directions as necessary. The rules for the game can include having to give away any picture a classmate asks for, or students can bargain and trade so that they eventually get two sets of five pictures that they really want. As an aid to less competitive students, two students at a time could ask for and give each other pictures in one encounter; or students can roam freely to gather pictures. Act as mediator if there are disputes as to what pictures someone "should" give their classmates.

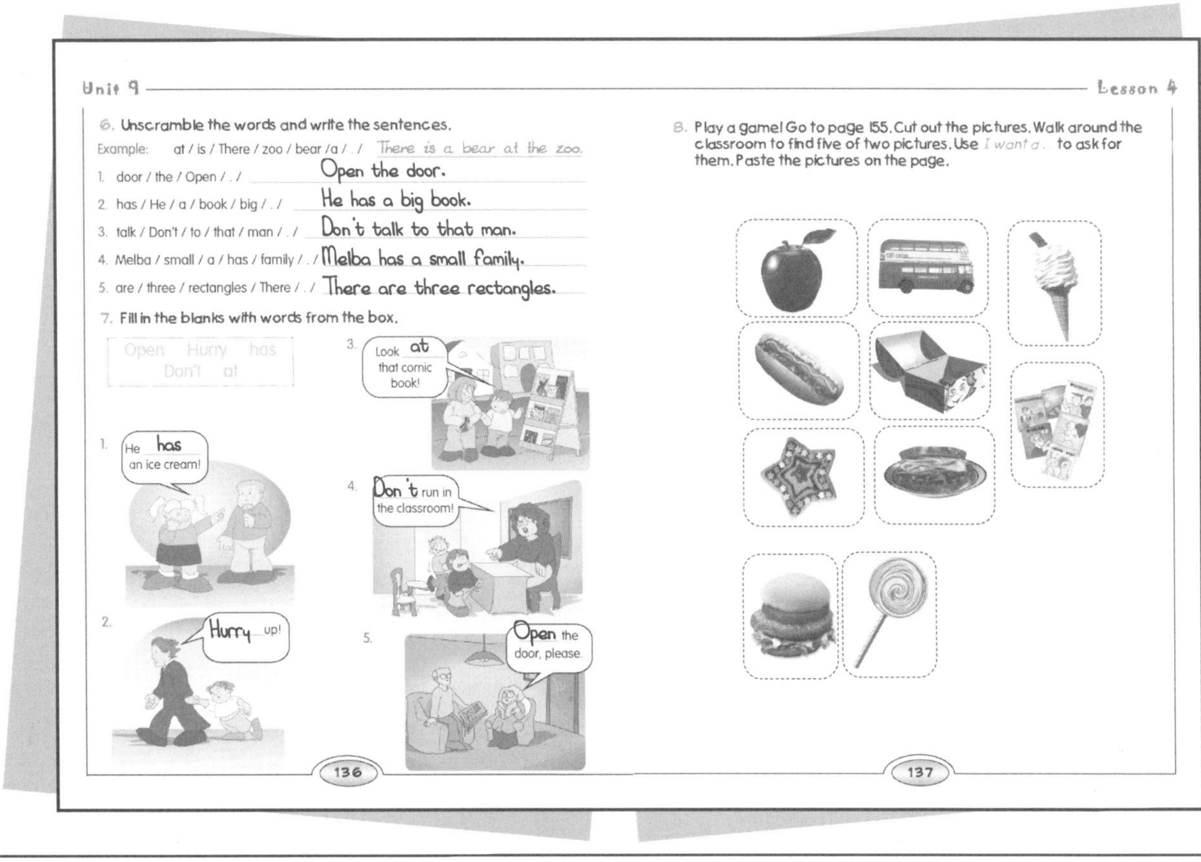
Unit 9 — Lesson 4

6. Unscramble the words and write the sentences.

Example: at / is / There / zoo / bear / a / . / There is a bear at the zoo.

1. door / the / Open / . / Open the door.
2. has / He / a / book / big / . / He has a big book.
3. talk / Don't / to / that / man / . / Don't talk to that man.
4. Melba / small / a / has / family / . / Melba has a small family.
5. are / three / rectangles / There / . / There are three rectangles.

7. Fill in the blanks with words from the box.

Open Hurry has Don't at

1. He has an ice cream!
2. Hurry up!
3. Look at that comic book!
4. Don't run in the classroom!
5. Open the door, please.

8. Play a game! Go to page 155. Cut out the pictures. Walk around the classroom to find five of two pictures. Use I want a . to ask for them. Paste the pictures on the page.

136 137

Fun and Games

A. **Teacher Says.** Play a simplified form of Simon Says, but have students follow your commands by moving the stick puppets. Assign the stick puppets to a group of six. Allow them to pick the puppet they want to be. Place your set of Unit 9 picture cards or word cards on the chalk ledge or a large flat surface. Demonstrate the game as follows: Call one student/puppet by name to go up to the blackboard. Give him or her a command such as the following: *Ken, sit under the bookstore.* or *Ken, don't touch the want card.* If "Ken" follows your commands correctly, he goes back to the group and they get a point. If "Ken" doesn't, the group loses a point. After everyone in the group has had a chance, assign the puppets to a new group of six. Use language from the lesson and practice both affirmative and negative commands. Play until a winning group of puppets is declared.

B. **Say singular or plural.** Be sure all students have their sets of picture-word cards for irregular nouns and are standing up. Divide the class into groups of five or six. Randomly show the singular side and the plural side of the cards , and have students hold up the exact same side of the card as quickly as possible. When everyone is holding up a card, name the card together loudly. Then check that everyone is showing the same side of the card . Any student who isn't, must sit down. Repeat the procedure faster and faster until only one student is left standing in each group.

C. **Families in restaurants.** Have students draw a two-scene cartoon of a family in a restaurant. They should write a dialogue using speech bubbles, similar to (but not copying) the scenes on page 134 in the Student Book.

Tapescript

Unit 9 Lesson 4 Page 135
Exercise 4: Listen and repeat. Then trace and say.

(Really pushing the b and v sounds)
baby /b/ /b/ /b/ baby
bike /b/ /b/ /b/ bike
vowels /v/ /v/ /v/ vowels
vet /v/ /v/ /v/ vet

Unit 9 Lesson 4 Page 135
Exercise 5: Listen and repeat. Write *b* or *v*.

Book. B-O-O-K. Book.
Seven. S-E-V-E-N. Seven.
Ball. B-A-L-L. Ball.
Vowel. V-O-W-E-L. Vowel.
Notebook. N-O-T-E-B-O-O-K. Notebook.
Driver. D-R-I-V-E-R. Driver
Five. F-I-V-E. Five.
8. Baby. B-A-B-Y. Baby

Unit 9 Test

Name______________________________ Date______________

1. Draw a very big store that sells everything. Draw and label all the things the store has. Give your store a name.

2. Fill in the blanks with the correct words from the word box.

wants	chocolate	chair	ice cream	to	box	Don't	candies

1. ______________________ eat in the classroom.
2. Talk ______________________ your family in the restaurant.
3. Sit on the ______________________. Don't sit on the hamburger!
4. There are three ______________ in the ______________.
5. I want an ______________. He ______________ an apple.
6. Where is the ______________________? It's in my mouth!

3. Write plural or singular nouns.

Example: ice cream ice creams

1. lollipop ______________________
2. sandwiches ______________________
3. feet ______________________
4. man ______________________
5. children ______________________
6. baby ______________________

Unit 10 Review

Objectives

Students will:
- review language from Units 6-9
- listen for a purpose

Unit 10 Review

1. Listen and read.

Melba: Look at the animals!
Natalie: Oh yummy! Chocolate!
Melba: There's a lion!
Steve: There are three giraffes!
Natalie: I have cookies, too!
Melba: There are two birds.
Steve: There is an elephant and a baby elephant!
Natalie: Look! A lollipop!
Melba: I have a sandwich and an apple.
Steve: And I have a sandwich and a banana.
Natalie: And I'm sick! Can we go home?

2. Listen and repeat. Write the numbers.

One lion(s) Two bird(s) Three giraffe(s) Two elephant(s)

3. Look at the picture and complete the sentences.

1. There are fifteen balloons.
2. There are two girls.
3. There is one lion.
4. There is one boy.
5. There one twelve ducks.

4. Listen and write the numbers.

monkeys 14 seals 12 bears 1 zebras 9

138 139

Materials

Best Friends Student Book 1 pages 138-145

Other Materials

picture and word cards from Units 6-9, stick puppets, picture-word cards for living room, kitchen, bedroom, crayons or colored pencils, large sheets of paper

Passive Vocabulary

cookie

Review

Ask students to look at the scene on pages 138 and 139 in their Student Book. Review vocabulary and structures as you talk about the scene. Say *Where are the children? They're at the zoo. Look at the giraffes. Look at the lion. There is a mother elephant. She is happy. Look, there is a baby elephant.* (Point to Natalie in the main scene.) *Natalie has a lollipop.* (Point to Steve and Melba in the circle.) *Melba has a sandwich. Steve has a sandwich and a banana.* (Point to Natalie in the circle.) *Look at Natalie. She is not happy. She is sick.* Repeat the statements several times and ask students to repeat with you as they point to the appropriate parts of the scene.

Play the audio for **Exercise 1.** Point to each line of dialogue and trace from left to right with a finger under the words. Ask students to listen the first time and trace with you.

Play the audio for **Exercise 2.** Play the dialogue several times as students try to concentrate on the numbers. To practice spelling, remind them to write the number words, not the numerals. In the case of *lion(s),* students should be able to write the number word *one* in place of the indefinite article *a.* Then play the dialogue a final time for students to check their answers. Encourage them to knock on their desks or stamp their feet at the mention of a number word.

For **Exercise 3,** present a few examples contrasting *There is* and *There are* by making statements about page 138 and asking students to repeat: *There is a lollipop. There is one lollipop. There is a banana. There is one banana. Steve has a sandwich, and Melba has a sandwich. There are two sandwiches. Melba, Steve, and Natalie... There are three children at the zoo.* Notice that in sentence 3, students have to include two words in the blank: *is* and *one.* Then have students do the exercise individually. Check answers as a class.

Note that for **Exercise 4,** some students may feel disconcerted when they listen to the audio and don't actually see in the scene the animals that they are listening for. It may take some time for them to realize that the speakers are talking about other parts of the zoo.

Play the tape several times before students write their answers. Again, encourage them to write the number words. Play the audio a final time to go over the answers together. Speak along with the audio and stress the number words.

Play the audio for **Exercise 5**. Read the words in the word box together. Tell students that there is one word in the word box that they don't need (*cloudy*), and one word that they have to repeat (*hot*). Or if their level is very good, elicit the word *sweaty* by pantomiming shaking sweat from your brow. Students shouldn't need an example done for them, but they may want to work in pairs. Check the exercise by having individual students tell you the answers.

For **Exercise 6**, students should be familiar enough with matching activities to do the exercise without any preview. When they are done, check answers by having individuals read aloud the answers as follows: First, he or she says, e.g., *Number 1, flag.* Then that student goes around the room and points to the picture of the flag in everyone else's books. When the student returns to his or her desk, the student can either sit down or attempt to spell the word by saying *flag, F-L-A-G, flag.*

For **Exercise 7**, explain the directions if necessary. When students are done, depending on their level, individuals can either say aloud just the missing letters, or attempt to spell out the entire word, similar to the activity done with Exercise 6. You or a volunteer can write what students spell out on the board as well. Then write the missing letters on the board (if a student hasn't already done so) and say *These are vowels. There are eight missing vowels.* Elicit the number of vowels in the words in Exercise 6 by pointing to the word *flag,* saying *a,* and writing it on the chalkboard. Have students follow your lead to eventually add the vowels. Say *There are thirteen vowels in Exercise 6*

For **Exercise 8**, review the rooms of the house with picture-word cards for living room, kitchen, and bedroom, and demonstrate vocabulary related to bedtime rituals. (Ken is a typical child trying to postpone going to bed). Show the Ken stick puppet and place the three picture cards on the chalk ledge with the picture side facing out (the bedroom should be some distance away from the other two

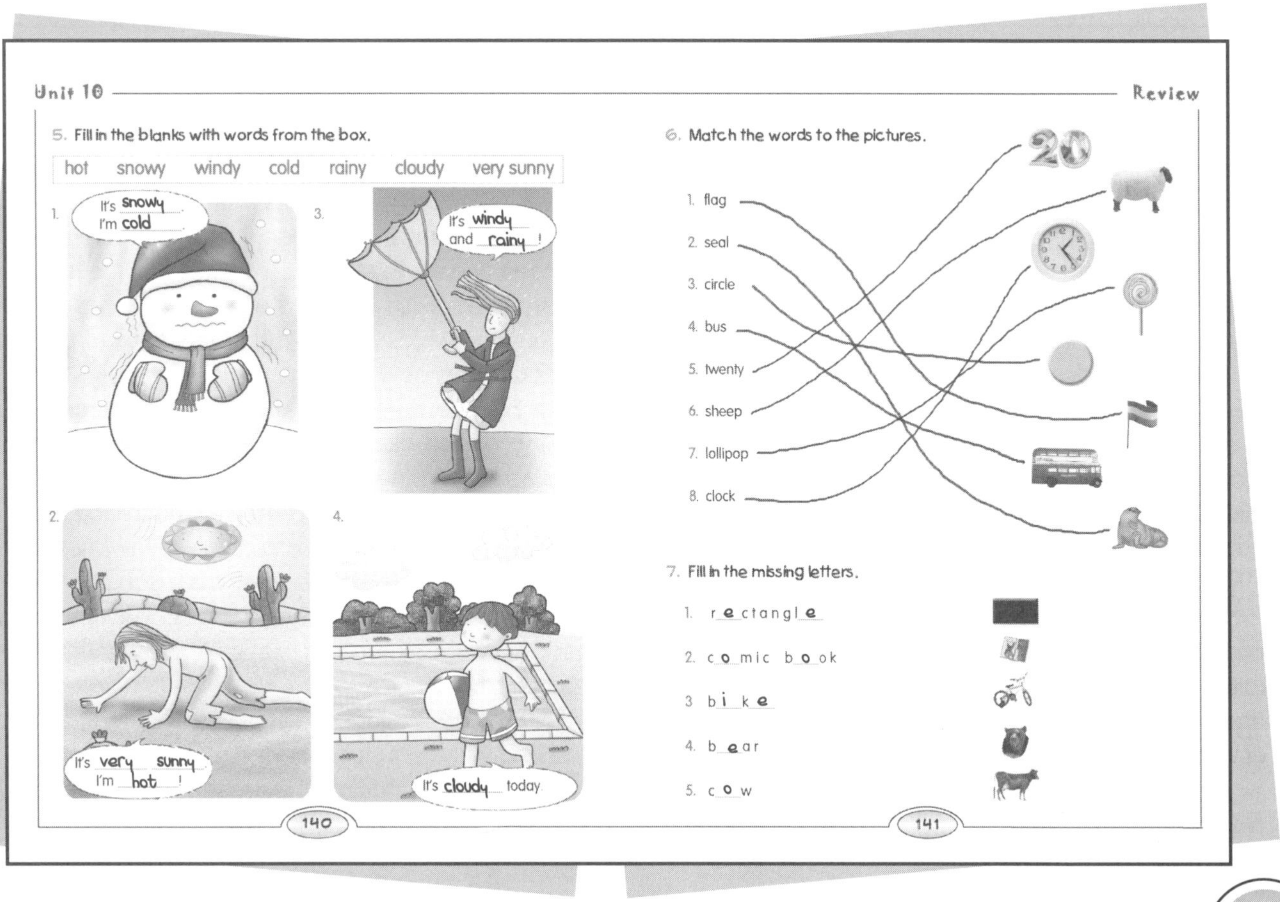

rooms). Demonstrate that Ken doesn't want to go to bed by moving him to the bedroom card and saying *This is Ken's bedroom.* Make Ken shake his head no (you do the same). Then move Ken from the bedroom card to the other two cards. Make Ken dance happily and say *Oh, the living room! Oh, the kitchen!* Move him back to the bedroom card and say in a very sad tone of voice *Oh, my bedroom.*

Then ask students to look at the picture on page 142 in their Student Book. Play the audio the first time for students to just listen. Students should understand the meaning of *Play* and *cookie* from the context and art in the scenes. Play the audio again and have students point to each speech bubble, tracing from left to right.

For **Exercise 9,** play the tape several times as students follow and repeat. After practicing Ken's lines and depending on students' ability, you could assign the roles of the two characters for students to read aloud and/or role-play. Encourage them to use appropriate tones of voice and *yummy* and *I love you* gestures.

For **Exercise 10,** call students' attention to the list of words. Read the first one aloud, then point to one of the cars on the toy train and say *square.* Ask students to make a check next to the word and that part of the train. Repeat the procedure for *baby,* saying the word several times as you search for a baby in the scene. Make it apparent that you don't see one. Have students work in the same manner as they try to establish (or not) a one-to-one correspondence between the words in the list and the items in the scene. Check answers as a group.

For **Exercise 11,** review the verb forms *have* and *has* by drawing on the blackboard a simple cat head and two sandwiches. Moving one of the stick puppets close to the cat as you say, for example, *This is Mariana. She has a cat.* Move two of the stick puppets near the sandwiches and say *This is Steve. This is Natalie. They have sandwiches.* Then have students fill in the blanks. When everyone is done, check answers by reading the sentences aloud together one at a time.

For **Exercise 12,** students should work individually. Check by asking individual students for the answers.

Play the audio for **Exercise 13** several times. The first time, ask students to listen as you pantomime the actions and point on yourself to the parts of the body mentioned: *clap hands, stomp feet, shout hurray!, do all three.* Play the audio again, encouraging students to pantomime all the gestures with you. Play the song as often as necessary for students to follow the song correctly. Finally, ask them to sing along as they make gestures.

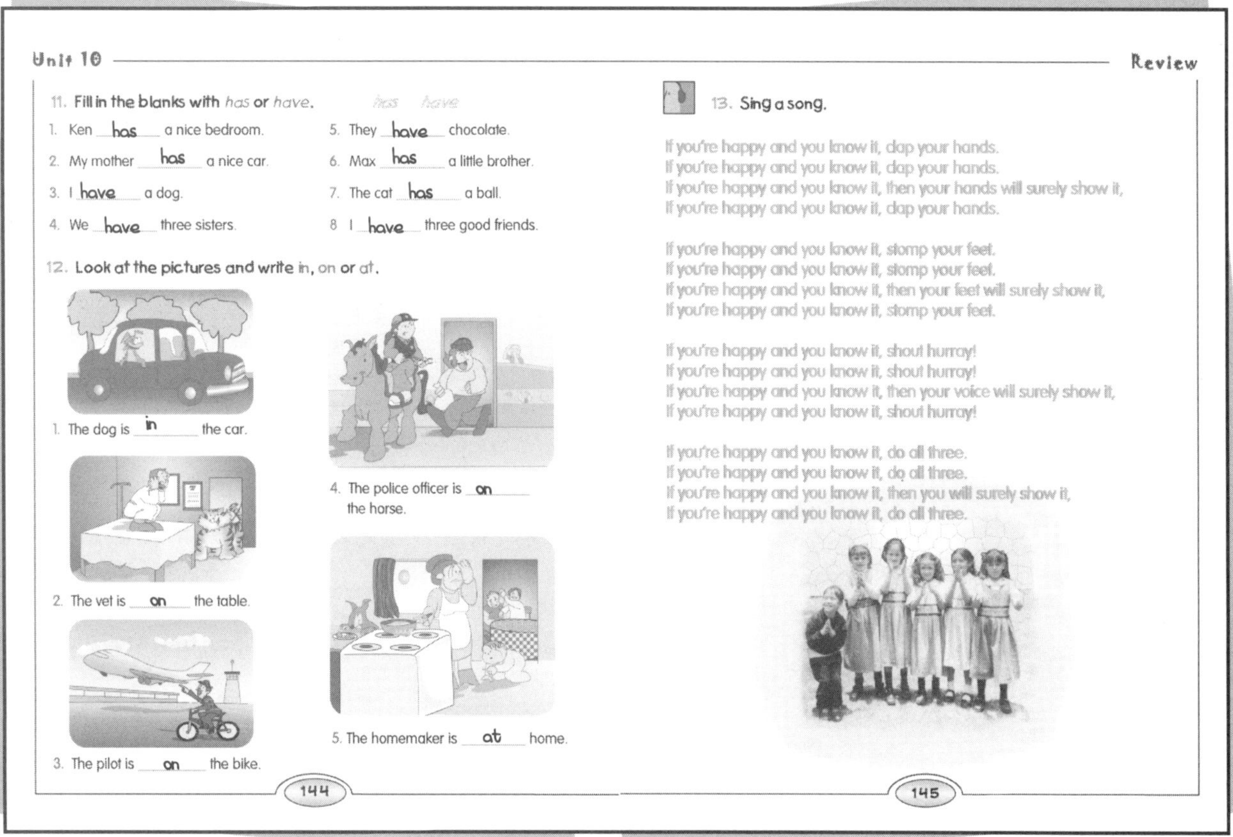

Unit 10 — Review

11. **Fill in the blanks with** *has* **or** *have*. has have

1. Ken has a nice bedroom.
2. My mother has a nice car.
3. I have a dog.
4. We have three sisters.
5. They have chocolate.
6. Max has a little brother.
7. The cat has a ball.
8. I have three good friends.

12. **Look at the pictures and write** *in*, *on* **or** *at*.

1. The dog is in the car.
2. The vet is on the table.
3. The pilot is on the bike.
4. The police officer is on the horse.
5. The homemaker is at home.

13. **Sing a song.**

If you're happy and you know it, clap your hands.
If you're happy and you know it, clap your hands.
If you're happy and you know it, then your hands will surely show it,
If you're happy and you know it, clap your hands.

If you're happy and you know it, stomp your feet.
If you're happy and you know it, stomp your feet.
If you're happy and you know it, then your feet will surely show it,
If you're happy and you know it, stomp your feet.

If you're happy and you know it, shout hurray!
If you're happy and you know it, shout hurray!
If you're happy and you know it, then your voice will surely show it,
If you're happy and you know it, shout hurray!

If you're happy and you know it, do all three.
If you're happy and you know it, do all three.
If you're happy and you know it, then you will surely show it,
If you're happy and you know it, do all three.

144 145

Fun and Games

A. **Categories.** Be sure all students have their sets of picture-word cards for Units 6—9. Play the following game: Write on the board the category headings *Weather* and *Transportation.* Ask each student to pull out the picture-word cards that fall under these categories. Divide the class into two teams, the Weather team and the Transportation team. When you say *Come to the chalkboard!*, the first person on each team runs to the board with one card from their assigned category and places it on the chalk ledge under the correct heading, with the word side of the card facing out. The first student to do it correctly wins a point for his or her team. Continue until all cards are properly categorized and everyone on each team has had a chance to play. (Some cards may have to be repeated.) The game can be played with other categories. Other team names and heading suggestions are: *Classroom objects/Zoo animals, Shapes/Farm animals, Food/Occupations. Stores/Shapes* (again) A variation on the game is to ask team members to write the category words on the board under the correct heading. The first student to do it correctly wins a point for his or her team.

B. **Picture dictation.** Distribute crayons or colored pencils and large sheets of paper to each student. Using vocabulary from Units 6—9, dictate what to draw. The sillier the ideas, the more fun students will have. Students can take their time. Some ideas are: *There is a mess at the zoo. There is a rainy classroom. There are seventeen purple bus candies. There are three animal flags. There are hamburgers in a bookstore, A sheep has an ice cream. Two men have a red and blue zebra.* Go around the room checking that everyone is basically doing the same drawing. For extra fun, have students come up with a silly idea of their own and draw it. They should keep their drawings if they are going to do Activity C below.

C. **Label the pictures.** Students who did Activity B should label the pictures they drew, following as closely as possible your dictation from memory or based on what they see; do not repeat the dictation, but give hints with key words. Accept one-word or incomplete answers

Tapescript

Unit 10 Page 138
Exercise 1: Listen and read.

Melba: Look at the animals!
Natalie: Oh yummy! Chocolate!
Melba: There's a lion!
Steve: There are three giraffes.
Natalie: I have cookies, too!
Melba: There are two birds.
Steve: There is an elephant and a baby elephant!
Natalie: Look! A lollipop!
Melba: I have a sandwich and an apple.
Steve: And I have a sandwich and a banana.
Natalie: And I'm sick! Can we go home?

Unit 10 Page 138
Exercise 2: Listen and repeat. Write the numbers.
(See Exercise 1 above.)

Unit 10 Page 139
Exercise 4: Listen and write the numbers.
Melba: This zoo is good. I love monkeys. There are fourteen monkeys.
Steve: There are twelve seals, too.
Natalie: There's one bear.
Melba: Let's go see the zebras. There are nine zebras.
Steve: They're beautiful!
Melba: Okay, let's go.

Unit 10 Page 142
Exercise 8: Listen and read.
Ken: Look at my game.
Mother: Play one game. Then good night.

Ken: I want a cookie, please, Mommy.
Mother: Okay. One cookie! Then good night.

Ken: This apple is yummy.
Mother: Eat your apple. Then good night.

Ken: Okay. Good night. I love you.
Mother: Good night. I love you, too.

Unit 10 Page 142
Exercise 9: Listen again. Say Ken's lines.
(Pause)
Mother: Play one game. Then good night.
(Pause.)
Mother: Okay. One cookie! Then good night.
(Pause.)
Mother: Eat your apple. Then good night.
(Pause.)
Mother: Good night. I love you, too.

Unit 10 Page 145
Exercise 13: Sing a song.

If you're happy and you know it, clap your hands.
If you're happy and you know it, clap your hands.
If you're happy and you know it, then your hands will surely show it,
If you're happy and you know it, clap your hands.

If you're happy and you know it, stomp your feet.
If you're happy and you know it, stomp your feet.
If you're happy and you know it, then your feet will surely show it,
If you're happy and you know it, stomp your feet.

If you're happy and you know it, shout hurray!
If you're happy and you know it, shout hurray!
If you're happy and you know it, then your voice will surely show it,
If you're happy and you know it, shout hurray!

If you're happy and you know it, do all three.
If you're happy and you know it, do all three.
If you're happy and you know it, then you will surely show it,
If you're happy and you know it, do all three.

Unit 10 Test: Review of Units 6–9

Name____ Date________________

1. Draw and color the people, animals, food, and weather at a zoo and on a farm. Label them. Write the number words.

2. Fill in the blanks with the correct words from the word box.

zebra	on	elephant	What	an	want	Don't	sandwich	rainy	apple	pilot

1. The bus driver is ____________________ the bus.
2. It's ____________________________ on the farm. The animals ____________________ umbrellas!
3. ______________________ open the window. It's snowy.
4. _________________________ are they? They're nurses.
5. He wants _________________________ ice cream. Chocolate, please!
6. You are a _________________________. You have a big plane.
7. Yummy! The teacher has a _______________________ and an ____________________________.
8. The ______________________ is black and white.
9. An ________________________ has four legs.

3. Write about your classroom.

____

____

____